Natural Resource Abundance, Growth, and Diversification in the Middle East and North Africa

Natural Resource Abundance, Growth, and Diversification in the Middle East and North Africa

The Effects of Natural Resources and the Role of Policies

Ndiamé Diop, Daniela Marotta, and
Jaime de Melo, Editors

THE WORLD BANK
Washington, D.C.

Contents

Figures

Tables

Acknowledgments

The authors are indebted to Alan Gelb, senior fellow at the Center for Global Development; Tony Venables, professor at Oxford University and director of the Centre for the Analysis of Resource Rich Countries; Olivier Cadot, professor at the University of Lausanne and director of the Institute of Applied Macroeconomics; and Lahcen Achy, of the Carnegie Endowment for Peace, Beirut, for agreeing to peer review this work and for their excellent comments and suggestions. We are also grateful to Caroline Freund, chief economist in the Middle East and North Africa Region of the World Bank; Jean-Pierre Chauffour, regional trade coordinator, Middle East and North Africa Region; and Michael Ross, professor at the University of California, Los Angeles-UCLA, as well as the participants in the 18th Economic Research Forum Conference in March 2012 in Cairo for useful comments.

The authors thank Manuela Ferro and Bernard Funck, respectively director and sector manager of the Poverty Reduction and Economic Management Department in the Middle East and North Africa Region of the World Bank, for their useful comments, guidance, and encouragement during the course of preparing this volume.

This book would not have been possible without the financial support of the Multi-Donor Trade Trust Fund, managed by the World Bank Trade

Department. We thank Bernard Hoekman, director of the Trade Department, for supporting the funding of this activity. Last but not least, we would like to thank a large number of colleagues in MENA and the Trade Department for the discussions we have had around the issues covered in this volume.

Contributors

Ndiamé Diop
Ndiamé Diop is a lead economist at the World Bank. He has worked for more than six years in the Economic Department of the Middle East and North Africa Region, as lead economist for Jordan and Lebanon (2010–12), the Bank's resident representative in Tunisia (2007–10), and senior economist (2005–06). Before that, he was senior economist in the Bank's Trade Department, undertaking applied research on international trade and related policy reform issues in developing countries. Mr. Diop has published in the areas of trade, growth, competitiveness, and macroeconomics.

Daniela Marotta
Daniela Marotta is a country economist at the World Bank. She has worked for the past five years in the Economic Department of the Middle East and North Africa Region on issues related to international trade and foreign direct investment, firm productivity and innovation, and poverty and inclusion analysis. Before taking her current position, she worked for the Latin America and Caribbean Region of the World Bank, as economic advisor to the British government, as business consultant at Andersen consulting group, and in academia. Dr. Marotta has a PhD in economics from the University of Pavia in Italy, an MSc from

University College of London, and an undergraduate degree from Bocconi University, Milan.

Jaime de Melo

Jaime de Melo is a senior fellow at the FERDI (Fondation pour les Études et Recherches sur le Développement International) in Clermont-Ferrand, France. From 1993 to 2012, he was professor at the University of Geneva and associate at CERDI (Centre d'Etudes et de Recherche sur le Développement International), University of Auvergne. From 1972 to 1976, he worked at the U.S. Agency for International Development, and from 1976 to 1980, he taught at Georgetown University. He then held various positions in the Research Department at the World Bank before joining the faculty at the University of Geneva in 1993. He studied at the Johns Hopkins University where he earned a PhD in economics.

Marcelo Olarreaga

Marcelo Olarreaga is a professor of economics at the University of Geneva and a research fellow at the Centre for Economic Policy Research (CEPR) in London. Before joining the University of Geneva, he worked as an economist in the Research Department of the World Bank and in the Economics Research Division of the World Trade Organization. He has also been an invited professor at CERDI (France), the Graduate Institute (Switzerland), INSEAD (France), Institute CLAEH (Uruguay), SciencePo-Paris (France), Universidad de la República (Uruguay), and the University of Antwerp (Belgium).

Cristian Ugarte

Cristian Ugarte is currently finishing a PhD in development economics at the University of Geneva, where he also works as a teaching assistant in econometrics, development, and trade theory. He has worked for several years as consultant to the World Bank, the African Development Bank, the International Labour Organization, and other institutions on issues related to microfinance, poverty, trade, competitiveness, growth, and development.

Celine Carrère

Celine Carrère joined the University of Geneva in 2011 as associate professor. She is also affiliated with the Centre for Economic Policy Research (CEPR) in London and the Foundation for International Development Study and Research (FERDI) in Clermont-Ferrand, France. After receiving her PhD in economics at CERDI in France (2005), she was an assistant professor of economics at HEC Lausanne, Switzerland (2005–07) and then research fellow at National Centre for Scientific Research (France) from 2007 to 2011. She is currently doing research on developing countries' exports, regional integration, preferential market access, and the impact of infrastructure and transport costs on trade.

Julien Gourdon

Julien Gourdon has been an economist at CEPII (Centre d'Etudes Prospectives et d'Informations Internationales), Paris, since August 2011. He holds a PhD in economics from CERDI, France (2007). He was an economist at the World Bank from 2006 to 2011, working for the Middle East and North Africa Region and in the International Trade Department. A specialist in international trade and development economics, his main topics of interest are trade policies, exports competitiveness, the impact of international trade on income inequalities, and the impact evaluation of trade assistance projects.

Ali Zafar

Ali Zafar is currently senior economist in the Africa Region of the World Bank. He has been a macroeconomist for more than 10 years, with operational experience in 5 regions of the World Bank, including the Middle East and East Asia. He has participated in more than 30 missions to the developing world and provided policy advice to authorities on key economic issues. His work has focused on macroeconomic policy, public finance, and competitiveness. He has also been an adviser to the UNDP in New York, Sudan, and Yemen. He has published extensively on exchange rate, trade, and macroeconomic issues, and is currently working with a team to finalize a book on competitive industries around the world and assess the lessons from Asian labor-intensive manufacturing for the rest of the developing world. He has an undergraduate degree in economics from Princeton University and a graduate degree from the University of Michigan in Ann Arbor.

Chapter Abstracts

Chapter 1

MENA countries set for themselves three interrelated policy shift goals in the 1990s: a shift from economies dominated by the public sector to economies led by the private sector; a move from closed economies to more globally integrated ones; and a transition from oil-dominated to more diversified economies. This chapter examines the pattern of structural transformation in MENA and summarizes the role of various factors examined thoroughly in the rest of the volume.

Chapter 2

Economic performance in MENA has shown significant progress recently, featuring higher growth rates, less growth volatility, and increased market shares for its exports than in the past despite competition from fast-growing countries and exporters such as China and India. MENA's catching up is encouraging against the backdrop of a generally disappointing performance over the past 50 years, particularly for the resource-rich countries. Nonetheless, with the exception of Oman, MENA countries have failed to climb the economic ladder and remain in either the lower-middle- or the upper-middle-income group. This chapter examines the correlates of this overall disappointing performance. At the macro level, MENA countries have been unable to maintain depreciated (undervalued) real exchange rates for long periods, yet such undervaluation has proved important to offset the market failures and poor institutional environment that severely hit the dynamic non-resource-intensive traded sectors. In addition, the volatility of the real effective exchange rate in MENA has been greater than in comparable groups of countries, contributing to the lack of development of new activities outside the resource sectors and to short-lived export spells. Further, despite some progress toward reducing tariffs on industry, MENA countries have fared poorly in most indicators describing the domestic microeconomic environment, giving the impression of an environment in which trade is not facilitated and of an unfinished reform agenda. Improved domestic regulatory policies along with improved public sector governance reflected in better values for key indicators would help MENA achieve greater integration into the world economy.

Chapter 3

This chapter shows that services sectors in resource-rich MENA countries have been declining as a share of gross domestic product (GDP) and of nonmining GDP as per capita incomes increase. This negative relationship between the share of services in GDP and income per capita is opposite to global patterns and is linked to the large rents generated by natural resources in these countries. A large number of services sectors can now be moved offshore or produced by temporary movement of service providers, implying that countries need to be competitive to maintain domestic production. Rents from natural resources inflate wages and nontradable prices, thereby appreciating the real exchange rate and discouraging domestic production of tradable services. As the chapter highlights, the negative effect of rents is compounded by the negative impact of policy and regulatory restrictions on entry, and of business conduct on the development of services sectors. These restrictions create rents captured by "protected incumbents" or increase the real cost of producing services—in both cases inflating the price of services. Resource-rich countries need to reduce these restrictions, build strong human capital, and improve their institutions to create an enabling environment for diversification in the long run. Meanwhile, they offer formidable export diversification opportunities to resource-poor MENA, provided that these countries reduce their own regulatory restrictions to investments in exporting service industries, improve their backbone services (such as telecom), and proactively engage resource-rich countries in reducing barriers to labor mobility within the region.

Chapter 4

This chapter explores the presence of systematic differences between the patterns of diversification in MENA and the rest of the world. The relationship between economic diversification and income per capita is non-monotonic: at early stages of development, countries typically diversify as income increases and new economic opportunities emerge, but at later stages the production bundle becomes more concentrated as income rises. This empirical regularity does not fit the observed pattern of development and diversification in MENA countries. At their early stages of development, production becomes more concentrated as income rises, and then less concentrated after reaching a certain income-per-capita threshold. This chapter explores the correlates of these different patterns of diversification, starting from the role of relative endowments in natural resources and then investigating the role of Dutch Disease associated with a strong appreciation of the real exchange rate in contrast with the role of weak links in the economy. The weak link argument is recent—it shows that complementarities in production and linkages among sectors can lead to either multiplier or weak link effects. When the links are weak, low productivity in one sector can reduce productivity throughout the economy, depending on the degree of substitutability among inputs. In a setup with low substitutability, weak links will result in a less diversified production bundle as downstream sectors are hurt by higher input prices and factor prices. We test econometrically the relevance of the Dutch Disease versus weak links in explaining MENA's peculiar pattern of diversification.

Chapter 5

This chapter shows that from a historical perspective, fiscal policy has not contributed significantly to diversification in MENA, because it has been more oriented toward food and fuel subsidies (consumption) rather than toward public goods such as infrastructure (investment). Even at that, fiscal policy has not been well targeted and has been particularly ineffective at promoting redistribution. Fiscal policy in resource-rich countries of MENA has also suffered from a lack of transparency and accountability. The recent oil boom in the Gulf

Cooperation Council (GCC) countries has led to an impressive buildup of sovereign wealth funds, which have helped mitigate deficits and cushion these countries through crises, but transparency on the governance of these funds has been limited. Nevertheless, over a longer period, the three regions in MENA—the GCC oil exporters, the Maghreb countries in the northwest of Africa, and the Mashreq countries located in the Middle East—have all improved their overall fiscal management, although they have all neglected infrastructure investments.

Chapter 6

The benefits of regional integration in the MENA region have been debated for a long time, mainly in terms of the classic potential trade-creation effects emanating from the elimination of tariffs and nontariff barriers among regional partners. In this chapter, the authors emphasize the different characteristics of the regional partners in terms of their resource endowments and consider wealth distribution effects within the region. The MENA region has resource-rich and resource-poor members. As argued in one recent study, the proximity of resource-rich and resource-poor countries creates an opportunity, through regional integration, to even up wealth distribution among these countries. Preferential trade liberalization is typically more beneficial than unilateral nondiscriminatory most-favored-nation trade liberalization for the resource-poor country, because the country gains access to the rents in the resource-rich country. This would imply that integration between the resource-rich labor-importing and the resource-poor labor-abundant countries might be beneficial only for the resource-poor countries in MENA. The authors test the extent to which economic diversification is achieved at the expense of trade diversion and, consequently, at the expense of broader economic efficiency. Results suggest that significant trade creation is associated with regional integration within MENA, with no evidence of trade diversion in resource-poor countries. But there is evidence of trade diversion in both labor-abundant and labor-importing resource-rich countries. Hence, while further intraregional trade integration is an important avenue for enhancing diversification of resource-poor MENA countries, resource-rich countries have no strong incentive for further preferential regional integration from a purely economic standpoint, and this may explain their relative reluctance to engage in this type of scheme.

Abbreviations

ADR	average distance ratio
AVE	ad valorem equivalent
BOT	build-operate-transfer
COMTRADE	United Nations Commodity Trade Statistics Database
CPI	consumer price index
ECO	Economic Cooperation Organization
EU	European Union
FTA	free trade agreement
GCC	Gulf Cooperation Council
GDP	gross domestic product
GNI	gross national income
H	high (income)
HS	Harmonized System
ICT	information and communication technology
IMF	International Monetary Fund
L	low (income)
LM	lower-middle (income)
LPI	Logistics Performance Index
MENA	Middle East and North Africa
NTB	nontariff barriers

NTM	nontariff measures
OECD	Organisation for Economic Co-operation and Development
OLS	ordinary least squares
OPEC	Organization of the Petroleum Exporting Countries
OTRI	Overall Trade Restrictiveness Index
PAFTA	Pan-Arab Free Trade Agreement/Area
PPP	purchasing power parity
QIZ	qualified industrial zones
REER	real effective exchange rate
RER	real exchange rate
RPLA	resource-poor labor-abundant
RRLI	resource-rich labor-importing
SDR	special drawing rights
SWFs	sovereign wealth funds
TFP	total factor productivity
TRI	Trade Restrictiveness Index
TTRI	Tariff-only Trade Restrictiveness Index
UAE	United Arab Emirates
UM	upper-middle (income)
UNIDO	United Nations Industrial Development Organization
WDI	World Development Indicators
WTO	World Trade Organization

Note: U.S. dollars are used unless otherwise indicated.

CHAPTER 1

An Overview of Diversification in MENA: Rationale, Stylized Facts, and Policy Issues

Ndiamé Diop and Daniela Marotta

In the early 1990s, most Middle East and North Africa (MENA) countries acknowledged the failure of the old state-led import-substitution model of development and set for themselves three interrelated policy shifts to sustainably boost growth and create jobs outside of the bloated public sector (Nabli et al. 2007). These shifts were from a public-sector-dominated economy to a private-sector-led economy; from closed economies to globally integrated ones, and from oil-dominated economies to more diversified ones.

This agenda has remained unfinished. Regarding the first shift, the private sector does have a larger role in MENA today than before. However, as shown by the World Bank report "From Privileges to Competition," it is far from being a strong engine of growth (World Bank 2009). Governments have, by and large, failed to establish rule-based modes of interaction with the private sector. Private-sector reforms were initiated, but sclerotic state institutions have continued discretionary interventions in businesses, resulting in an uneven playing field for the private sector. Reforms took place in a weak institutional context of nepotism in most cases, resulting in limited domestic competition and maintenance of market entry barriers, thus undermining innovation and small and medium enterprise growth. MENA's situation illustrates the view that economic institutions evolve very slowly and in accordance with the social order and the balance of power in economic and political interests (North, Wallis, and Weingast 2009). In this view, the ongoing Arab Spring could present an opportunity to foster a more genuine institutional change, if citizens and other nonstate institutions are truly empowered.

Turning next to global integration, recent studies unambiguously point to an unfinished agenda both at the macro level and with regard to regulatory reforms. In a recent volume, Lopez-Calix, Walkenhorst, and Diop (2010) show that "while MENA has increased its pace of trade integration reforms, compared to fast-growing East Asia and ECA [Europe and Central Asia], it has not fully exploited the benefits of participating in global production networks, increasing global trade in services, the rise of China and India, and regional integration." At the micro level, Freund and Bolaky (2008) find that the 12 MENA countries included in their large sample of 126 countries have among the most regulated economies. On the reasons for this slow pace of integration reforms, most studies strongly suggest that oil rents, remittances, and foreign aid act together to lessen the pressure for reform (Diwan and Squire 1993; Hoekman 1995; Shafik 1995; Nabli 2004; WEF and OECD 2005; and Havrylyshyn 2010). In the same vein, drawing on the Doing Business data from a large sample of 133 countries, Amin and Djankov (2009) find that the proclivity to undertake microreforms that reduce unjustified regulatory restrictions is much lower in countries whose exports are concentrated in abundant natural resources.

This volume aims to complement the picture by focusing on the third goal, diversification away from oil, and its relation to MENA's pace of structural transformation. Has MENA managed to diversify away from natural-resource-based sectors toward manufacturing and services over the past 30 years? More specifically, what is the role of natural resource abundance and macroeconomic policies in the region's economic diversification patterns? What is the impact of natural resource rents and real exchange rates on diversification toward manufacturing and tradable services? Has fiscal policy been supportive of economic diversification? Beyond Dutch Disease,[1] do weak links (input sectors with low productivity) play a role in limiting diversification? To what extent can resource-poor but more diversified MENA countries benefit from complementarities with the resource-rich MENA countries through trade?

The Facts: MENA Economies' Low Level of Diversification

Typically, as countries become richer, the share of agriculture declines, giving way to a rise in the share of manufacturing and services. This often happens because of technological advances that increase agricultural productivity and drive resources out of agriculture toward manufacturing and services (Baumol 1967; Chenery and Syrquin 1975). At the same time, Engel's Law stipulates that as household income increases, the percentage of income spent on food decreases while the proportion spent on other goods and services increases.[2] Thus supply and demand forces suggest that as income rises the share of agriculture in overall GDP (gross domestic product) should decline while nonagricultural GDP increases.

MENA's production structures have, however, undergone little diversification over the past 30 years. Contrary to global trends, the relative size of the manufacturing sector hardly increased at all in MENA countries while the relative size of the services sector actually shrank between 1980 and 2010 (figure 1.1). Agriculture contracted, as it did in other regions, but did not give way to vibrant and innovative manufacturing and services sectors. While MENA's difficulty in expanding manufacturing is well documented, the contraction of services as a share of GDP is particularly striking.

The pattern of change in the services sectors share in GDP is sharply differentiated within MENA (figure 1.2). This share has increased

Figure 1.1   Changes in the Composition of GDP, 1980–83 to 2007–10

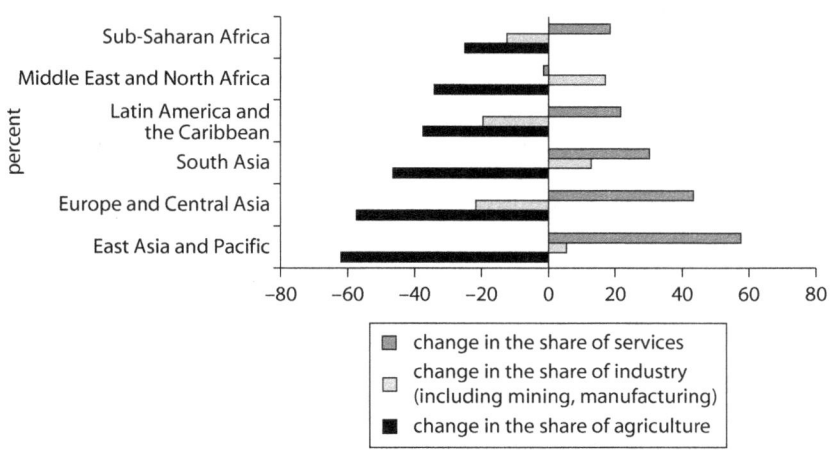

- change in the share of services
- change in the share of industry (including mining, manufacturing)
- change in the share of agriculture

Source: World Development Indicators, World Bank.

Figure 1.2   Services Share in GDP by Level of Income

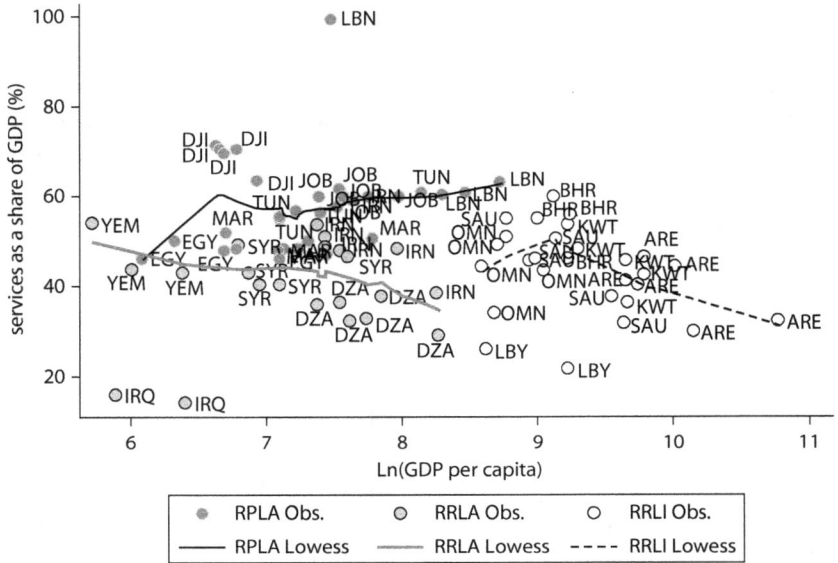

Source: Authors' calculations.
Note: The figure is showing averages over five-year periods. RPLA = resource-poor labor abundant;
RRLA = resource-rich labor abundant; RRLI = resource-rich labor-importing; Obs = observations; Lowess = locally
weighted scatterplot smoothing = fitting trend. Lowess (band width = 0.8) excludes Iraq, Libya, and Qatar.

modestly in resource-poor countries (Jordan, Lebanon, Morocco, and Tunisia), but it has decreased in those countries that are resource rich (Algeria, Bahrain, Islamic Republic of Iran, Iraq, Kuwait, Oman, Qatar, Saudi Arabia, and the Republic of Yemen). (See box 1.1 for a description of the typology used in this volume.) There is a clear positive correlation between services shares in GDP and per capita GDP for the resource-poor group, implying that resource-poor countries conform to theoretical expectations. In contrast, for the resource-rich country group, the share of services in GDP decreases with per capita GDP. In other words, the observed decline of services in GDP for MENA is driven by the resource-rich countries. The United Arab Emirates constitute a notable exception, because it has experienced a dramatic increase in the share of services in the economy (+32 percent) and a moderate shift toward manufacturing over the past 30 years.

The declining share of services in GDP in resource-rich countries is not an artifact reflecting the large and growing share of mining (including oil and gas) in overall GDP. For the countries for which data are

Box 1.1

How Is MENA Performance Captured and Benchmarked in This Volume?

MENA countries differ along several dimensions: resource endowments, internal market size, policies, and so forth. These differences caution against generalized observations and justify looking for suitable countries against which to compare individual countries' performance. Throughout this volume, we capture country performance through three classifications.

First, countries are classified according to the three-grouping classification: resource-poor labor-abundant (RPLA): Arab Republic of Egypt, Jordan, Lebanon, Morocco, and Tunisia; resource-rich labor-abundant (RRLA): Algeria, Islamic Republic of Iran, Iraq, Libya, Syrian Arab Republic, and Republic of Yemen; and resource-rich labor-importing (RRLI): Bahrain, Kuwait, Oman, Qatar, Saudi Arabia, and United Arab Emirates.[a] This last group corresponds to the members of the Gulf Cooperation Council (GCC) countries.[b] The GCC holds about 40 percent of global oil reserves. Its total GDP is about $1 trillion. Oil accounts for about half of the GCC's total GDP, 80 percent of government revenues, and 75 percent of total exports. Whenever relevant, we drop GCC countries (6 countries) from the analysis and refer to the RRLA countries as resource-rich countries (6 countries) and compare them with the RPLA or what we refer to as resource-poor countries (5 countries).

This classification captures only some of the diversity in the region, however. For example, in the GCC grouping, two of the countries (Bahrain and Qatar) have a population of around 1 million, two (Kuwait and Oman) have a population of 3 to 4 million, one (United Arab Emirates) has a population of around 7 million, and one (Saudi Arabia) has a population of 25 million. Hence, we develop four additional country classifications, which we also use to compare MENA countries with other developing countries. First, to account for the importance of market size and the exploitation of economies of scale, we create a group of LARGE developing countries with a population over 20 million (48 in the world, 6 of which are in MENA).

Second, we build an OIL group that includes all the major oil exporters in the world (18) and the region (10); these are countries whose oil exports account for 80 percent or more of total merchandise exports. Third, although they are not included in the OIL group, Morocco, Syria, and Tunisia have natural resources and qualify as "point-source natural resource" countries in the classification proposed

(continued next page)

Box 1.1 *(continued)*

by Hausmann, Pritchett, and Rodrik (2005).[c] This classification distinguishes natural-resource-rich countries according to whether these resources are "diffuse" (such as in the United States) and do not give rise to rents or are "point source" (such as phosphates in Morocco) that give rise to rents. The resulting group, POINT source (43 countries, 8 MENA countries), is large and includes half of the MENA countries, including Egypt.

Fourth, to analyze "income mobility" (that is, changes in income category through sustained growth), we include MENA countries in the World Bank's four-group classification: low-income (L), lower-middle-income (LM), upper-middle-income (UM), and high-income (H) categories in an extended sample that also includes Organisation for Economic Co-operation and Development (OECD) countries (but excludes the former socialist countries of Europe and Central Asia). The list of countries in each grouping is given in appendix table A1 at the end of this book.

a. This three-group classification was introduced in World Bank (2004, chapter 2).
b. The GCC was founded in 1981. Regional integration picked up around 2000, with a quasi-common market status achieved in 2008.
c. The objective of this classification is to capture the idea that natural riches produce institutional weaknesses (the "voracity effect" associated with the attempt at rent-capture by different social groups; see Tornell and Lane 1999). Point source natural resources such as oil, minerals, and plantation crops are extracted from a narrow economic base while "diffuse" natural resources are extracted from a large base. While this voracity effect extends to all sources of rents (natural monopolies, foreign aid, nontariff barriers, financial elites), over the long haul, it makes sense to include a classification of countries along this dimension.

available, the observation of a shrinking share of services in nonmining GDP over time is confirmed. In contrast, the share of services in nonmining GDP in resource-poor countries is either increasing or stagnant. Figure 1.3 illustrates this contrast, with the share of services in nonmining GDP declining in Saudi Arabia and Kuwait but increasing in Tunisia and Jordan.

In oil-rich MENA, the mining sector is large and has gotten bigger in relative size over time, suggesting that diversification away from oil is still an elusive goal. In 2010, mining accounted for 37 percent of GDP (up from 28 percent in 1990), 85 percent of merchandise exports, and between 65 percent and 95 percent of government revenues (90–95 percent in the six GCC countries and 60–80 percent in non-GCC resource-rich countries). The size of the mining sector in resource-rich economies of the region is largest in the GCC, where it represents almost half of GDP (48 percent). This high concentration of production is

Figure 1.3   Share of Services in Nonmining GDP

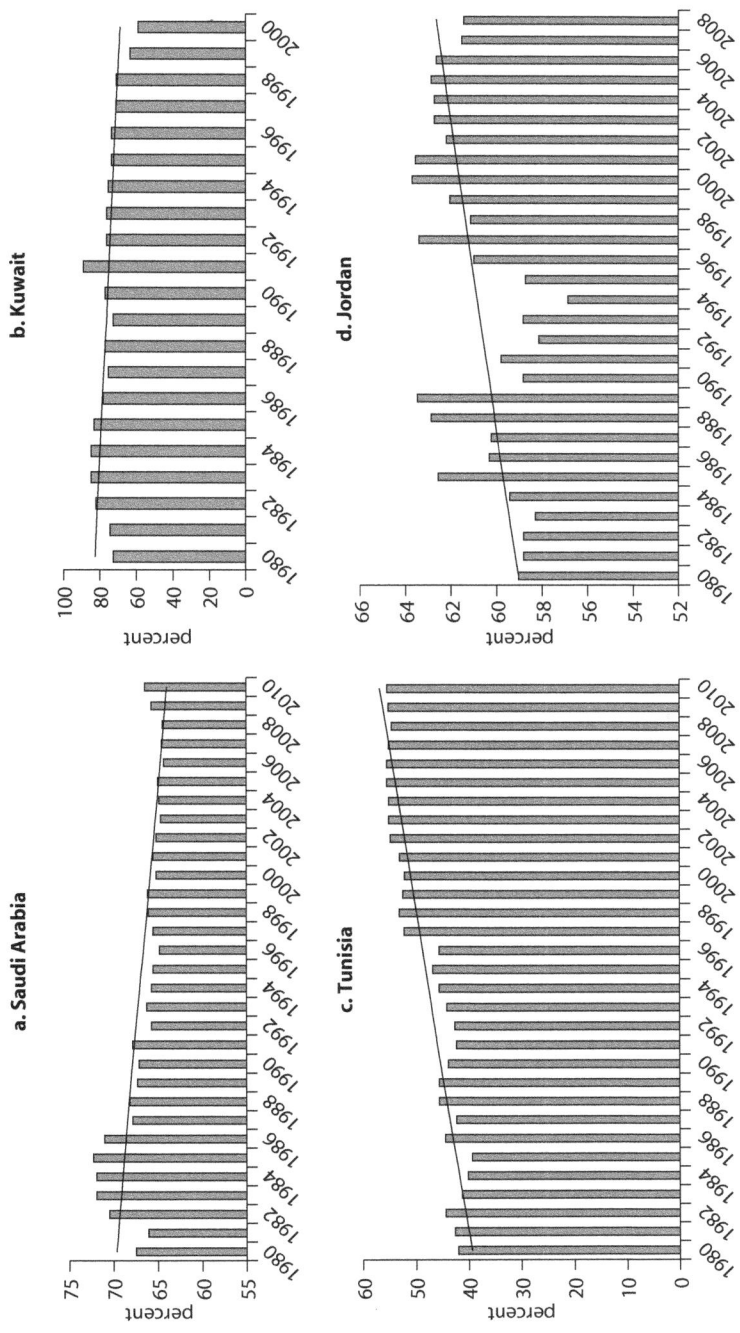

a. Saudi Arabia

b. Kuwait

c. Tunisia

d. Jordan

Source: World Development Indicators.
Note: Data for Kuwait are not available afer 2000.

reflected in the composition and dynamics of exports. Figure 1.4 shows that export diversification across MENA countries in 1998–2008 occurred through exports of existing processed and primary industrial products (oil-related) to existing markets. More specifically, export growth in resource-rich MENA was driven by exports of existing processed and industrial goods (mainly crude and refined oil) to existing and new markets mainly in Asia, the European Union (EU), and within the GCC. Product diversification (export of new products) occurred exclusively within the industrial sector. For resource-poor MENA, export growth was driven by existing primary and processed industrial goods as well as by consumer goods to existing markets mostly in Europe. The

Figure 1.4   Drivers of Export Growth (Excluding Oil Products), 1998–2008

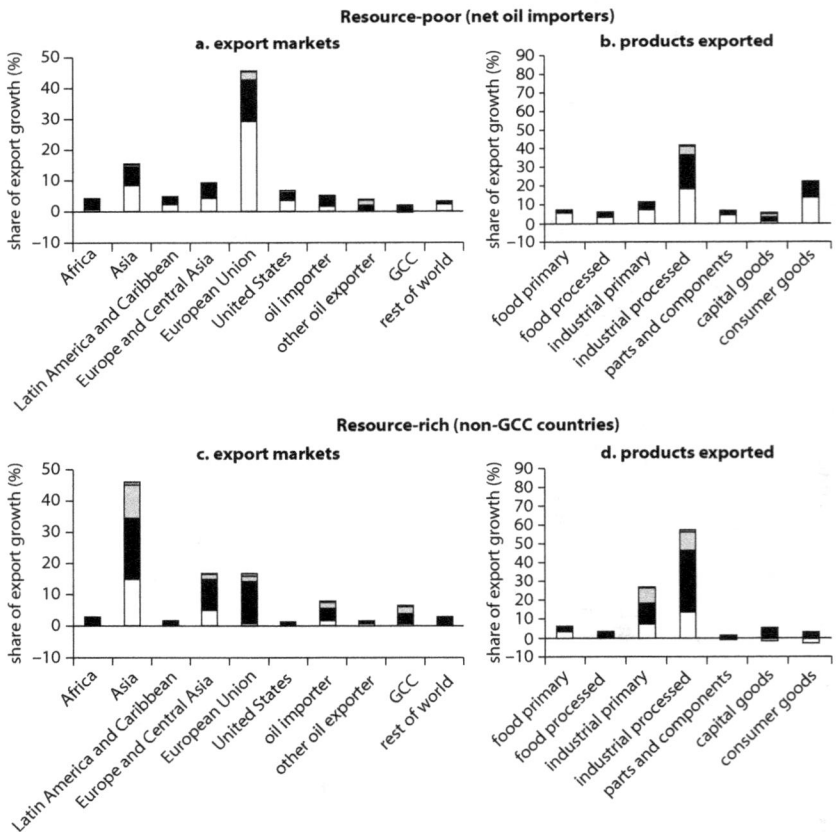

(continued next page)

Figure 1.4 *(continued)*

Resource-rich (GCC countries)

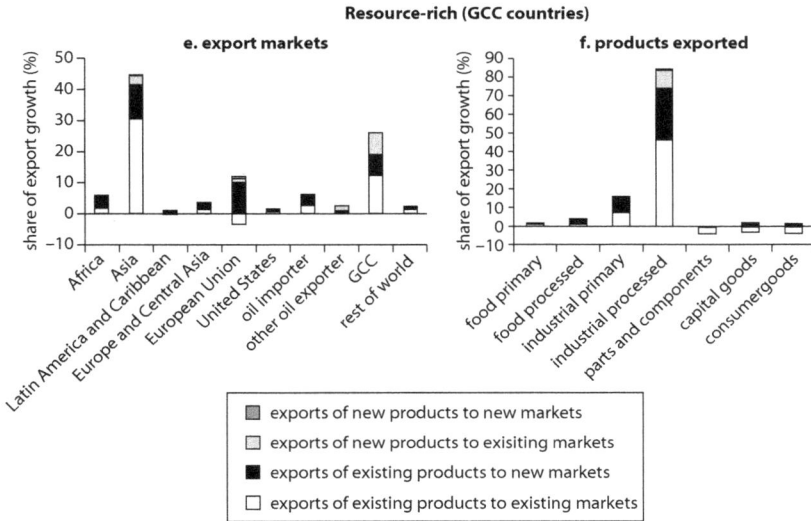

e. export markets

f. products exported

- ☐ exports of new products to new markets
- ☐ exports of new products to exisiting markets
- ■ exports of existing products to new markets
- ☐ exports of existing products to existing markets

Source: Staff calculations based on Comtrade.

extent of growth in exports of new products was limited both in sectors and in markets (mostly to MENA oil exporters and the EU).

Limited Diversification, Natural Resource Rents, and Growth Volatility

A mirror image of the overdominance of the oil and gas sector in MENA is the very large share of natural resource rents in GDP compared with other regions. In 2010, rents from natural resources reached 24 percent of GDP in MENA, against about 14 percent in Sub-Saharan Africa and Eastern Europe and 5–7 percent in East Asia, South Asia, and Latin America and the Caribbean (figure 1.5).[3]

MENA's natural resource dependence also induces large, oil-price-driven fluctuations of production and growth.[4] Indeed, MENA's growth exhibits the highest level of volatility among the regions of the world (figure 1.6). The volatility of growth in the six members of the GCC is twice as high as the volatility in the other resource-rich MENA countries (Algeria, Islamic Republic of Iran, Iraq, Libya, Syrian Arab Republic, and Republic of Yemen) and four times as high as in the resource-poor countries of the region.[5] Compared to the rest of the world, the volatility in growth in the

Figure 1.5   Natural Resource Rents in 2010, by Region

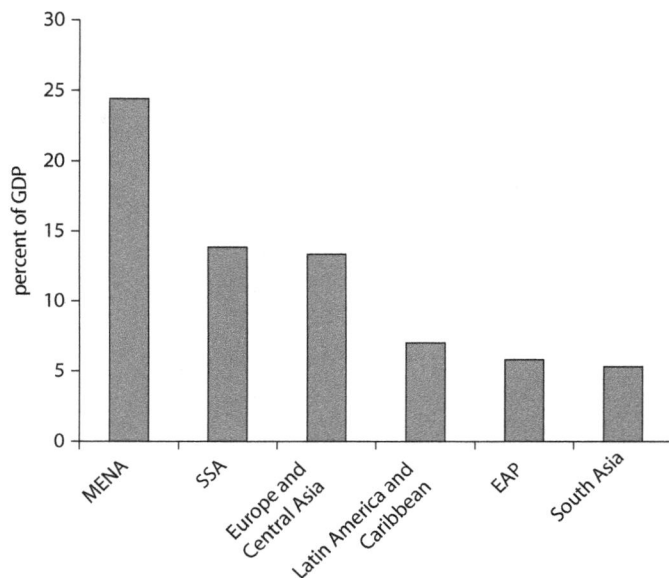

Source: World Development Indicators.

GCC and other resource-rich MENA countries is higher than that observed across all other World Bank income classification groups (except the low-income group) in 1982–2010. Likewise, MENA oil exporters' volatility is higher than that of the world's other major oil exporters.

Output volatility is bad for long-term growth and diversification, in part because reversals in growth trends are sharper and more frequent. Volatility also is bad for investment and capital accumulation and may harm productivity growth. In a recent paper, Furth (2010) finds that differences in terms of trade volatility account for 25 percent of the cross-country variations in growth from 1980 to 2007. Using a broad sample of countries from 1960 to 2000, Aghion et al. (2009) find negative growth effects of terms of trade volatility, measured in five-year periods, under fixed exchange rate regimes. Ramey and Ramey (1995) link higher output growth rate volatility to lower average output growth. Consistently, MENA trails significantly behind East Asia and South Asia in its long-term per capita growth. Between 1980 and 2010, MENA grew by a mere 1.3 percent a year in per capita terms, compared to 4 percent in South Asia and 6.9 percent in East Asia.

Figure 1.6   Growth Volatility, by Region

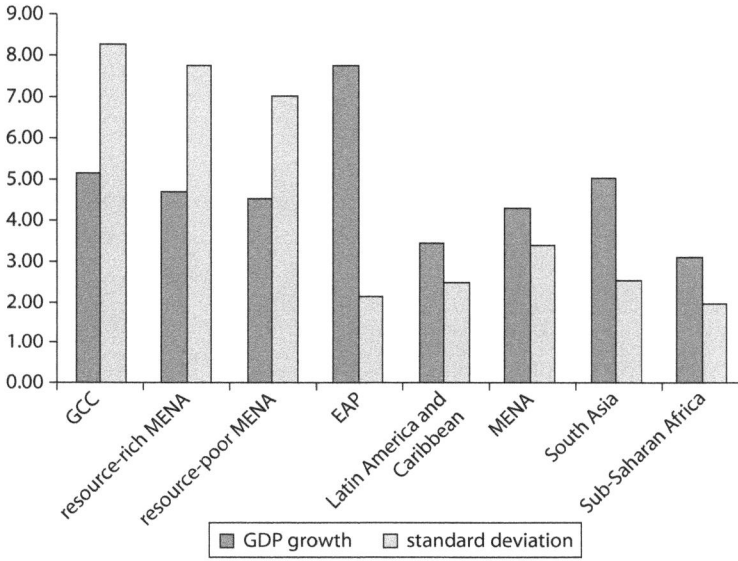

Source: World Development Indicators.
Note: Growth volatility is measured as the standard deviation of GDP per capita growth in 1970–2008.

The link with diversification is straightforward. As shown by McMillan and Rodrik (2011), growth requires both new activities and ongoing structural changes. MENA's slow growth implies that the expansion of new activities or structural change, or both, is limited. Asia's high growth is both a cause and a consequence of its structural shift from agriculture (where productivity is low) to services and manufacturing (where productivity is higher).

Why Is Greater Diversification Desirable in MENA?

Many reasons motivate countries' drive for diversification. One key objective is job creation. For countries abundantly endowed with natural resources, diversification away from resource-based sectors is crucial to widen the scope for job creation. In natural-resource-rich countries of MENA, arable land and water are scarce, and agriculture is expected to remain a minor source of labor absorption. The public sector, the largest employer in the region (29 percent of total employment), has reached a saturation point in almost every MENA country. Going forward, rapid job creation will have to come from the private sector. Thus for resource-rich MENA countries, finding ways to develop manufacturing and services sectors is crucial for widening the scope of job creation.

Another rationale for greater diversification is to reduce macroeconomic volatility. Indeed, as noted, the concentration of activities in resource-rich MENA is associated with volatility; so the natural policy response has been to push for export diversification. Empirically, Di Giovanni and Levchenko (2008) and Loyaza et al. (2008) show for instance that export concentration is associated with greater volatility of the real exchange rate, which in turn is associated with greater volatility in GDP growth. A higher concentration of activities and volatility of the real exchange rate can also be a channel for a resource curse (Lederman and Maloney 2008; Hausmann and Rigobon 2002). The latter can undermine long-term growth through various channels: if large rents are generated by few activities, the ensuing "easy life" can lead to lower investment in human capital, contributing to less learning and innovation (Gylafson 2001); macroeconomic volatility (Hausmann and Rigobon 2002); institutional weaknesses as groups attempt to capture rents (Mehlum, Moene, and Torvik 2006); corruption in nondemocratic contexts (Bhattacharya and Hodler 2010); and possibly conflicts (Collier and Hoeffler 2004).[6] Finally, as discussed later, if real exchange rates become overvalued, they undermine tradable manufacturing and services.

For natural-resource-poor countries where economic activities are less concentrated, diversification is often seen as an important ingredient in sustaining long-term growth. Strong empirical evidence shows that diversified economies perform better over the long term (Lederman and Maloney 2007). Some authors suggest that countries can increase their growth rate through externalities associated with diversifying into products where learning by doing is large (Matsuyama 1992) or into "rich-country products," that is, more sophisticated products (Hausmann, Hwang, and Rodrik 2007). Rodrik (2011a, 2011b) argues that manufacturing industries generally produce goods that can be rapidly integrated into global production networks, facilitating knowledge transfers and adoption. The "monkey-tree" argument put forth by Hidalgo et al. (2007) is similar: some products, such as electronics or mechanics, tend to be exported along with a large range of different products; in contrast, other commodities, such as oil, tend to be exported alone. This is because the skills and assets used to produce many manufacturing products can be much more easily deployed in a large range of other manufactures than those used to extract oil, for instance.

Thus diversifying into manufacturing may open up more possibilities for boosting exports through the "extensive margin," that is, exports of new products as opposed to exporting the same products more intensively or through "intensive margin." In turn, this diversification is associated with greater economies of scale and opportunities to reap the benefits of global integration thereby boosting long-term growth.

This volume intends to shed light on the causes and consequences of limited diversification in MENA (and thus growth) and to identify potential policy remedies. Much of the recent literature on the determinants of MENA's economic performance has focused on weaknesses in the areas of private sector development and trade integration. Although the limited dynamism of the private sector and integration to the global economy are important, they are not the whole story. Natural resource management and macroeconomic policies also play a decisive role in the economy through their impact on the incentive framework and the overall environment for private sector activity. In examining diversification, the volume does not focus on diversification within the resource sector (such as moving from oil extraction to natural gas and petrochemical) but, rather, on diversification toward manufacturing and services, where the scope for creating jobs is the highest in most countries. An explicit attempt to capture MENA's diversity in resource abundance and market size is also made throughout this volume.

The Role of Rents and Real Exchange Rates

At the macrolevel, growth and diversification in most MENA countries were impaired by frequent overvaluation of the real exchange rate (RER). The importance of the real exchange rate—the relative price of tradables to nontradables ($RER = P_T/P_N$)—in the growth process cannot be underestimated. It operates directly by increasing the relative profitability of tradables, which in turn is associated with higher growth (Prasad, Rajan, and Subramanian 2007; Rodrik 2009). As Rodrik argues, it also operates indirectly by helping compensate for market failures and poor governance (in rule of law, property rights, or contract enforcement), which undermine the competitiveness of tradable sectors in developing countries. A key example is the penalty arising from weak institutions that result in lower appropriability of returns to investment in tradables. Investment in tradable sectors depends more on these governance and institutional factors. An increase in the relative price of tradables therefore boosts the competitiveness of the tradable sector at the margin, contributing to higher growth.

MENA countries have experienced a sustained undervaluation of their real exchange rates, as shown by an event analysis, discussed in chapter 2, that identifies the systematic events preceding growth accelerations. This approach is particularly useful for developing countries, where growth patterns are much less stable than those portrayed in the standard growth models.[7] In an event analysis study, Hausmann, Pritchett, and Rodrik (2005) analyzed 83 growth episodes over the period 1957–1992, using the Penn World Tables.[8] Of the 83 episodes, 8 were from the MENA region (years in parenthesis): Algeria (1975), Egypt (1976), Jordan (1973), Morocco (1958), Tunisia (1968), and Syria (1969, 1974, and 1989). Hausmann, Pritchett, and Rodrik found that compared with the seven years before the growth episode, the acceleration period was correlated with increases in investment and trade shares in GDP and a sharp depreciation of the real exchange rate. Investment and trade (imports and exports) shares of GDP were close to 15 percent higher before the acceleration period, and contributed up to one-fifth of the growth acceleration. Rodrik (2009, figure 10) shows that around the event year when acceleration starts, the RER is undervalued by around 20 percent, and that undervaluation lasts throughout most of the decade following the start of the growth acceleration. The event analysis literature thus points to the importance of trade for growth and of the RER for the growth of trade, particularly of manufactures.

Between 1980 and 2010, the real exchange rates in MENA were overvalued frequently in a large number of countries, and there is evidence that this overvaluation has hurt MENA's competitiveness in manufacturing. In Morocco, Oman, Saudi Arabia, and Syria, the RER was overvalued most of the time during the period of analysis.[9] Overvaluation was much more widespread during the first periods, with the number of countries with overvalued RER peaking at 13 of 17 during the 1980–85 period and dropping to 5 of 17 in the 2000–05 period. In any case, since the early 1970s, no MENA country experienced a period of 10 consecutive years of undervaluation. MENA countries do not exhibit the kind of undervaluation (or lack of overvaluation) identified with extended past growth episodes found to be critical in sustaining growth acceleration around the world. Importantly, strong evidence shows the presence of a Dutch Disease phenomenon that undermines the competitiveness of the manufacturing sectors in MENA's resource-rich economies and even a few resource-poor ones (such as Morocco), as discussed in chapter 2 and in Havrylyshyn (2010) and Lopez-Calix, Walkenhorst, and Diop (2010).

Natural resource rents and RER overvaluation have undermined MENA's services sectors as well. The analysis in chapter 3 suggests that the declining share of services in the nonmining GDP of resource-rich countries is linked to the large rents generated by natural resources in those countries. At first sight, this finding appears paradoxical. Indeed, that domestic service sectors can be developed in resource-rich countries has been taken as granted for a long time. This belief was underpinned by at least two combined theoretical considerations. First, Engel's Law effects in consumption imply that demand for services tends to increase with income because of higher income elasticity of demand for services relative to agricultural products (Chenery and Syrquin 1975; Chenery, Robinson, and Syrquin 1986). At the same time, services sectors— implicitly assumed to be largely nontradable in earlier Dutch Disease models—would be positively affected by an appreciation of the real exchange rate subsequent to a natural resource boom (Corden and Neary 1982; Corden 1984).

While Engel's consumption effects do operate in resource-rich MENA (see chapter 3), the largely nontradable status of services implicit in the earlier Dutch Disease literature is no longer valid. A large number of services sectors have now become "off-shorable" or can be produced by temporary movement of service providers, implying that countries need to be competitive to maintain domestic production. Rents from natural resources tend to inflate wages and prices of nontradables in resource-rich countries, thereby raising the real exchange rate and discouraging domestic production of tradable goods and services. This explains why resource-rich MENA countries have become large importers of tradable services and why only domestic production of nontradable services (such as real estate, retail trade, hotels, and restaurants) has really developed.

Unfortunately, microeconomic regulations on business have tended to compound the problem, rather than compensate for it. Restrictions on business entry, licensing, and business conduct are indeed significant and correlate negatively with the share of services in GDP. The MENA region, in particular the resource-rich countries, stands out for heavy and discretionary restrictions on services sectors compared with the rest of the world. These restrictions either create rents within the services sector that are captured by "protected incumbents" or increase the real cost of producing services—in both cases inflating the price of services and further reducing competitiveness of tradable services sectors.

It is therefore recommended that resource-rich economies strive to reduce production costs and to offset the negative effect of rents on production in the nonresource tradable sectors. This can be achieved by reducing regulatory restrictions on entry and competition in these sectors. Experience from resource-rich countries around the world also shows the importance of investing in human capital and strengthening institutions (see Gelb 2011 for a summary). Finland, the Republic of Korea, and Norway are examples of countries that have invested to build a high-quality human capital base and have successfully diversified into high-tech manufacturing and services. Similarly, strong evidence shows that institutions matter for diversification. Gelb (2011, 67) argues that manufacturing sectors are "heavily dependent on strong contract enforcement, a rule of law and generally strong business environment." These arguments equally apply to services, if not more strongly so. Institutions that prevent or reduce rent seeking are also important, as the example of Botswana shows (Acemoglu, Johnson, and Robinson 2005).

If the increased tradability of services makes it challenging for resource-rich MENA to maintain domestic production of services, it offers formidable opportunities to resource-poor countries of the region. Indeed, given their cultural proximity and common language, these countries are well placed to capture a share of the large and growing market of tradable services in resource-rich MENA. To capture these opportunities, however, resource-poor countries will need to undertake autonomous reforms to improve their competitiveness and work with resource-rich countries to reduce barriers to labor mobility within the region. More specifically, they will need to reduce their own restrictions to entry and competition in professional services, improve their backbone services (such as telecom and transport), and proactively engage resource-rich countries in reducing barriers to trade and mobility through specific bilateral agreements.

The Role of Weak Links in Output Concentration

An influential paper by Imbs and Wacziarg (2003) suggests a U-shaped relationship between economic development and economic concentration. At early stages of development, economic concentration falls as income per capita rises, but starts increasing once income per capita reaches a certain threshold (around $10,000, according to Imbs and Wacziarg). This U-shaped relationship is confirmed by recent evidence by Carrere, Strauss-Kahn, and Cadot (2009) for export diversification.

MENA contradicts this empirical regularity. Chapter 4 empirically confirms, for MENA, an *inverted U-shaped* relationship between income per capita and concentration: at early stages of development, economic concentration increases with income per capita and only starts falling with income per capita at relatively high levels of economic development. More specifically, MENA countries start to diversify only after GDP per capita reaches $17,000 to $22,000. Since most MENA countries are below this income threshold, concentration of production is the most common pattern observed in the region—in contrast with what is observed, on average, in the rest of the world.

To explain these differences in the development process, two alternatives have been tested. MENA is a resource-rich region and subject to Dutch Disease–type phenomena (à la Corden and Neary 1982). It is also a region where some sectors have notoriously low levels of productivity, and these weak links (Jones 2011) can lead not only to lower levels of growth but also to a higher concentration of production. It was found that weak links contribute to a more concentrated production bundle than the Dutch Disease does. Moreover, after controlling for these two variables, the differences in development patterns between MENA and the rest of the world become smaller.

The weak link argument is recent. Jones (2011) extends Hirschman's "linkage" concept[10] and shows that complementarities in production and linkages between sectors can lead to either multiplier or weak link effects. When the links are weak, low productivity in one sector can reduce productivity throughout the economy depending on the degree of substitutability among inputs. In situations with low substitutability, weak links will result in a less diversified production bundle as downstream sectors are hurt by higher input prices and factor prices.

This result has some interesting policy implications, at least in terms of the timing of industrial policy reforms. Policies aimed at diversifying the production process should first try to address the region's weak links. Otherwise resources may be wasted in trying to diversify into sectors that are not economically viable. Although more research is needed in this area, the findings in this volume suggest that if governments first address the existing weak links in their economy, diversification may naturally follow. If addressing weak links may sometimes seem like a daunting task requiring large infrastructure investments with a long-term objective, it is important to note that one characteristic of weak links is that they are nontraded goods. If there is an easily imported substitute, then the low productivity of the domestic input sector is no longer a drag on growth. Thus, when restrictive trade policies are the ones limiting the tradability of input sectors, liberalization may be sufficient to address those weak links. Liberalization of input sectors for easier access to imported inputs or greater efficiency of domestic inputs is important for addressing weak links and encouraging diversification.

Fiscal Policy and Output Concentration

Beyond rents, Dutch Disease, and weak links, has fiscal policy played a role in the poor record of diversification of MENA? This question is not trivial, since fiscal policy can affect diversification through several channels. For instance, today's investments in education and core infrastructure are crucial for tomorrow's private sector capacity and return on investment. Consistently, fiscal management and the composition of public expenditures matter. If public finance is tied up by high subsidies and short-term public consumption, fiscal space for investing in human capital and infrastructure may be limited. At the same time, large expenditures on subsidies, in particular on energy, tend to distort investment incentives in favor of energy- and capital-intensive sectors, at the expense of labor-intensive industries. Finally, fiscal policy can adversely affect diversification if it crowds out private investment, or if private investment is discouraged when fiscal policy generates or is unable to manage volatility.

Taking a historical view, fiscal policy in the MENA region has not contributed significantly to diversification, because it has been more oriented toward food and fuel subsidies (consumption) than toward public goods such as infrastructure (investment), which has historically been neglected in most MENA economies. Much of government expenditure in MENA has historically gone to fuel and food subsidies that—while keeping prices low—have had little impact on the poor because of ineffective targeting mechanisms. In Saudi Arabia and the United Arab Emirates, subsidies represent 8 percent of GDP. Subsidies are generally not well targeted, making them a costly way to protect the poor. For instance, in Jordan, where the top two deciles capture 40 percent of the subsidies for food and fuel, the government spends 5 dinars to channel 1 dinar of subsidy to the poor (Coady, El Said, and Flamini 2011).

Although higher public investment in infrastructure and education would theoretically be good for diversification, existing literature finds a weak and short-lived relationship between public spending and private investment in MENA. For instance, Agenor, Nabli, and Yousef (2005) find that public infrastructure expenditure has had a small and short-lived impact on private investment in Egypt, Jordan, and Tunisia. Chapter 5 shows that gross fixed capital formation in the private sector seems more closely correlated with the environment for private investment than with any metric of government capital spending. In Egypt, from 1982 to 2009, there was a secular decline in investment expenditure by the state, but an increase in private capital. In Jordan, the relationship between public and private capital is similarly ambiguous, leading to difficulty in finding any significant correlation. Overall, there seems to be little empirical evidence for either crowding in or crowding out over the long run, but there may be particular spending in individual countries that can play a catalytic role. In brief, there is no evidence that MENA's limited output diversification is driven by a lack of public investment.

Further, another challenge with fiscal policy in MENA has been a lack of transparency and accountability in most economies. In the wake of the recent oil boom in the GCC countries, there has been an impressive buildup of sovereign wealth funds (SWFs), which have helped mitigate deficits and cushion these countries through crises. The overall assets of the SWFs are estimated to be more than $1.3 trillion. Overall, while the details of the SWF stocks are not publicly available, the available estimates suggest that the Abu Dhabi Investment Authority has more than $600 billion and Saudi Arabia has more than $400 billion (the Saudi fund is technically a monetary account and not an SWF).[11] However, it must be noted that these funds suffer from a lack of accountability and transparency, in part a reflection of the lack of clear fiscal rules and open governance structures among the GCC countries. Truman (2007) finds that many wealth funds, particularly in the MENA region, involve large official holdings of cross-border assets, which are often unknown to the citizens of the countries and to market participants. In a similar vein, Elbadawi and Soto (2011) find that the resource-rich but largely democracy-deficient MENA region has been a fiscal-rules-free region, and that fiscal rules can be valuable fiscal stabilization instruments, especially with the nascent democracies demanding more accountability. A more open approach to information on the SWFs will increase the accountability and transparency of these revenues.

The long-term challenge for the MENA region is to ensure that fiscal policy is used to promote growth and diversification. The GCC countries will need to implement policy reforms to accelerate non-oil growth and create sustained employment opportunities for a rapidly increasing labor force. For oil importers in the Mashreq and Maghreb, reorientation of public expenditure from subsidies that do not aid the poor to both conditional cash transfers and effective public investment programs must be encouraged. Through fiscal policy targeted toward infrastructure, MENA countries can help lay the foundation for successful diversification.

Natural Resources and Incentives for Regional Trade Reforms

As noted, the MENA region contains both resource-rich and resource-poor countries. At the same time, as recently argued by Venables (2009), the proximity of resource-rich and resource-poor countries gives an opportunity to even out wealth distribution within the group of countries through regional integration. Indeed, the resource-poor countries have a strong incentive for preferential trade liberalization with their resource-rich counterparts next door, as a way to get access to the rents. However, this can be done only at the cost of trade diversion in the resource-rich country, with a loss of efficiency there. This would imply that integration between the resource-rich labor-importing and the resource-rich labor-abundant countries might be beneficial only for the resource-poor labor-abundant group of countries in MENA.

Chapter 6 tests this hypothesis by looking at the extent to which economic diversification is achieved at the expense of trade diversion and consequently of broader economic efficiency among RRLI and RPLA countries of MENA. The main prediction of Venables (2009) is that the resource-rich countries are more likely to experience trade diversion. This prediction is supported by data for MENA that show a decline in non-oil imports from the rest of the world of around 38 percent in the case of resource-rich members of the Pan Arab Free Trade Area, and no trade diversion at all in the case of resource-poor countries.[12] Resource-rich countries of MENA generally export only a few products and have a highly concentrated export bundle.

Hence, while further intraregional trade integration is an important avenue for enhancing diversification of resource-poor MENA countries, resource-rich countries have no strong incentive, from a purely economic standpoint, for further preferential regional integration. This may explain their relative reluctance to engage in this type of scheme. Future discussions of regional trade agreements should take this into account. In this context, trade liberalization on a most-favored-nation (MFN) basis may be the best option for furthering global integration.

In conclusion, several policy recommendations emerge from this volume. First, policy makers in the region should strive to avoid real exchange rate overvaluation through consistent fiscal policies, flexible exchange rates, and adequate product and factor market regulations. Overvalued real exchange rates often lead to Dutch Disease and undermine the competitiveness of the non-oil tradable activities in the manufacturing and tradable services sectors. Countries with an export-oriented growth model, in particular, should pay attention to the trend in their real exchange rates. Further, MENA is bound to remain a large consumer of services because of its financial wealth from natural resource extraction. But the worldwide revolution in technology, transportability, and tradability that has occurred over the past 20 years has made a large number of services tradable. What proportion of the services consumed in MENA will be produced locally and what proportion will have to be imported now depends on competitiveness factors, of which the real exchange rate is an integral part. Reforms aimed at reducing regulatory restrictions that constrain business activities in most services sectors are equally crucial.

Second, reforms aimed at reducing competition barriers in upstream input industries are crucial to prevent real exchange rate overvaluation and boost diversification. Indeed, there is strong evidence that weak links act to constrain production in MENA. Competitiveness hinges in part on the ability to purchase good-quality inputs at the lowest cost possible. China's competitiveness, for example, is based in part on the availability of a large domestic input market. Because weak links hurt only when the inputs are imported at a high cost, trade liberalization for easier access to imported inputs is as important as fostering domestic competition for greater efficiency of domestic inputs.

Further, countercyclical fiscal policies are needed to reduce instability and create a favorable environment for diversification. There is no fiscal rule in any country of MENA. Discretion is the rule, due to a lack of political incentives or institutions that impose constraints on policy makers. Therefore, fiscal policy has been procyclical most of the time in most MENA countries and certainly in all resource-rich ones since the early 1970s. It will be crucial for MENA countries to develop institutional mechanisms that constrain fiscal policy discretion. In the resource-poor countries, reforms aimed at creating fiscal space to invest in core infrastructure and human capital will be equally crucial for enabling diversification. Indeed, in these countries, public finances are tied up by large subsidies and short-term consumption expenditures, resulting in limited fiscal space to invest in growth-enhancing areas.

Finally, while regional trade integration is desirable for political, social, cultural, and economic reasons, an MFN liberalization (that is, a liberalization of trade vis-à-vis all countries) is the best option for resource-rich countries of the region. Indeed, these countries have little incentive for a preferential liberalization because it leads to trade diversion.

Notes

1. The term Dutch Disease refers to the adverse effects on Dutch manufacturing of the natural gas discoveries of the 1960s, essentially through the subsequent appreciation of the Dutch real exchange rate

2. Engel's Law was introduced by Ernest Engel in 1857.

3. Box 2.1 in chapter 2 summarizes the literature on political economy of rents in general and in MENA in particular.

4. Burnside and Tabova (2009) show that five global risk factors, including three commodity price indexes, and country-specific exposure to each factor can account for 70 percent of the variation in growth volatility.

5. The GCC was formed in May 1981 to encourage policy coordination, integration, and unity among the member states. An explicit attempt to capture MENA's diversity in resource abundance and market size is made throughout this volume.

6. Brunschweiler and Bulte (2009) contest this result, suggesting that conflict increases dependence on resource extraction (captured by the share of primary exports), while resource abundance (measured by resource stocks) is associated with a reduced probability of civil war.

7. Event analysis refers to a situation when the data is reordered around an "event," which serves as the base year rather than the usual calendar year. In Hausmann, Pritchett, and Rodrik (2005), data is centered around the year when the event (growth acceleration) occurred. Jerzmanowski (2006) also studies extreme growth events using a Markov-switching model that distinguishes four different growth regimes and finds that institutional quality helps determine the transition between these states. His study does not focus on regions, however, so it is not helpful in detecting a MENA specificity.

8. Growth episodes are defined as an increase in GDP per capita growth of at least 2 percentage points for an eight-year period, with a postacceleration growth of at least 3.5 percent a year.

9. Estimates for Lebanon and Iran reflect periods of conflict.

10. In a classic work, Hirschman (1958) developed the concepts of backward and forward linkages and analyzed their importance for economic growth. In his own words: "The setting up of an industry brings with it the availability of a new expanding market for its inputs whether or not these inputs are supplied initially from abroad." This enhanced market exerts a backward pressure for establishing industries that supply the new entrants. He calls this process *backward* linkage effects. Similarly, forward linkage effects are created when one industry uses another industry's outputs as its inputs. The sum of the two linkage effects gives the total linkage effect, which can be seen as the growth in new industries induced from establishing an industry.

11. These buildups in the SWFs have been aided by unprecedented and relatively high oil prices, which have persisted since the 2008–09 financial crisis. Currently, at more than $100 a barrel in mid-2012, the price levels are much higher than the $35–50 price range assumed by the GCC authorities during the budget planning process.

12. The Pan-Arab Free Trade Agreement was signed in 1996 and entered into force in 1998. It was signed by Bahrain, Egypt, Iraq, Jordan, Kuwait, Lebanon, Libya, Morocco, Oman, Qatar, Saudi Arabia, Syria, Tunisia, United Arab Emirates, and Republic of Yemen.

References

Acemoglu, D., S. Johnson, and J. Robinson. 2005. "Institutions as a Fundamental Cause of Long-Run Growth." In *Handbook of Economic Growth*, vol. 2, ed. P. Aghion and S. Durlauf, 385–472. Amsterdam: North-Holland.

Agenor, P-R., M. K. Nabli, and T. Yousef. 2005. "Public Infrastructure and Private Investment in the Middle East and North Africa." Policy Research Working Paper 3661, World Bank, Washington, DC (July).

Aghion, P., P. Bacchetta, R. Rancire, and K. Rogoff. 2009. "Exchange Rate Volatility and Productivity Growth: The Role of Financial Development." *Journal of Monetary Economics* 56 (4): 494–513.

Amin, M., and S. Djankov. 2009. "Democracy and Reforms." Policy Research Working Paper 4835, World Bank, Washington, DC.

Baumol, W. J. 1967. "Macroeconomics of Unbalanced Growth: The Anatomy of Urban Crisis." *American Economic Review* 62 (June): 415–26.

Bhattacharya, S., and R. Hodler. 2010. "Natural Resources, Democracy and Corruption." European Economic Review 54 (4): 608–21.

Brunnschweiler, C., and E. Bulte. 2009. "Natural Resources and Violent Conflict: Resource Abundance, Dependence and the Onset of Civil Wars. " *Oxford Economic Papers* 61 (4): 651–74.

Burnside. C., and A. Tabova. 2009. "Risk, Volatility, and the Global Cross-Section of Growth Rates." Working Paper 15225, National Bureau of Economic Research, Cambridge, MA.

Carrère, C., V. Strauss-Kahn, and O. Cadot. 2009. "Trade Diversification, Income and Growth: What Do We Know?" CERDI Working Paper E 2009.31, Centre d'Etudes et de Recherche sur le Développement International, Clermont-Ferrand, France.

Chenery, H., S. Robinson, and M. Syrquin, eds. 1986. *Industrialization and Growth: A Comparative Study*. Oxford, U.K.: Oxford University Press for the World Bank.

Chenery, H., and M. Syrquin. 1975. *Patterns of Development, 1950–1970.* Oxford, U.K.: Oxford University Press for the World Bank.

Coady, D., M. El Said, and V. Flamini. 2011. "Welfare Impact of Price Subsidy Reform in Jordan." International Monetary Fund, Washington, DC (September).

Collier, P., and A. Hoeffler. 2004. "Greed and Grievance in Civil War," *Oxford Economic Papers* 56 (4): 563–95.

Corden, W. M. 1984. "Booming Sector and Dutch Disease Economics: Consolidation and Survey." *Oxford Economic Papers* 36: 359–80.

Corden, W. M., and J. P. Neary. 1982. "Booming Sector and De-Industrialisation in a Small Open Economy." *Economic Journal* 92 (368, December): 825–48.

Di Giovanni, J. and A. A. Levchenko. 2008. "Trade Openness and Volatility." IMF Working Papers, International Monetary Fund, Washington, DC (June).

Diwan, I., and L. Squire. 1993. "Economic Development and Cooperation in the Middle East and North Africa." MENA Discussion Paper 9, World Bank, Washington, DC.

Elbadawi, I. A., and R. Soto. 2011. "Fiscal Regimes In and Outside the MENA Region." Documentos de Trabajo 398, Instituto de Economia. Pontificia Universidad Católica de Chile.

Freund, C., and B. Bolaky. 2008. "Trade, Regulations, and Income." *Journal of Development Economics* 87 (2, October): 309–21.

Furth, S. B. 2010. "Terms of Trade Volatility and Precautionary Savings in Developing Economies."

Gelb, A. 2011. "Economic Diversification in Resource Rich Countries." Center for Global Development, Washington, DC, www.imf.org/external/np/seminars .eng/2010/afrfin/pdf/GELB2.pdf.

Gylafson, T. 2001. "Natural Resources, Education and Economic Development." *European Economic Review* 45 (6): 847–59.

Hausmann, R., J. Hwang, and D. Rodrik. 2007. "What You Export Matters." *Journal of Economic Growth* 12 (1): 1–25.

Hausmann, R., L. Pritchett, and D. Rodrik. 2005. "Growth Accelerations." *Journal of Economic Growth* 10 (4): 303–29.

Hausmann, R., and R. Rigobon. 2002. "An Alternative Interpretation of the Resource Curse." Working Paper 9424, National Bureau of Economic Research, Cambridge, MA.

Havrylyshyn, O. 2010. "Does the Global Crisis Mean the End of Export-Led Open-Economy Strategies?" Paper prepared for World Bank Trade Department, Washington, DC.

Hidalgo, C. A., B. Klinger, A. L. Barabási, and R. Hausmann. 2007. "The Product Space Conditions the Development of Nations." *Science* 317 (5837): 482–87.

Hirschman, A. 1958. *The Strategy of Economic Development.* New Haven, CT: Yale University Press.

Hoekman, B. 1995. "The World Trade Organization, the European Union and the Arab World: Trade Policy Priorities and Pitfalls." CEPR Discussion Papers 1226, Centre for Economic Policy Research, London.

Imbs, J., and R. Wacziarg. 2003. "Stages of Diversification." *American Economic Review* 93 (1): 63–86.

Jerzmanowski, M. 2006. "Empirics of Hills, Plateaus, Mountains and Plains: A Markov-Switching Approach to Growth." *Journal of Development Economics* 81 (2): 357–85.

Jones, C. 2011. "Intermediate Goods and Weak Links in the Theory of Economic Development." *American Economic Journal: Macroeconomics* 3 (April): 1–28.

Lederman, D., and W. Maloney, eds. 2007. *Natural Resources, Neither Curse nor Destiny.* Stanford, CA: Stanford University Press.

Lederman, D., and W. Maloney. 2008. "In Search of the Missing Resource Curse." *Economia* (Journal of the Latin American and Caribbean Economic Association) 9 (1):1–51.

Lopez-Calix, J., P. Walkenhorst, and N. Diop, eds. 2010. *Trade Competitiveness of the Middle East and North Africa.* Washington, DC: World Bank.

Matsuyama, K. 1992. "Agricultural Productivity, Comparative Advantage and Economic Growth." *Journal of Economic Theory* 58 (2): 317–34.

McMillan, M., and D. Rodrik. 2011. "Globalization, Structural Change and Productivity Growth." Working Paper 17143, National Bureau of Economic Research, Cambridge, MA.

Mehlum, H., K. Moene, and R. Torvik. 2006. "Institutions and the Resource Curse." *Economic Journal* 116 (508): 1–20.

Nabli, M. 2004. "Jobs, Growth and Governance in MENA: Unlocking the Potential for Prosperity." World Bank, Washington, DC.

Nabli, M., et al. 2007. "Job Creation in a High Growth Environment: The MENA Region." MENA Working Paper 49, World Bank, Washington, DC.

North, D., J. J. Wallis, and B. R. Weingast. 2009. "Violence and Social Orders." Cambridge, U.K.: Cambridge University Press.

Prasad, E., R. Rajan, and A. Subramanian. 2007. "Foreign Capital and Economic Growth." *Brookings Papers on Economic Activity* 2007 (1): 153–209.

Ramey, G., and V. A. Ramey. 1995. "Cross-Country Evidence on the Link between Volatility and Growth." *American Economic Review* 85 (5, December): 1138–51.

Rodrik, D. 2009. "Growth after the Crisis." CEPR Discussion Paper 7480, Centre for Economic Policy Research, London.

———. 2011a. "The Future of Economic Convergence." Working Paper 17400, National Bureau of Economic Research, Cambridge, MA.

———. 2011b. "Unconditional Convergence." Working Paper 17546, National Bureau of Economic Research, Cambridge, MA.

Shafik, N. 1995. "Claiming the Future: Choosing Prosperity in the Middle East and North Africa." World Bank, Washington, DC.

Tornell, A., and P. R. Lane. 1999. "The Voracity Effect." *American Economic Review* 89 (1): 22–46.

Truman, E. 2007. "SWF: The Need for Greater Transparency and Accountability." Policy Brief, Peterson Institute for International Economics, Washington, DC.

Venables, A. J. 2009. "Economic Integration in Remote Resource Rich Regions." OxCarre Working Papers 022, Oxford Centre for the Analysis of Resource Rich Economies, University of Oxford, Oxford, U.K.

WEF (World Economic Forum) and OECD (Organisation for Economic Co-operation and Development). 2005. "Arab World Competitiveness Report, 2005." Geneva: WEF.

World Bank. 2004. "Trade, Investment, and Development in the Middle East and North Africa: Engaging with the World." World Bank, Washington, DC.

———. 2009. *From Privileges to Competition.* Washington, DC: World Bank.

CHAPTER 2

Resource Abundance and Growth: Benchmarking MENA with the Rest of the World

Jaime de Melo and Cristian Ugarte

The years 1995–2006 were for the Middle East and North Africa (MENA) a period of catching up to the rest of the world. During this period, export growth, excluding minerals and fuels, was higher in MENA than in the average developing country, leading to an increase in market share despite strong competition from Asia. MENA countries were also catching up along other dimensions, expanding the reach of export markets at a greater pace than competitors in Europe and Central Asia and East Asia and the Pacific. A catching up on the policy front took place as well, as protections—which started from higher averages than competitors—fell more rapidly than elsewhere, with the region's average applied tariff rate (the most-favored-nation, or MFN, rate) falling by a third during 2000–07, to 15 percent. Finally, this trade growth performance has been consistent with MENA's improved growth performance over the past 15 years. Growth increased from an average 3 percent in 1995 to 6 or 7 percent in the mid-2000s.

Has MENA's performance led to structural income change and mobility across the region (such as movement from low-income to high-income categories)? How much have policy, an abundance of natural resources, and luck driven MENA's recent performance? Have macroeconomic and microeconomic underpinnings of growth improved significantly? This chapter attempts to respond to these questions. It shows that MENA's recent good trade and growth performance should be analyzed against the backdrop of a generally disappointing performance over the past 50 years, especially for the resource-rich countries. This poor performance explains the slow structural change occurring in the region.

The next section of this chapter benchmarks MENA's growth and volatility performance against a large number of comparator developing countries over the past 50 years, distinguishing MENA countries by their abundance of natural resources. MENA's growth performance is first examined from an income mobility perspective; that is, whether growth has been strong and long lasting enough to lift MENA countries up the income ladder over time. To complement this analysis, MENA's performance is examined from the perspective of volatility. Overall, the section shows that although resource-poor MENA countries were at par with comparator groups except the high-growing Asian countries, MENA overall has failed to climb up the ladder, remaining either in the lower-middle- or in the upper-middle-income group (with the exception of Oman).

The chapter then examines the key macroeconomic correlates of MENA's long-term growth performance. The first part of this section builds on the "event analysis" literature,[1] which shows that for developing countries, sustained growth is accompanied by growth in trade and investment, which is preceded by a strong and sustained depreciation of the real exchange rate. Indeed, in developing countries, maintaining equilibrium or an undervalued real exchange rate often helps offset the market failures and poor institutional environment that undermine the competitiveness of non-resource-intensive tradable sectors. In the case of MENA, an estimation of equilibrium real exchange rates (RERs) in 1970–2005 shows that RERs were marginally overvalued for most of the time in most countries. This finding is consistent with the natural resource curse (Dutch Disease) thesis.

This chapter and the supporting evidence show that the combination of macro- and micropolicies in a generally weak institutional environment has produced this outcome. At the macrolevel, MENA countries have been unable to maintain a depreciated (undervalued) real exchange rate for long periods, which may be explained on distributional grounds. The region, but especially the resource-rich group, displayed greater volatility in macro-indicators than comparable groups until the middle 1990s, when performance started to pick up. For example, the Gulf Cooperation Council (GCC) countries, as well as the wider resource-rich group, adopted fewer countercyclical fiscal policies than did other resource-rich countries with comparable external shocks. As a result, the greater volatility of the real effective exchange rate in these MENA countries contributed to the lack of development of new activities outside the resource sectors, and to short-lived export spells.

Cross-country evidence shows that the positive correlation between openness and per capita income holds only for countries with good values for regulatory reform indicators. The Doing Business data also show that countries rich in natural resources are less inclined to carry out reforms than others. Despite some progress toward reducing tariffs on industry, MENA countries fare poorly in most indicators describing the domestic microeconomic environment, giving the impression of an environment in which trade is not facilitated and of an unfinished reform agenda. Improved domestic regulatory policies along with improved public sector governance, as reflected in better indicator values, would help MENA to achieve greater integration in the world economy.

Benchmarking MENA's Long-Term Growth and Volatility

In this section. Mena's growth performance is benchmarked against several comparator groups on to two main aspects of an economy: income mobility, or its ability to grow fast and climb up the development categories, and exchange rate and macroeconomic stability.[2]

Low-Income Mobility

From the 1960s to the mid-1980s, the region's growth model was government led, featuring high public spending and protected national markets. This growth strategy was mainly financed by high oil revenues in resource-rich countries, and workers' remittances and public borrowing in resource-poor countries. Figure 2.1 shows the trend of GDP (gross domestic product) growth rates over the longest period possible for a large sample of countries.[3] Two patterns stand out: on average, the resource-poor group performed as well as the resource-rich group within MENA. And, as expected, the resource-poor group experienced less growth volatility during the oil shocks of the 1970s and early 1980s than the resource-rich group.

Beyond these observations, one should note that for about 50 years, all MENA countries belonged to either the lower-middle- (LM) or the

Figure 2.1   MENA Long-Run Growth Performance

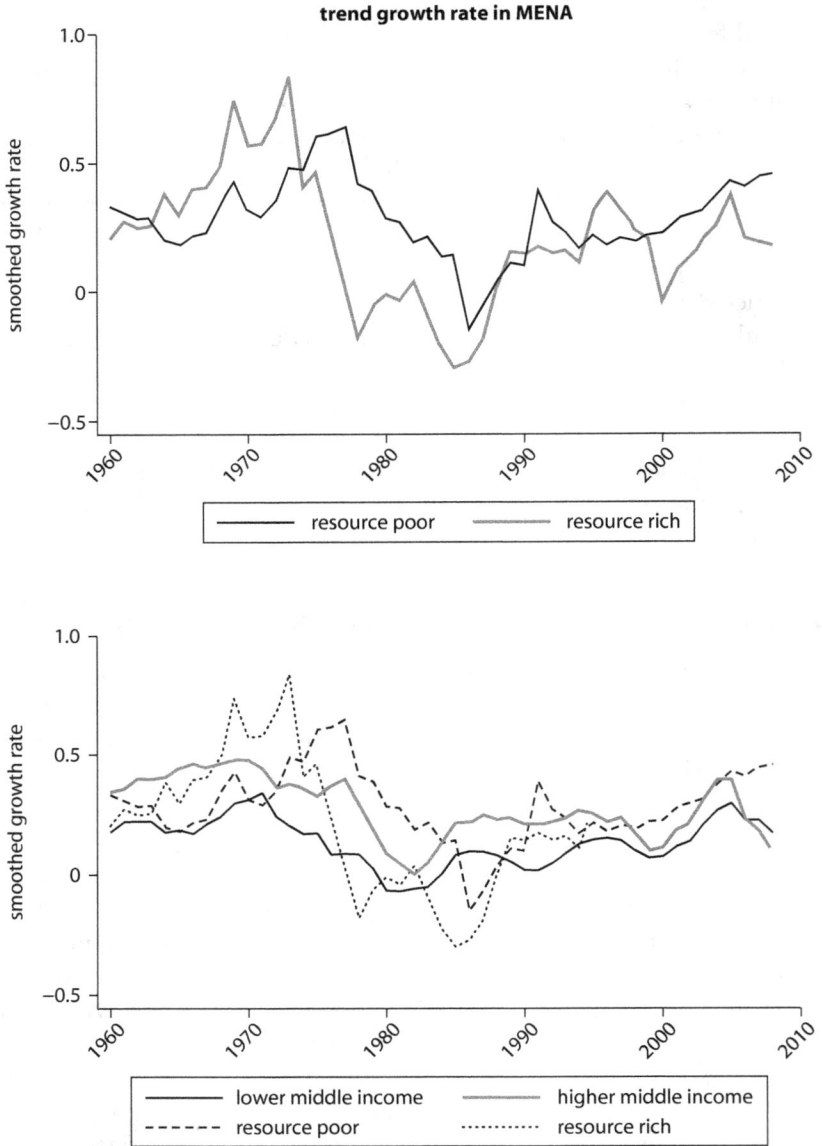

Source: Authors' calculations using WDI data.
Note: Sample is a five-year moving average of the growth rate.

upper-middle-income (UM) group (except for what is now the Republic of Yemen after 1982). Figure 2.1b compares the trend performance of MENA countries broken down into resource-poor and resource-rich groups, with the average growth for the samples of lower-middle-income (44) and upper-middle-income (25) countries. This comparison confirms the growth volatility of both resource-poor and resource-rich MENA compared with the UM and LM groups, but especially for the resource-rich MENA grouping. However, this greater growth volatility may result partly from the small sample size and the greater commonality of shocks in the resource rich and poor groups relative to the two larger samples.

Because of the large amount of missing data for several countries, table 2.1 takes a shorter time period, starting in 1982, using complete gross national income (GNI) series for 12 MENA countries. In table 2.1, MENA's performance is compared with that of 115 countries over the

Table 2.1   Per Capita Income Mobility, 1982–2010

1982↓	1996→	L	LM	UM	H	Total (1982)
L		16 (0/1/0) (YEM)				16 (0/1/0)
LM		19	23 (0/0/3) (EGY, MAR, TUN)	3		45 (0/0/3)
UM			8 (0/3/1) (DZA, IRN, SYR, JOR)	13 (1/0/0) (OMN)	5	26 (1/3/1)
H				1 (1/0/0) (SAU)	27 (2/0/0) (ARE, KWT)	28 (3/0/0)
Total (1996)		35 (0/1/0)	31 (0/3/4)	17 (2/0/0)	32 (2/0/0)	115 (4/4/4)
1996↓	**2010→**	**L**	**LM**	**UM**	**H**	**Total (1996)**
L		22 (0/1/0) (YEM)	13			35 (0/1/0)
LM			17 (0/1/4) (SYR, EGY, JOR, MAR, TUN)	14 (0/2/0) (DZA, IRN)		31 (0/3/4)
UM				12	5 (2/0/0) (OMN, SAU)	17 (2/0/0)

(continued next page)

Table 2.1   *(continued)*

1982↓ | 1996→	L	LM	UM	H	Total (1982)
H				32	32
				(2/0/0)	(2/0/0)
				(ARE, KWT)	
Total (2010)	22	30	26	37	115
	(0/1/0)	(0/1/4)	(0/2/0)	(4/0/0)	(4/4/4)

Source: Authors' calculations using WDI data.

Notes: All data are from the World Development Indicators and refer to gross national income (GNI) per capita data. The thresholds used in classifying countries by income level are those defined by the World Bank for 1982, 1996, and 2010. Former members of the Commonwealth of Independent States are excluded. In parenthesis, the number of countries in each cell belonging to the three country groups considered for MENA are in the following order: GCC (ARE, KWT, OMN, SAU); R-R (DZA, IRN, SYR, YEM); and R-P (EGY, JOR, MAR, TUN). Reading across a row gives the number of countries in the corresponding row at the beginning of period and down the corresponding column the number of countries at the end of the period. So there were 28 H countries in 1982 and 32 in 1996. The bottom of the table shows that of the 31 countries in the LM group in 1996, 14 moved to the UM group while 13 from the L group joined the LM group. Country abbreviations in this table and other tables and figures in this chapter are the three-digit ISO country codes.

period 1982–2010, split into two 14-year periods. Countries are classified into four income groups according to the World Bank's classification system: LM, UM, low income (L), and high income (H). The 12 MENA countries account for 10 percent of the sample of 115 countries.[4] Table 2.1 shows a clear underperformance of MENA countries. In the resource-poor group, no country moved up the ladder over the 28-year period, and one country, Jordan, moved down from UM to LM status.[5] Among the resource-rich group, two countries, Algeria and the Islamic Republic of Iran, moved down from UM to LM, but reverted to their original status in the second period. The Syrian Arab Republic descended from UM to LM status, and the Republic of Yemen remained in the low-income group.

Looking at the whole sample, one sees regression during the first subperiod (the "lost decade of the 1980s"), with 28 countries below the diagonal (implying movement down the income-group ladder). The second period shows a large improvement, with more than one-third of the countries in the L group moving up to the LM group, close to half moving from LM to UM status, and no country moving down the ladder.

For MENA countries, two patterns emerge during this 28-year time span. First, during 1982–96, 5 of the 28 countries that regressed were from the MENA region, which is twice as large as the share of MENA in the sample. Second, during the 1996–2010 period of higher growth, of the 32 countries that moved up a notch, only 4 came from MENA, again revealing underperformance. In sum, in both subperiods MENA countries underperformed, although MENA's performance improved in the post-1995 period compared with its own historical performance.

High Growth Volatility and High Real Exchange Rate Volatility

In addition to low levels of growth and no upward income mobility, MENA's growth exhibits a high level of volatility, again especially in the pre-1996 period. Table 2.2 shows two measures of volatility (coefficient of variation of growth and real effective exchange rate, REER) for MENA compared with a large number of developing-country income groups.[6] With an average annual growth rate of 1.4 percent, MENA underperformed relative to all but the low-income classification group in 1982–2010, with the Gulf Cooperation Countries and resource-rich groups mostly accounting for the poor performance (column 1). Despite the presence of high performer Oman in the GCC, the poor performance of this group stands out during the period. As discussed below and in chapter 5, the region's difficulty in managing volatility has contributed to lower growth.

The comparisons with the LARGE, OIL, and POINT groups in the bottom of the table confirm this picture. Populous countries in MENA

Table 2.2   Growth and Its Volatility, 1982–2010

Indicators	Mean growth[a] (1)	Coefficient of variation[b] (2)	Mean change in growth[c] (3)	REER volatility[d] (4)
(A) GNI per capita 1982				
Low (20)	2.03	2.99	4.55	49.46
Lower middle (52)	0.96	5.00	3.31	35.34
Upper middle (32)	1.90	2.36	3.63	21.44
High (33)	1.86	1.52	1.93	8.71
(B) GNI per capita 2010				
Low (24)	0.76	8.11	4.18	45.15
Lower middle (38)	1.72	3.62	3.72	33.96
Upper middle (32)	1.96	2.81	3.99	22.15
High (43)	2.24	1.87	2.44	11.12
MENA (17)	1.40	4.76	4.78	52.20
GCC (6)	0.51	11.31	4.59	27.48
Resource rich (6)	1.37	5.58	5.29	110.41
Resource poor (5)	2.28	2.81	4.50	23.66
MENA vs. comparators[e]				
LARGE (33)	2.04	2.44	3.15	46.49
LARGE MENA (6)	1.32	5.55	5.05	74.01
OIL exporters (6)	1.17	5.59	4.46	46.72

(continued next page)

Table 2.2 *(continued)*

Indicators	Mean growth[a]	Coefficient of variation[b]	Mean change in growth[c]	REER volatility[d]
	(1)	*(2)*	*(3)*	*(4)*
MENA OIL exporters (10)	0.97	7.23	4.82	65.79
POINT (34)	0.95	5.82	4.19	45.32
POINT MENA (10)	1.54	4.07	4.65	65.30

Source: Authors, using data from WDI Indicators.

Notes: Rows (A) and (B) give the composition of income groupings for the two definition years (1982 and 2010), with the classification in row B reflecting the outcome of the mobility during the period. The L group has a much lower growth according to the latter classification because it includes all the failed states that moved down the ladder during the period. Equally, the difference in the mean growth for the L and LM groups in rows A and B reflects the mobility shown in table 2.1, where nearly half (19) of the LM group joined the L group during the first period and one-third (13) moved up from L to LM status over the second period. The Commission for Growth identified 13 countries with stellar performance over the period since 1960. Oman is in that group.

a. Mean growth is the average growth rate over the period 1982–2010, that is, approximately 28 observations per country resulting in sufficiently large samples to give significantly different mean growth rates in each sample.

b. Standard deviation divided by the mean.

c. Mean change is the absolute mean change in growth rates observed between two years.

d. The standard deviation of the monthly real effective exchange rate is computed over the period 1980–2010. The sample is not exactly the same as those for columns 1 to 3.

e. See appendix A for a list of countries included in the comparator groups.

(more than 20 million) showed lower growth and higher volatility than the comparator LARGE group. Likewise, growth is lower and volatility is higher when the comparison is with the OIL group, where this time the two samples are of the same size. It is only when MENA countries are compared with the heterogeneous sample of POINT source countries, which includes many failed states, that MENA outperforms its comparator group with higher average growth and less volatility.

Columns 2 and 3 of table 2.2 show high growth volatility for MENA driven by the two groups of oil exporters (GCC and MENA OIL exporters), while the resource-poor group has low growth volatility. Particularly striking is the high volatility of growth in the GCC group, which is twice as high as volatility in the resource-rich group and four times as high as in the resource-poor group. This high volatility is confirmed in the detailed decomposition of growth volatility reported by Koren and Tenreyro (2010).[7] They show that in the GCC, the idiosyncratic component of volatility, which is large and mostly unavoidable in resource-rich countries, is no larger than the country-specific component of volatility, which reflects aggregate domestic policy. Being pegged to a currency (the special drawing rights for all countries except the

Omani, whose rial is pegged to the U.S. dollar) implies that the GCC countries have relinquished the use of monetary policy for stabilization purposes, potentially increasing volatility. Koren and Tenreyro (2010) also show that compared both with other countries at the same per capita income level, and also with a smaller group with high export shares of oil and gas products in total exports, the GCC group is an outlier along several dimensions of volatility, including the nonuse of countercyclical fiscal policy.[8]

Finally, column 4 reports the standard deviation of the REER over the period across the different country groupings. As expected, REER volatility falls as per capita income increases. Among MENA countries, the resource-rich and the GCC groups have much less volatility than the resource-poor group. Nonetheless, volatility is still three times higher than for the high-income group. Also, when the comparison is across the other three groupings (LARGE, OIL exporters, and POINT source), MENA countries always have a higher REER volatility than the comparator group. This suggests that the fundamentals of sound fiscal and monetary policies—a prerequisite for sustained performance—have been largely missing in the MENA region over the past 30 years.

Volatility of the REER can also hamper the development of non-resource-based activities. Gelb (1988) and others studying the resource curse argue that this volatility has resulted in a "volatility-induced inefficient specialization" pattern. Hausmann and Rigobon (2003) even suggest that volatility produces a vicious cycle. A volatile REER raises uncertainty and makes investments in nonresource tradables unattractive, leading to a concentrated export basket in the resource-based sector, which then causes volatility in the real exchange rate.

Table 2.3 describes a breakdown by decades of REER volatility for individual countries in MENA. REER volatility has fallen continually over the period. Taking REER volatility as a first approximation for instability (the REER should be flexible to maintain external balance, so this is not strictly a measure of macroeconomic instability), MENA countries improved in each of the past two decades compared with the 1980s, when no country in the region was in the bottom quartile, and half the group of MENA countries were in the fourth quartile. The GCC countries had low volatility in the 1990s and 2000s along with Morocco (and Tunisia in the 1990s). Except for the Arab Republic of Egypt (and conflict-torn Lebanon), all the countries with high volatility (beyond the interquartile range) are resource-rich countries, indicating another specificity for that group.

Table 2.3   Real Effective Exchange Rate Volatility by Period

Volatility	1980–89 (standard deviation)		1990–99 (standard deviation)		2000–10 (standard deviation)	
High	Syrian Arab Republic	(120.5)	Iran, Islamic Rep.	(52.6)	Libya	(97.9)
	Iran, Islamic Rep.	(116.5)	Libya	(46.1)	Egypt, Arab Rep.	(26.6)
	Libya	(66.2)	Algeria	(31.8)	Iran, Islamic Rep.	(21.9)
	Algeria	(66.2)	Egypt, Arab Rep.	(24.5)	Lebanon	(14.2)
	Oman	(38.7)	Lebanon	(23.0)	Bahrain	(13.9)
	Tunisia	(32.7)			United Arab Emirates	(5.6)
Low	0		Morocco	(5.3)	Jordan	(5.5)
			Tunisia	(1.9)	Kuwait	(5.3)
					Morocco	(3.5)
Mean	26.0		15.7		11.7	
Interquartile range	[7.3–32.7]		[5.3–18.8]		[5.8–13.4]	

Source: Authors' calculations using IMF data.
Notes: The standard deviation of the monthly real effective exchange rate from the IMF's International Financial Statistics data for each period is used as the measure of volatility for a sample of 16 countries over the period 1980–2010. High (low) volatile countries are those having a standard deviation higher (lower) than the third (first) quartile of values observed across countries. Extremely volatile countries (standard deviation higher than 200) were excluded from the sample.

Correlates of MENA's Growth Performance

A key focus of the empirical growth literature in recent years has been to capture the prerequisites for sustained growth acceleration. What are the characteristics of growth acceleration episodes? Are they similar across countries in the world? And have MENA countries experienced them?

Event analysis is useful to identify these characteristics, particularly for developing countries where growth patterns are much less stable than those portrayed in the standard growth models. In an early event analysis, Hausmann, Pritchett, and Rodrik (2005) studied 83 growth episodes over the period 1957–1992 using the Penn World Tables (PWT).[9] Of the 83 episodes, 8 (event years in parenthesis) were from MENA: Algeria (1975), Egypt (1976), Jordan (1973), Morocco (1958), Tunisia (1968), and Syria (1969, 1974, 1989). They found that compared with the previous seven years before the growth episode, the acceleration period was correlated with increases in investment and trade shares in GDP and a sharp depreciation of the real exchange rate of more than 20 percent. Investment and trade (imports and exports) shares in GDP were close to 15 percent higher than they were before the acceleration period, contributing up to one-fifth of the growth acceleration.

Using the same Penn data, Jones and Olken (2008) also studied the extremes of growth and collapse events using structural break techniques for time series data. They found an asymmetry between up and down breaks: growth collapses feature sharp reductions in investment in the midst of price instability, while growth take-offs are associated with large expansions in international trade (the latter finding is similar to that of Hausmann et al. 2005). Jones and Olken identified 73 breaks (30 up and 43 down) in 48 of the 125 countries with at least 20 years of data. Among these, 4 occurred in MENA.[10]

Real Exchange Rate Depreciation and Growth Acceleration
The event analysis literature thus points to the importance of trade for growth and of the RER for the growth of trade, particularly of manufactures. At the macrolevel, the importance of the RER—the relative price of tradables to nontradables (RER = P_T/P_N)—in understanding growth operates directly and indirectly: directly by increasing the relative profitability of tradables, which in turn is indirectly associated with higher growth (Rajan and Subramanian 2007; Rodrik 2008).[11]

Since undervaluation of the real exchange rate has been characteristic of growth accelerations,[12] we examine whether MENA country RERs are more often undervalued or overvalued. Following Rodrik (2008), the equilibrium RER over the period 1970–2005[13] was estimated using the latest PWT 7.0 tables, taking five-year averages for a panel of eight periods (country and period fixed effects included).[14] We obtain:

$$\ln RER = 1.35 - 0.09 \ln GDP_{PC} \quad R^2 = 0.12 \quad (2.1)$$
$$\underset{(15.5)\quad(-9.5)}{}$$

So a 10 percent increase in income is accompanied by close to a 1 percent fall (that is, appreciation) of the equilibrium RER.[15] Following Rodrik (2008), we take the log of the difference between the actual RER and the one estimated in equation 2.1, so that a positive (negative) value implies undervaluation (overvaluation), with a zero value for the indicator corresponding to an equilibrium RER.

The results for MENA are reported in table 2.4, where column 1 gives the average deviation over the periods (from five to eight depending on the country), and column 2 gives the percentage of periods with overvaluation

Table 2.4   Deviations from Estimated Equilibrium Real Exchange

Country	Mean deviation of the RER in percentage	Percentage (number) of periods with overvaluation
GCC		
Bahrain (8)	4.7	50 (4)
Kuwait (5)	0.6	80 (4)
Oman (8)	−18.1	63 (5)
Qatar (5)	10.4	20 (1)
Saudi Arabia (5)	−9.0	80 (4)
United Arab Emirates (5)	6.4	20 (1)
Resource rich		
Algeria (8)	−9.0	75 (6)
Iran, Islamic Rep. (8)	13.3	25 (2)
Iraq (8)	2.7	63 (5)
Libya (5)	−1.9	60 (3)
Syrian Arab Republic (8)	−17.9	63 (5)
Yemen, Rep. (5)	6.1	40 (2)
Resource poor		
Egypt, Arab Rep. (8)	9.4	50 (4)
Jordan (8)	−2.4	63 (5)
Morocco (8)	−24.3	100 (8)
Tunisia (8)	−1.4	63 (5)

Source: Authors' calculations using PWT and WDI data.
Note: Residuals from equation 2.1: A negative value in column 1 means an overvalued RER on average during the whole period (up to eight five-year periods 1970–2005). In 1970, 7 of 11 countries with data had an overvalued RER; in 1985, 13 of 17 countries; and in 2005, 5 of 17.

for each country. Most countries are overvalued about half the time, while a few countries (Morocco, Oman, Saudi Arabia, and Syria) are overvalued most of the time.[16] Further, except for the Islamic Republic of Iran and the Republic of Yemen, the estimates suggest that resource-rich countries are overvalued for most periods. Also, overvaluation was much more widespread during the early periods, peaking with 13 of 17 overvalued during 1980–85 and dropping to 5 of 17 in the last period (2000–05).

Referring to his previous work on growth accelerations discussed above, Rodrik (2008, figure 10) shows that, around the event year when acceleration starts, the RER is undervalued by around 20 percent and that this undervaluation lasts throughout most of the decade following the start of the growth acceleration. Figure 2.2 traces the deviation of MENA countries from the estimated relation in equation 2.1 for one year, 1985 with two lines showing the 20 percent limit. It is clear that the distribution of observations outside the band is on the bottom of the figure, indicating significant overvaluation. We checked whether any country

Figure 2.2   Estimated Equilibrium Real Exchange Rates

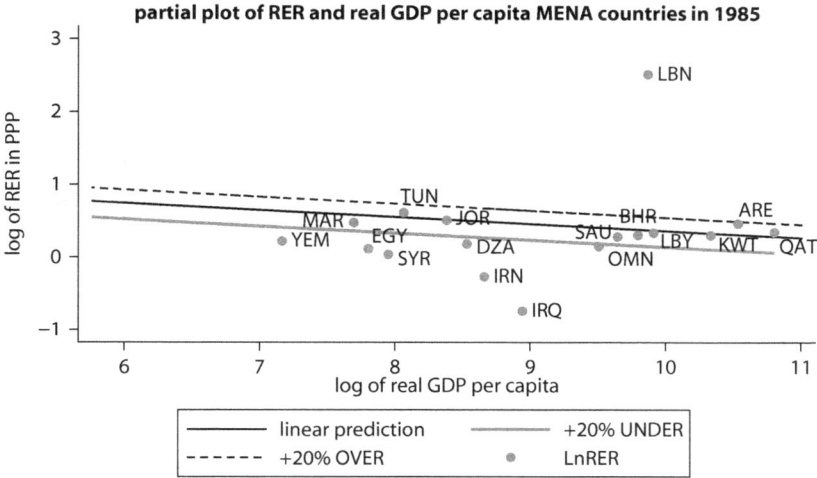

partial plot of RER and real GDP per capita MENA countries in 1985

Source: Authors' calculations using PWT and WDI data.
Note: Partial plot of estimates in equation 2.1 Points under the line indicate overvaluation of the RER relative to the PPP (purchasing power parity) equilibrium prediction.

had two adjacent episodes (that is, 10 years of undervaluation), but that was never the case. MENA countries do not exhibit the kind of under-valuation identified with extended past growth episodes.

If an overvalued RER is a penalty for manufacturing and for a dynamic services sector, this should show up in comparisons of MENA's shares of manufactures and services relative to other countries at similar income levels. Chapter 3 estimates predicted shares in both cross-section and panel. It turns out that dummy variables for MENA countries are never significant when total exports are considered (so MENA's openness accords with the norm). When sector shares are considered, however, the sizes of the manufacturing and service sectors in the economy diverge markedly from the estimated shares in both cross-section and panel esti-mates. In the resource-rich labor-abundant (RRLA) group, the manufac-turing and services sectors are undersized, and their export shares in these sectors are also lower than predicted. However, this association is muted when the share of rents in GDP is taken into account, suggesting the presence of the resource curse syndrome, as widely discussed in the lit-erature on growth in MENA (box 2.1).

If an undervaluation of the real exchange rate is found to precede and to be associated with episodes of significant export growth, one should

Box 2.1

MENA in the Natural Resource Curse Literature

The manifestations of the natural resource curse are perhaps the most invoked reason give for the overall underperformance of the Middle East and North Africa (MENA) in the past 50 years (see, for example, World Bank 2004, chap. 2). Three channels for the deleterious effects of natural resource abundance have been emphasized. First, natural resources are often concentrated in sectors that may be associated with lower productivity growth and fewer spillovers. Second, natural resources are often extracted from a narrow economic base ("point source" sectors—see below), giving rise to rents. These rents and the ensuing "easy life" for the elite in turn are associated with lower investment in human capital, contributing to less learning and innovative capacity (Gylafson 2001). These aspects are central to the Dutch Disease aspect of the curse, whereby manufacturing (and tradable services) activities are depressed through an appreciated real exchange rate during resource booms, which is exacerbated when, during busts, countercyclical fiscal policies are not operative and exchange rate policies are rigid.[a] Third is the high level of export concentration leading to higher price volatility and hence to macroeconomic volatility.[b] However, this vulnerability to changes in a country's terms of trade is not particular to natural resource abundance but more to a country's overall openness to trade.[c]

These channels have been explored in a vast cross-sectional growth literature. Early findings revealed a robust negative conditional correlation between growth and the share of primary exports. More recent contributions have pointed out the weaknesses of the early estimates, relying on trade-based proxies (that is, primary exports measured by the share of oil and minerals in total exports) for relative endowments (Lederman and Maloney 2008). These proxies are outcome variables that reflect resource dependence rather than resource abundance and, as such, do not capture resource abundance, resulting in a lack of resource curse effects when better proxies for resources (such as "resource stocks") are used (see the critique in Lederman and Maloney 2007, 2008). Moreover, case studies of high growth rates by resource-abundant countries (Botswana, Indonesia, and Oman, to name a few) cast doubt on the early findings, a conclusion that also appears in this chapter in the mobility analysis.

Less easily apprehended is a fourth channel by which natural riches engender institutional weaknesses as groups attempt to capture rents (Mehlum, Moene, and Torvik 2006). This curse-via-politics is largely endogenous to the political

(continued next page)

Box 2.1 *(continued)*

environment and not likely to be improved by governments in power that have a vested interest in blocking institutional change.[d] Resource riches can also be the cause of conflicts.[e]

In the Arab world, curse-via-politics effects could have been important, but this channel has probably been operative in the destiny of nations before the ascendance of oil in the world economy. It is striking that the MENA region was a powerful engine of progress through several millennia, mostly through trade (World Bank 2004, box 3.1), and that it was the most technologically advanced region of the world about 1,000 years ago, just about the time that Islamic legal institutions were introduced. Five hundred years later, that technological leadership was erased, and the Arab region lagged behind both Western Europe and China, a decline that has continued ever since.[f]

Several studies have uncovered a positive correlation between natural resources (proxied by resource rents or the share of exports of fuels and minerals) and an index of corruption (Isham et al. 2005; Leite and Weidman 2002 in cross-section). However, Bhattacharya and Hodler (2010) show that this correlation becomes negative when the sample is split into democratic and nondemocratic groups, thereby justifying why some resource-rich countries such as Canada, Iceland, and Norway have avoided the curse. With panel data covering the period 1980–2004, Isham et al. (2005) show that the relationship between natural resources and corruption depends on the quality of democratic institutions, the curse applying only in nondemocratic environments.

Insofar as the inertia in MENA's institutions is linked to deep-rooted legal developments, there might be a MENA "specificity" on the institutional side. Two other pieces of recent evidence are relevant to the natural resource curse and reforms. Freund and Bolaky (2008) relate business regulations to per capita income over a large sample of 126 countries in which all 12 MENA countries in the sample are among the 50 percent most regulated economies. They find that increased trade is positively correlated with income only for countries that are among the 50 percent least regulated, indicating that domestic policies that impede factor mobility blur the positive relation between trade openness and income. This finding supports the policy prescription that trade and regulatory reform are complementary and should go hand-in-hand. Given the multiple possibilities for regulatory capture in high-rent environments, this may explain why all the MENA countries in the sample are in the most regulated group. Drawing on the Doing Business data for a large sample of 133 countries, Amin and Djankov (2009) find

(continued next page)

Box 2.1 *(continued)*

that the proclivity to undertake microreforms that reduce regulation is much lower in countries whose exports are concentrated in abundant natural resources.

a. The Dutch Disease model is examined in Corden and Neary (1982). Gelb (1988) and many others have applied it in the context of oil windfalls.

b. A higher volatility of the real exchange rate is typical of natural-resource-abundant countries and can also be a channel for a resource curse (Lederman and Maloney 2008; Hausmann and Rigobon 2003).

c. As put by Lederman and Maloney (2008), Costa Rica's microchips are as vulnerable to exogenous developments in world market conditions as Chile's copper.

d. Acemoglu, Johnson, and Robinson (2005) present the view that institutions evolve very slowly, largely as a result of a change in the balance of power between parties with opposing wealth.

e. Collier and Hoeffler (2004) were the first to give evidence that conflicts were more likely to be driven by greed to get hold of the rents, than by grievance for ethnic or religious reasons. Brunnschweiler and Bulte (2009) contest this result, suggesting that conflict increases dependence on resource extraction (captured by the share of primary exports) while resource abundance (measured by resource stocks) is associated with a reduced probability of civil war. MENA has had its share of conflicts, but over the past 30 years, the count is no higher than in other regions.

f. The technology estimates are from Comin, Easterly, and Gong (2010, table 5). The importance of legal institutions is developed by Kuran (2010).

not underestimate the difficulty of effecting such an undervaluation. Gaining competitiveness by exchange rate manipulation could well be politically infeasible. For example, in Egypt, oil is heavily subsidized. In Morocco, fuel subsidies represented 18 percent of government expenditures (3.7 percent of GDP in 2010). As noted by Augier et al. (2011), these subsidies are a reward to gas-guzzling cars and to negative externalities, and they complicate fiscal management because of their high built-in volatility.

Oil subsidies are prevalent throughout MENA. They have a high elasticity to the exchange rate, which makes it difficult to raise the competitiveness of manufacturing activities through a devaluation of the exchange rate. Unless compensation can take place, a devaluation would have large redistributive effects that would make devaluation politically unsustainable.

Barriers to Trade: Policy-Related and Others
Given the importance of trade in growth acceleration episodes, it is important to review MENA's barriers to trade, in addition to the evolution of the RER examined above. Past appraisals of trade policies and barriers to trade in MENA suggest limited reforms, even though all the

indicators reviewed here indicate progress in reducing barriers to trade. Reducing government intervention is not the only key to success. Much recent literature and experience suggests that a comprehensive competiveness-based approach to exports and growth is also a necessary ingredient. Governments must still overcome market failures, particularly with regard to information externalities and to collective action and coordination challenges. The evidence reviewed here suggests that MENA still has an unfinished agenda. In particular, trade and regulatory barriers are widespread and trade costs high. Both impede the pace of regional and global integration.

As shown here, MENA's reduction in protection has not been accompanied by the hoped-for improvement in openness. Reasons for this outcome are explored below. As a general observation, most Latin American countries that opened up their economies were disappointed by their subsequent export performance compared with the rapid growth in exports experienced by the Asian countries in the 1960s. Wood (1997) argued that Latin American wages were not sufficiently low to compete with the low-wage South Asian exporters and China.

If this diagnostic is correct for MENA—if the region is not able to compete in the high-tech sectors because of lack of skills or in the labor-intensive sector because of relatively high wages, it suggests that the best option for MENA is to participate in outward processing. Such a strategy, however, would require improvements in hard and soft infrastructure, hence the importance of monitoring closely the evolution of trade cost indicators relative to those of competitors.

Tariffs and nontariff barriers. Despite recent progress in reduced protection, the opening of MENA countries to world trade remains an unfinished agenda.[17] Augier et al. (2011) report recent data on nontariff measures (NTMs) for 2010 for 29 countries. Except for Egypt, which has NTM frequency and coverage ratios of 90 percent, the other four MENA countries in the sample (Lebanon, Morocco, Syria, and Tunisia) have ratios around the average valued for the sample. Figure 2.3 shows that the frequency ratios are down, with a shift away from old-style control-and-command measures such as quantitative restrictions, prohibitions, and anticompetitive measures, toward technical regulations—sanitary and phytosanitary and technical barriers to trade—which have replaced all other forms of nontariff barriers.

As pointed out by Augier et al. (2011), this shift could be taken as a modernization of nontariff barrier apparatus, marking a shift from

Figure 2.3   Frequency Ratios, Core NTMs, 2001–10

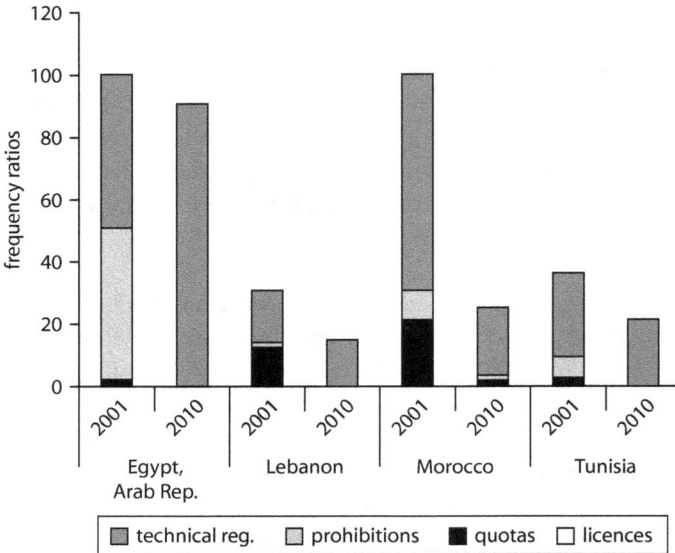

Source: Augier et al. (2011, figure 2). Data from World Bank/UNCTAD NTM data.

protectionist measures to regulatory ones. Whether that is so remains to be determined by case studies on the ground. On the other hand, the shift could also hide the increasing use of technical regulations as barriers to trade, through complex designs that end up being discriminatory de facto although not de jure.

Augier et al. (2011) also estimated product-level price-gap comparisons between a country and the average for the sample for products with a core NTB in which the authors control for tariffs and other country effects such as differences in cost-of-living indexes. Simple average estimates of price gaps for products with NTMs are 87 percent for Morocco and 37 percent for Tunisia. These are high. Their econometric estimates suggest that NTMs are more restrictive than tariffs.

The impression of an unfinished agenda is also apparent from inspection of the policy indicators affecting trade, displayed in table 2.5. The table is split into two groups of indicators: trade policy indicators in columns 2–5 and trade-supporting indicators in columns 6–9. Overall, individually and by group, MENA countries have poor (that is, high) rankings. Three patterns stand out. First, the indicators are best for the GCC and worst for RRLA countries. Second, the rankings for trade

Table 2.5 Policy Indicators Affecting Trade in MENA

Country	TAR-AGR 1990–95/ 2006–09	TAR-MAN 1990–95/ 2006–09	TTRI Value (rank: 125) 2006–09	OTRI Value (rank: 102) 2008	LPI (rank: 164) 2006–09	Doing Business (rank: 183) 2006–09	Trading across borders (rank: 183) 2010	Rule of law (rank: 213) 2009
RPLA	n.a.	n.a.	58.4	67.3	79.6	102	60.6	102.6
Egypt, Arab Rep.	35.8/54.6	23.6/9.2	3.3 (68)	10.0 (59)	94	106	21	97
Jordan	—/16.7	—/10.0	4.6 (108)	11.3 (66)	80	100	77	81
Lebanon	—/11.4	—/5.1	1.9 (50)	—	33	107	95	145
Morocco	66.5/26.7	63.9/10.8	1.8 (48)	14.1 (75)	131	128	80	106
Tunisia	29.6/38.6	28.0/21.0	0.9 (18)	11.7 (69)	60	69	30	84
RRLA	n.a.	n.a.	29	9	119.2	133.6	135.4	169.2
Algeria	25.4/21.5	21.3/15.9	0.7 (9)	1.5 (4)	135	136	124	156
Iran, Islamic Rep.	—/28.5	—/24.6	1.9 (49)	2.7 (14)	104	137	131	171
Iraq	—/0	—/0	—	—	156	153	179	210
Libya	—/0	—/0	—	—	137	—	—	161
Syrian Arab Republic	—/15.8	—/12.8	—	—	80	143	120	132
Yemen, Rep.	—/7.0	—/5.3	—	—	103	99	123	185
GCC	n.a.	n.a.	49.8	16.8	41	38.5	50	77
UAE	—/4.7	—/4.2	3.6 (71)	3.5 (20)	24	33	3	76
Bahrain	—/7.7	—/3.9	2.6 (58)	3.3 (19)	32	20	33	77
Kuwait	—/3.1	—/4.2	—	—	36	61	113	73
Oman	8.2/4.9	5.1/3.7	1.4 (31)	3.1 (16)	60	65	87	66
Qatar	—/5.9	—/4.1	1.8 (47)	—	55	39	46	81
Saudi Arabia	11.8/3.0	12.4/4.1	1.7 (42)	2.6 (12)	39	13	18	89

Sources: Columns (1–2) WITS: Applied tariffs; columns 3–5: World Trade Indicators; column 6: Doing Business; column 7: World Governance indicators.

Notes: For all ranks, a higher value means a worse ranking. TAR-AGR = Applied tariffs in agriculture; TAR-MAN = Applied tariffs in manufactures. — = missing data. n.a. = not applicable.

policy barriers are usually better than for the trade-supporting indicators. Third, the rankings are generally poor relative to the lower-middle- and upper-middle-income comparator averages.

This still relatively high level of tariff protection is reflected in the values and rankings of the Trade Restrictiveness Index (TRI) for the MENA countries (table 2.5, column 3), and also for the regional average when compared with other middle-income countries. On a regional basis, the overall Tariff-only Trade Restrictiveness Index (TTRI) is still the second-highest in the world after South Asia. When nontariff measures are included, the Overall Trade Restrictiveness Index (OTRI) for the MENA region (based on the countries listed in column 4 in table 2.5) is the highest in the world. This high value is mostly attributable to the high ad valorem equivalent (AVE) of nontariff measures for the countries in the RPLA group. The barriers to trade in MENA particularly penalize exports from Sub-Saharan Africa (40 percent) and Latin America (57 percent).

Because reforms are often complementary, improvements in the trade-supporting indicators (columns 5 to 9) are needed if trade is to be an engine of growth in MENA. To partake in the rapid growth of offshoring in services (such as back-office work processes, call-center operators, legal research, and so forth), restrictions to trade in services must not be higher than they are in competing countries. Likewise, to participate in the global production networks, where different stages of production take place in different locations, a country needs state-of-the-art supply and logistics chains (high-performance transport, customs, and communication) and efficiency in the full range of backbone service sectors). Except for the GCC, none of the MENA countries has good scores on these trade-supporting indicators.

The pervasiveness of nontariff measures is compounded by the relatively poor ranking in the indicators capturing the regulatory environment: the Logistics Performance Index (LPI)(column 6), the Doing Business indicators (column 7), the trading across border indicator (column 8) and the rule of law indicator (column 9). By and large, both resource-rich and resource-poor countries have low rankings, according to most of these overlapping indicators that capture the regulatory environment.[18] Taken together, these rankings are consistent with rigid economies and an unfriendly business environment where, as shown by Freund and Bolaky (2008), more trade is not associated with a rise in per-capita income (as is the case in the flexible economies).

Trade costs and trade facilitation. MENA manufactures and non-oil exports, especially those of the resource-rich group, have underperformed (see the estimates in annex table 2A.1). Two broad categories of factors have been advanced so far: macroeconomic policies and the unfavorable regulatory environment. In the standard gravity model, after controlling for other factors, this lack of trade integration would be reflected in a high value for a regional dummy variable. To test whether this is the case, we estimate a gravity model augmented by a proxy for trade facilitation, which captures the unfavorable environment reflected in the indicators in table 2.5. The proxy is the time-to-export from the factory to the port (broken down into number of days for documentation, transit time, port handling, and customs clearance, available for three years from the Doing Business database).[19]

The model estimated for non-oil and nonmineral bilateral exports is:

$$LnEX_{ijt} = \alpha_1 X_{it} + \alpha_2 LnDIST_{ij} + \alpha_3 Z_{ij} + \alpha_4 TIME\_EXP_i$$
$$+ \alpha_4 DUMR + \mu_j + \varepsilon_{ijt} \tag{2.2}$$

where EX_{ijt} are bilateral exports of manufactures (excluding oil and minerals) from i to j, X_{it} is a vector of exporter-specific variables that includes GDP, population, and an indicator of remoteness, $DIST_{ij}$ is distance between partners, Z_{ij} are the usual bilateral controls (contiguity, common language, former colony), $TIME\_EXP$ is the time to get a standardized container from factory gate on board to the ship, $DUMR$ is a regional dummy (the Organisation for Economic Co-operation and Development, or OECD, membership is the omitted dummy), and μ_j captures all time-invariant importer-specific characteristics.[20]

Results are reported in table 2.6. All the controls have expected magnitudes and expected significance levels. Of interest is the negative coefficient for the MENA dummy in column 1, which implies that MENA exports about 39 percent less ($e^{-0.89} - 1 = -0.39$) than expected relative to the excluded OECD, after having taken into account the effects of all the other controls. Interestingly, East Asia star performers export 630 percent more than the OECD does, followed by South Asia. All other regions export less on a bilateral basis than the reference group, but what comes out of the estimates is that MENA is the region that deviates the most from the expected trade volume.

Adding the time-to-export variable (column 2) to capture the effects of trade facilitation lowers only slightly the coefficient value for the dummy. Unlike the results by Freund and Rocha (2011) for Sub-Saharan Africa, where introducing the time-to-export variable takes away much

Table 2.6   Correlates of Bilateral Non-Oil Exports

Ln(Aggregate non-oil exports)	(1) All	(2) Time exp.	(3) Log time	(4) MENA	(5) MENA
Ln(GDP)	1.30***	1.21***	1.15***	0.55***	0.43***
	[0.01]	[0.01]	[0.01]	[0.05]	[0.05]
Ln(Population)	−0.15***	−0.06***	−0.00	−0.13***	−0.14***
	[0.01]	[0.01]	[0.01]	[0.03]	[0.03]
Ln(Distance)	−1.64***	−1.65***	−1.66***	−1.96***	−1.97***
	[0.01]	[0.01]	[0.01]	[0.08]	[0.08]
Time to export		−0.02***		−0.08***	
		[0.00]		[0.01]	
Ln(Time)			−0.63***		−2.32***
			[0.03]		[0.15]
MENA	−0.89***	−0.83***	−0.74***		
	[0.04]	[0.04]	[0.04]		
SSA	−0.44***	−0.45***	−0.48***		
	[0.04]	[0.04]	[0.04]		
LAC	−0.20***	−0.26***	−0.21***		
	[0.04]	[0.04]	[0.04]		
EAP	1.99***	1.94***	1.91***		
	[0.04]	[0.04]	[0.04]		
SAS	0.38***	0.29***	0.30***		
	[0.06]	[0.06]	[0.06]		
ECA	−0.66***	−0.51***	−0.47***		
	[0.03]	[0.04]	[0.04]		
Contiguity	0.80***	0.80***	0.79***	−0.34	−0.33
	[0.07]	[0.07]	[0.07]	[0.26]	[0.26]
Partner fixed effects	Yes	Yes	Yes	Yes	Yes
Observations	53,359	52,458	52,458	4,808	4,808
R-squared	0.702	0.706	0.707	0.607	0.615

Source: Authors.
Notes: Aggregate non-oil exports are equal to total exports minus exports in HS 2-digit sectors 26 (oil) and 27 (ores and minerals). All exports are gross exports. MENA, SSA, LAC, EAP, SAS, and ECA are dummy variables for regions: Middle East and North Africa, Sub-Saharan Africa, Latin America and the Caribbean, East Asia and Pacific, South Asia, and Europe and Central Asia. The reference region is OECD. Other control variables included in the regression are common language, colony, landlocked, and remoteness. The estimates for unreported control variables are always statistically significant with the expected sign. Standard errors in brackets. *** p<0.01, ** p<0.05, * p<0.1.

of the significance for the Africa dummy (not shown), this is not the case for MENA manufacture exports. Nor are the results affected by the shift to a log specification for the time-to-export variable (column 3), or by an estimation carried out on total exports (not reported here).

The estimates for the MENA subsample of 12 countries are given in columns 4 and 5. Even though MENA countries are not landlocked, the coefficient of the distance variable increases significantly, suggesting higher-than-average, distance-related trade costs. The contiguity coefficient is not significant, probably reflecting conflicts in the region as well as a lack of trade facilitation at the regional level. In MENA, the average time to get merchandise from the factory gate to the port is 20 days (less than in the other regions except OECD because of the low values for inland transit, since MENA countries are not landlocked). According to the estimates in column 4, a reduction in time-to-export of 10 percent (that is, two days) would increase trade volume by 8 percent.

Breaking down the time-to-export into each one of the three components[21] also results in negative and significant coefficient values for each component. When the respective coefficient values between the estimates for the whole sample and for the MENA sample are compared, the coefficient value for time related to customs and ports is much higher for the MENA sample (–0.21) than for the whole sample (–0.05). While interpretation of the results is subject to endogeneity problems (trade facilitation may stimulate trade, but trade is also likely to influence trade facilitation), the large estimated values for the customs and ports components suggest benefits from trade facilitation.

As shown in figure 2.4, unlike most other countries and regions, the average distance of trade for MENA countries has fallen from 7,000 kilometers to 6,000 kilometers over a 30-year period. Referring again to the gravity trade model, this decline could result from two developments. One is that the region is losing ground and lagging relative to competitors (as suggested by the comparative performance along the indicators in table 2.5). If so, then costs related to international trade are increasing relative to those of competing partners, and countries would trade more with closer partners to minimize trade costs (or other countries are taking their place because their trade costs are falling more rapidly).

An alternative possibility is that MENA countries have decreased trade-related costs mostly on a regional basis, through reductions in tariff and nontariff barriers or in creased trade facilitation resulting from the implementation of regional trade agreements. If so, with relative trade-related costs falling faster on a regional basis, countries would trade more with close partners, thereby reducing the average distance of trade.[22]

The prediction that a fall in border-related costs should lead countries to increase the volume of international (relative to internal) trade is largely borne out by the data: over the past 30 years, international trade has increased by 300 percent while world production has increased by 75 percent. According to the gravity model, in a frictionless world,

Figure 2.4   Average Distance of Trade and Trade Costs

MENA and comparators, 1970–2006

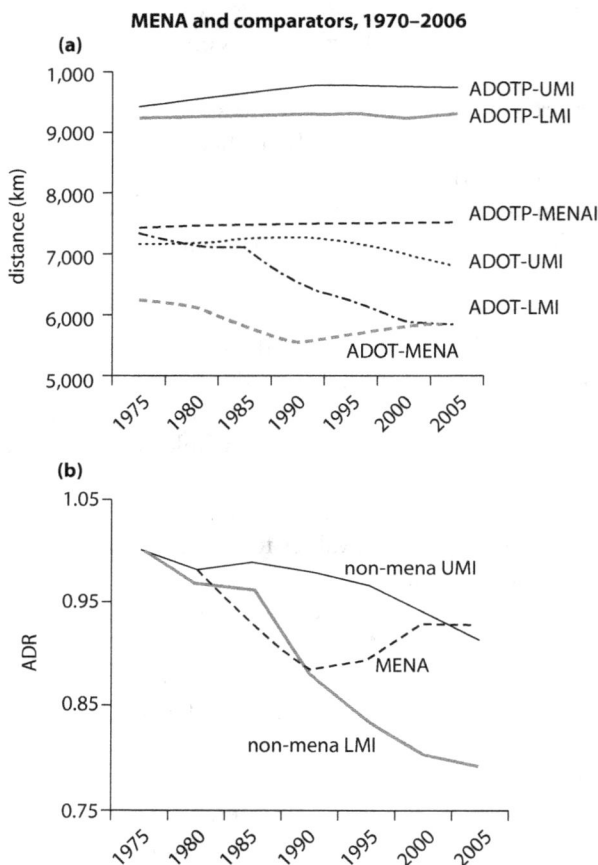

Source: Authors' calculations based on Carrère, de Melo and Wilson (2010).
Note: Country averages over five-year periods during 1970–2004 and a two-year period, 2005–06. The 10 MENA countries are United Arab Emirates, Algeria, Egypt, Jordan, Kuwait, Morocco, Oman, Saudi Arabia, Syria, and Tunisia. UMI = upper middle income. LMI= lower-middle income. ADOTP = Potential average distance of trade in a frictionless world. ADOT = actual average distance of trade. ADR = average distance ratio. ADR = ADOTP/ADOT = trade cost. ADR is normalized to 1 in 1970.

potential trade would be proportional to the trading partners' GDP. Multiplying by the distance between the partners and summing over all partners gives the gravity-predicted average distance of trade for country i, denoted here as the potential distance of trade $(ADOT_i^p)$. This measure (which takes a maximum value when all countries are of the same size) will increase when there is less dispersion in the group and over a long period when there is convergence in incomes.

A reduction in all costs related to distance (including better information about distant markets) should lead countries to increase their trade
with distant partners. On the other hand, if the relative costs associated
with distance increase, countries should trade with closer partners. Since
what counts is the evolution of distance-related costs across all partners,
trade costs could be falling for all trading partners, but those for which
trade costs are falling the least would see a regionalization of their trade.
Then if the gravity model is an adequate description of bilateral trade, the
ratio of actual trade $(ADOT_i)$ to potential $(ADOT_i^p)$, here called the average distance ratio (ADR_i), is an indirect measure of trade costs: falling
values of the ratio (that is., a regionalization of trade) then reflect an
increase in relative trade costs.

Figure 2.4 reports these measures for the average of the 10 MENA
countries with data over the period 1970–2004 along with the corresponding average for the upper-middle- and lower-middle-income
groups (UMI, LMI), since all MENA countries except the Republic of
Yemen belong to one of these two groups (see table 2.2). To iron out
fluctuations, each point is a five-year average. For all countries, potential
trade is greater than actual trade, suggesting cost minimization in bilateral
trade patterns by choosing closer partners (with lower trade costs).
MENA countries' potential (or frictionless) trade is about 2,000 kilometers less than the corresponding estimate for the comparator groups,
reflecting a higher dispersion in GDPs across the partners. Over time, the
potential distance of trade increases slightly for the UMI group, reflecting
a higher growth for distant partners. For the MENA and LMI groups, the
potential distance of trade remains flat.

More interestingly, the indicator of trade costs in the bottom half of
the figure (the ADR is normalized to 1 in 1970) shows a sharp fall of
around 10 percent in the average distance of trade for the two comparator groups. This drop could be either because the trade costs associated
with physically close partners are falling more rapidly (as, for example,
with deep integration), or because the costs of barriers to trade have not
gone down as rapidly as they have for the high-income countries, whose
ADR (not shown here) stayed constant throughout the 30-year period.
However, for MENA, the fall in the ADR is reversed starting in the early
1990s, which is the period when the regionwide preferential trade agreements were put in place (along with others outside the region).

Since the average potential distance of trade stays constant, a change
in the composition of trading partners must have taken place. If new
partners (extensive margin) are geographically close, then one would

observe a regionalization of trade. A regionalization of trade would also be observed if existing trade were redirected toward geographically close partners or if trade among geographically close partners were growing faster.

Figure 2.5 gives the breakdown between existing (intensive margin) and new partners (extensive margin). It shows that until 2005, the new partners are closer. This is in line with the results in Carrère, Gourdon, and Olarreaga (2011), who find that trade increased following the signing of preferential trade agreements. It also shows that new partners have an increasing weight in total import value. Thus the regionalization of trade has taken place at the intensive margin and the increasing trend in regional trade noted by Shui and Walkenhorst (2011, table 10.3) has been in new products.

Exports, Diversification, and Survival

MENA countries have lower shares of manufacturing exports than comparator countries. The causes behind this symptom are not clear: is it a matter of volume of trade, lack of diversity, the difficulty in maintaining

Figure 2.5   Average Trade Distance of MENA Countries with Traditional and New Trade Partners

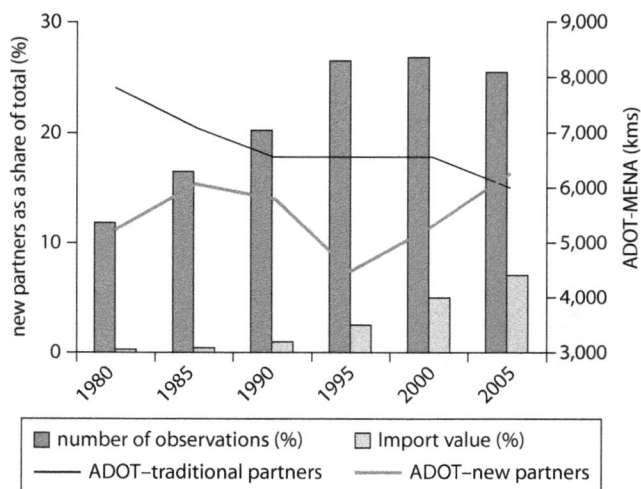

Source: Authors' calculations based on Carrère, de Melo, and Wilson (2010).
Notes: Country averages over five-year periods during 1970–2004 and a two-year period, 2005–06. UMI = upper middle income. LMI = lower-middle income. ADOTP = potential average distance of trade in a frictionless world. ADOT = actual average distance of trade. ADR = ADOTP/ADOT = trade cost.

export spells for new products, or perhaps, as pointed out above, the bad luck of being in the most crowded region for factor endowments? This section explores the extent to which low productivity levels could be a barrier to exporting. It also looks at what contributes to the survival of new exports, since an export surge cannot last if survival rates are low.

Low firm productivity. Many firm-level studies support the view that increased openness to world markets stimulates productivity levels in stronger firms and encourages weaker firms to leave the market, thereby reallocating resources from weaker to stronger firms. The firm-level studies also show that access to imports (made possible by foreign exchange earnings from exports) boosts growth by granting access to capital goods and inputs from many competitive sources (this is probably a reason why investment rates shoot up after trade liberalization). However, we do not know if it is exporting that improves productivity at the plant level or rather that exporters self-select into exporting based on higher productivity, even if interviews from case studies suggest that quality matters for exporting to rich markets.[23]

At the microlevel, much effort has focused on the correlates of the low level of productivity (technical efficiency) in MENA manufacturing. A typical finding is that, compared with other middle-income countries, MENA manufacturing firms have lower technical efficiency, lower productivity, and higher labor costs across a wide range of manufacturing sectors. This is the finding of a recent study by Kinda, Plane, and Veganzones-Varoudakis (2011), reported in table 2.7,[24] which shows a lesser performance for MENA countries relative to other middle-income countries across nearly all industries; this finding again suggests a MENA specificity.

Kinda, Plane, and Veganzones-Varoudakis (2011) also find that in most sectors, lower technical efficiency is positively correlated with below-average indicator values for the regulatory and legal environment captured by the Investment Climate Assessment indicators (quality of infrastructure, experience and education of labor force, and different dimensions of the government-business relationship). Given the poor rankings of most MENA countries in trade and regulatory indicators, this result is not surprising. In sum, as concluded by several studies and reports (Nabli 2007; World Bank 2004; World Bank 2009), over the past three decades, investment has lagged, manufacturing exports have not diversified, and a largely inefficient manufacturing sector has developed.

Table 2.7 Firm-Level Productivity, MENA and Non-MENA

	Textile	Leather	Garment	Agroprocessing	Metal, machinery products	Chemicals, pharmaceuticals	Wood, furniture	Nonmetal, plastics
Labor Productivity (LP) (US dollars at current exchange rate)								
Non-MENA	10.08***	6.80***	6.65*	14.9	16.0	18.5	7.5	11.1**
MENA	7.93	4.91	4.96	15.2	15.6	18.6	7.3	8.8
Unit labor costs								
Non-MENA	0.37***	0.46***	0.69	0.46	0.44**	0.33*	0.58**	0.54
MENA	0.49	0.82	0.63	0.42	0.50	0.43	0.68	0.48
Technical efficiency								
Non-MENA	44.6**	63.9***	62.3	44.5***	60.6***	40.8	48.3***	61.6***
MENA	42.8	54.7	64.8	40.3	44.4	42.5	37.5	49.8

Source: Kinda, Plane, and Veganzones-Varoudakis (2011, table 4).

Note: Number of firms per industry: 360 (leather) to 1,601 (garments). MENA countries: Algeria, Egypt, Lebanon, Morocco, Saudi Arabia. NON-MENA: (LAC) Brazil, Ecuador, El Salvador, Guatemala, Honduras, Nicaragua; (AFR) Ethiopia, South Africa, Tanzania, Zambia; (SAS) Bangladesh, India, Pakistan, Sri Lanka; (EAP) China, Philippines, Thailand. * 10 percent significance. ** 5 percent significance. *** 1 percent significance.

Export diversification and survival. Is product diversity (in terms of products, partners, or both) correlated with superior performance? At the macrolevel, concentration of activities is associated with volatility,[25] so the natural policy response—which has been part of the package of reforms advocated for MENA countries—has been to push for export diversification (export growth at the extensive margin, either from existing products to new markets or from new products). But the evidence at the microlevel is still inconclusive. Some have pointed out that productivity increases are primarily achieved through interindustry spillovers and that these are more likely in certain product groups—that is, in the product-space language, in the "denser" part of the "forest," where there are greater opportunities for cross-product linkages. Along these lines, Hausmann, Hwang, and Rodrik (2007) find that, after controlling for intervening factors, notably per capita income, countries with a more sophisticated (that is, more diversified) export bundle subsequently grow faster.

These results have not remained unchallenged. For example, Harrison and Rodriguez-Clare (2009) suggest that the links between diversity and productivity have not yet been established, and that quality upgrading (which is essential to remain competitive in rapidly evolving markets) rather than product diversity may be the key to success. Also, the evidence is mixed about whether productivity increases come through learning from exporting, or whether initially, at least, the highest-productivity firms that self-select into exporting (increases in productivity that might come from first exporting at the regional level).

Figure 2.6, adapted from Cadot, Carrère, and Strauss-Kahn (2011), estimates an index of concentration in relation to income per capita at the HS-6 level for 156 countries over two periods: 1990–95 and 1996–2007 (period averages). Their estimates show that diversification takes place mostly at the extensive margin (new products to old or new partners) rather than at the intensive margin (old products to existing or new partners). As can be seen from the figure, this decrease in concentration takes place until income per capita reaches about $22,000. The fit is quite tight, and the relationship is stable over the two periods, with a slightly more concave estimated curve for the second period.

It is worth noting that all oil exporters in the resource-rich and GCC groups are far above the estimated line, while the resource-poor countries are either on or below the estimated line (meaning they are more diversified). This is undoubtedly related to the small size of the industrial sectors in resource-rich countries, and it once more reveals a specificity for the oil exporters even though the root causes of lack of diversification vary

Figure 2.6 Export Diversification and per Capita Income

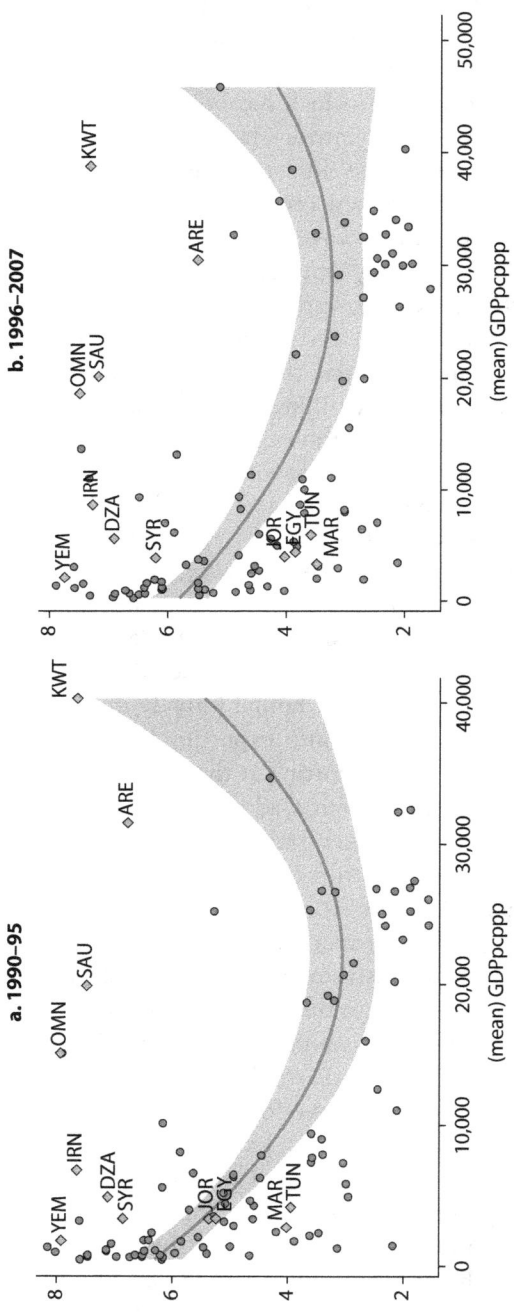

a. 1990–95

b. 1996–2007

Source: Authors' calculations from Cadot, Carrère, and Strauss-Kahn (2011).

across countries. But moving to new products is not just a matter of passive factor accumulation: as emphasized by Hausmann and Rodrik (2003), it also requires having the capabilities associated with the new products, capabilities that depend on what you already export. According to the measures developed by Hidalgo and others (2007), these capabilities are limited for exporters of hydrocarbons.

Algeria's exports are very concentrated, as Hausmann, Klinger, and Lopez-Calix (2010) show, even when one excludes oil and minerals. They reject real exchange rate appreciation and volatility as potential explanatory factors. They recognize that high protection and rent-seeking might have played a role, as well as a business-unfriendly environment, but they argue that (partial) correlation between Doing Business indicators and the product diversity of the export bundle still shows that Algeria's non-oil export basket is very concentrated, once controlling for the value of the Doing Business indicator. Using a measure of the connection of products showing that the product space has a core-periphery structure, they find that hydrocarbons are poorly connected to the rest of the product space, suggesting that diversification for oil exporters will be inhibited because new activities are not closely related in the product space (see their figure 4.9). Thus the pattern in figure 2.6 suggests that exporters of hydrocarbons have an inherent difficulty in diversifying.

There is, however, an intriguing observation behind the quadratic shape of the concentration curve in figure 2.6. Cadot, Carrère, and Strauss-Kahn (2011) show that the search for new products (called "discoveries" by some and "export entrepreneurship" by others), which disappears after the turning point, coincides with a change in the export bundle to more closely resemble the comparative advantage of countries (as measured by the distance from their endowments). This would suggest that there is level of development beyond which a country's comparative advantage settles. So, among MENA countries, the oil exporters might be closer to their long-term comparative advantage, because high diversification characterizing the middle part of the development process would be an "out-of-equilibrium" stage between two states, characterized by specialization according to comparative advantage. But it could also reflect weak links because of the size of their industrial sector, as suggested in chapter 4 of this book.

Typically, export spells are of very short duration in low-income countries. The issue then is what accounts for (is correlated with) this lack of duration of new products. From a policy point of view, knowing this is as important as (if not more important than) what lies behind the discovery phase. Having shown that 80 percent of new exports die within a year, Besedes and Prusa (2006) suggest that higher survival rates are essential for achieving faster export growth. This conjecture finds support in Brenton, Pierola, and Von Uexkull (2009), who show that poorly performing countries are not inferior to stronger countries in introducing new trade flows, but rather that they experience much lower rates of survival. The authors find that a strong positive association between export survival rates and per capita income as well as the probability that the death of an export flow diminishes the longer the export flow survives. More recently, Besedes and Prusa (2010) show that differences in survival rates and the deepening of existing relationships are important drivers in accounting for long-run differences in performance.

Figure 2.7 compares the survival rates of exports for the MENA group with those for the sample of upper-middle- and lower-middle-income groups used earlier in the chapter, using HS-4 level data to remove the large errors in measurement for low-income countries in the more disaggregated data.[26] This gives us 1,240 product categories over the years 1998–2007.[27] Survival rates increase with income per capita (see Brenton, Saborowski, and Von Uexkull 2010, figure 1). Since MENA countries mostly belong to the middle-income groups, we compare survival rates with those of the UM and LM group averages. Survival rates are lower for the MENA group than for both the LM and UM groups.[28] This low survival of exports is indeed another MENA specificity.

Figure 2.7   Kaplan-Meier Survival Rates

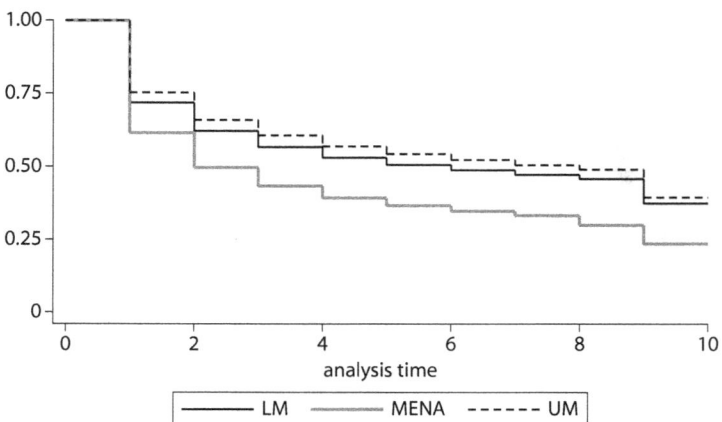

Source: Authors' calculations using International Trade Dataset at the Product Level (BACI).
Note: See text for an explanation of this figure.

We now use the standard Cox proportional hazard model to estimate the correlates of the hazard rates and estimate:

$$\lambda_i(t) = \lambda_0(t)\exp(z_i(t)'\beta) \tag{2.3}$$

where $\lambda_0(t)$ is the baseline hazard rate, and $z_i(t)$ is a vector of covariates that has a proportional impact on the hazard function.[29]

Results are reported in table 2.8 for the high- and middle-income group of countries in the first two columns, and for 15 MENA countries in the last two columns. For the control comparator group (columns 1 and 2), greater distance between the partners reduces the duration of the export spell (that is, increases the hazard rate). Volatility does not affect the hazard rate.[30] Surprisingly, this is not the case for the MENA group of countries, for which distance does not affect the hazard rate. Contiguity and common language are associated with longer duration. Interestingly, for the MENA group, misalignment is associated with a significantly lower export spell.

It is difficult to arrive at unambiguous conclusions given data truncation problems (the time series data is only over a 10-year period) and the fact that some of the coefficient values change when the sample group is altered. Nonetheless, since earlier evidence shows that diversification and duration of export flows are associated with superior long-run export growth, the evidence suggests that MENA countries are disadvantaged by the short duration of their export flows.

Table 2.8   Correlates of Hazard Rates for 4-Digit Export Flows

Variable	High- and middle-income countries		MENA countries	
	Coefficient	p-value	Coefficient	p-value
Log(Distance)	1.078	0.000	0.984	0.024
Contiguity	1.007	0.170	0.876	0.000
Common language	1.010	0.003	0.884	0.000
Colony	0.931	0.000	1.013	0.605
Log(Total bilateral trade)	0.800	0.000	0.884	0.000
Volatility	1.007	0.000	1.004	0.000
Misalignment	1.028	0.000	1.118	0.000

Source: Authors' calculations using International Trade Dataset at the Product Level (BACI).
Note: The dependent variable is the hazard rate of export flows at the HS 4-digit level excluding oil and minerals (HS-2 digit: 26 and 27). Coefficients are presented in exponential form so a coefficient of 1.07 (0.93) means that, holding the other covariate values constant, the hazard rate is 7 percent higher (lower) than the baseline estimate. Total bilateral trade is calculated for the first year of the spell. Volatility is the monthly volatility in the exporter's real effective exchange rate with respect to the partner's volatility. Misalignment is the exchange rate between exporter and importer in the year the trade relationship starts relative to the period average (1998–2007).

Conclusion

MENA's recent performance has shown progress, with higher growth rates, less growth volatility, and increased market shares for its exports despite the competition from fast-growing countries and exporters such as China and India. This catching up is encouraging against the backdrop of a generally disappointing performance over the past 50 years, especially for the resource-rich countries. Over the past 50 years, performance has been better for the resource-poor countries, which have quite closely tracked comparator groups except the high-growing Asian countries, while resource-rich labor-abundant countries have lagged. With the exception of Oman, MENA countries have failed to climb up the ladder, remaining either in the lower-middle- or upper-middle-income group.

This chapter and the supporting evidence have shown that the combination of macro- and micropolicies in a generally weak institutional environment produced this outcome. At the macrolevel, MENA countries have been unable to maintain a depreciated (undervalued) real exchange rate for long periods; such an undervaluation helps to correct the market failures and poor institutional environment that hits hardest the dynamic non-resource-intensive traded sectors. The region, especially the resource-rich group, displayed greater volatility in macro-indicators than comparable groups until the mid-1990s, when performance started to pick up. For example, for the GCC, but also for the resource-rich group, countercyclical fiscal policies have been less effective than in other resource-rich countries with comparable external shocks. As a result, the volatility of the real effective exchange rate has been greater than in comparable groups, and volatility contributed to the lack of development of new activities outside the resource sectors and to short-lived export spells.

Cross-country evidence shows that the positive relation between openness and per capita income holds only for countries with good indicator values for regulatory reform. The Doing Business data also show that countries rich in natural resources are less inclined to carry out reforms than others. Despite some progress toward reducing tariffs on industry, MENA countries fare poorly in most indicators describing the domestic microeconomic environment, giving the impression of an environment in which trade is not facilitated and of an unfinished reform agenda. Improved domestic regulatory policies, along with improved public sector governance (reflected in better indicators values), would help MENA to achieve greater integration in the world economy.

Annex 2A Trade, Structural Change, and Natural Resources

This annex examines patterns of structural change from traditional sectors toward high-productivity sectors, that is, shifts out of agriculture and the informal sector into the other sectors of the economy where the production of most high-productivity tradables takes place. For countries in the Middle East and North Africa (MENA), the low-productivity sectors include not only agriculture, but most rent-generating sectors in oil and minerals, many public sector services, and some nontradable services.[31]

If development entails a resource shift toward manufactures and services, then there should be a positive correlation between the shares of manufacturing and services in GDP and per capita income. Likewise, if exports from these sectors reflect high productivity and the exploitation of spillovers, one would expect a positive correlation between the shares of exports of manufactures and per capita income. By the same token, one would also expect a positive correlation between the export shares of services and per capita income. Controlling for factors associated with exports, does this positive association hold, and is there a MENA specificity?

Patterns of growth and structural change are examined by fitting trade and production shares against per capita GDP, y_{it}, and control variables, z_{it} (such as population, the share of rents in GDP, an index of trade costs, conflicts, and/or time and country fixed effects).[32] Endogeneity issues are ignored because the only objective is to see if MENA countries or groupings are "different" from average development patterns. The typical estimated equation is:

$$\theta_{it}(t) = \alpha + \beta y_{it} + \gamma z_{it} + \varepsilon_{it}; \quad i = 1, \dots n, t = 1, \dots T \qquad (2A.1)$$

We expect that the shares will be positively correlated with per capita GDP. Dummy variables for MENA countries are included to detect regional specificity (that is, the effect of omitted variables). Data availability for the control variables determines the sample size. We start with trade shares and then move on to predictions of manufacturing and services shares in GDP.

The first exploration takes a large sample of countries to try to identify the correlates of the trade share in GDP, taking first the overall trade share, then the share of manufacturing exports (excluding oil and minerals) in GDP as the regressand. To ease comparisons, the same set of regressors is used with a dummy variable for MENA added to the list of regressors, starting in each case with per capita income (column 1 in table 2A.1) and adding one regressor at a time. For the correlates of the overall trade share (only reported in figure 2A.1), per capita income always enters positively. Except for population, which is always negatively related to the trade share, adding regressors improves the overall fit only marginally even though the share of rents in GDP, the average rate of protection, and the number of conflicts have the expected signs.[33] Noticeably, the Logistics Performance Index (a higher value of the index means better physical infrastructure) is not significant, although that is because it is significantly positively correlated with per capita income. When taken jointly, the control variables (in addition to per capita income and population) are statistically significant. In conclusion, the MENA dummy variable is never significant, so there is no MENA specificity in the overall openness of the countries in the region, and to borrow from World Bank (2004, figure 2.3), contrary to what was said in that report regarding the trade share in GDP, one cannot say that MENA "failed to ride the wave."

This conclusion is confirmed in the partial scatter plot of the trade share against per capita GDP in annex figure 2A.1a after having netted out the other control variables, where except for conflict-stricken Lebanon, all MENA countries are bunched around the predicted line.

However, when the same set of regressors is applied to the share of manufacturing trade (excluding oil and minerals) in GDP, a MENA specificity does appear (see table 2A.1). The sample is smaller, the fit less good and less stable, and there are obvious endogeneity problems with two-way causality between protection and trade and between the infrastructure index and trade. The significance of per capita income disappears when the average rate of protection for manufactures is introduced in column 3 because of the significant negative correlation between protection of industry and per capita income in the sample. However, the significance of the MENA dummy remains for all specifications.

The partial scatter plot in figure 2A.1b suggests that the specificity is related to the distinction between the resource-rich and resource-poor groups. Most resource-rich members, except for Bahrain and United Arab Emirates, which are above the line, fall on or below the predicted relation while all the resource-poor countries are close to or above the regression line. Particularly significant is Algeria's low non-oil trade share. Hausman, Klinger, and Lopez-Calix (2010) argue that

Table 2A.1 Correlates of Trade Shares in GDP

Ln(Non-oil exports as % of GDP)	(1) Income	(2) L-lock	(3) Pop.	(4) Protect.	(5) Rents	(6) Conflict	(7) LPI
Ln(GDPpc)	0.16***	0.18***	0.18***	0.05	0.05	0.04	−0.25**
	[0.05]	[0.06]	[0.06]	[0.07]	[0.08]	[0.08]	[0.10]
Landlocked		0.15	0.16	0.06	0.04	0.03	−0.02
		[0.19]	[0.19]	[0.18]	[0.18]	[0.18]	[0.18]
Ln(Population)			0.01	−0.02	−0.02	0.01	−0.12**
			[0.04]	[0.04]	[0.04]	[0.05]	[0.06]
Average tariff				−0.03*	−0.03	−0.03	−0.02
				[0.02]	[0.02]	[0.02]	[0.02]
Ln(Rents)					−0.01	−0.01	0.00
					[0.01]	[0.01]	[0.01]
Number of conflicts						−0.01*	−0.01
						[0.01]	[0.01]
LPI index							0.79***
							[0.20]
MENA	−0.86***	−0.83***	−0.83***	−0.72***	−0.70***	−0.69***	−0.56**
	[0.24]	[0.24]	[0.24]	[0.24]	[0.25]	[0.25]	[0.25]
Constant	2.60***	2.54***	2.51***	3.13***	3.06***	3.05***	1.65***
	[0.13]	[0.15]	[0.18]	[0.29]	[0.29]	[0.29]	[0.48]
Observations	124	124	124	122	121	121	113
R-squared	0.142	0.147	0.147	0.167	0.175	0.195	0.304

Source: Authors' calculations.

Note: The results are estimated in cross-section regressions for year 2005. "Average tariff" is a simple average of applied MFN tariffs on manufactures. "Rents" is the share of total rents in GDP (2004). Total number of conflicts by country is calculated over the period 1980–2005. Conflicts are counted yearly. LPI is the Logistics Performance Index. Standard errors in brackets. *** p<0.01, ** p<0.05, * p<0.1.

Figure 2A.1 Predicted Trade Shares in GDP

a. total trade

b. non-oil trade

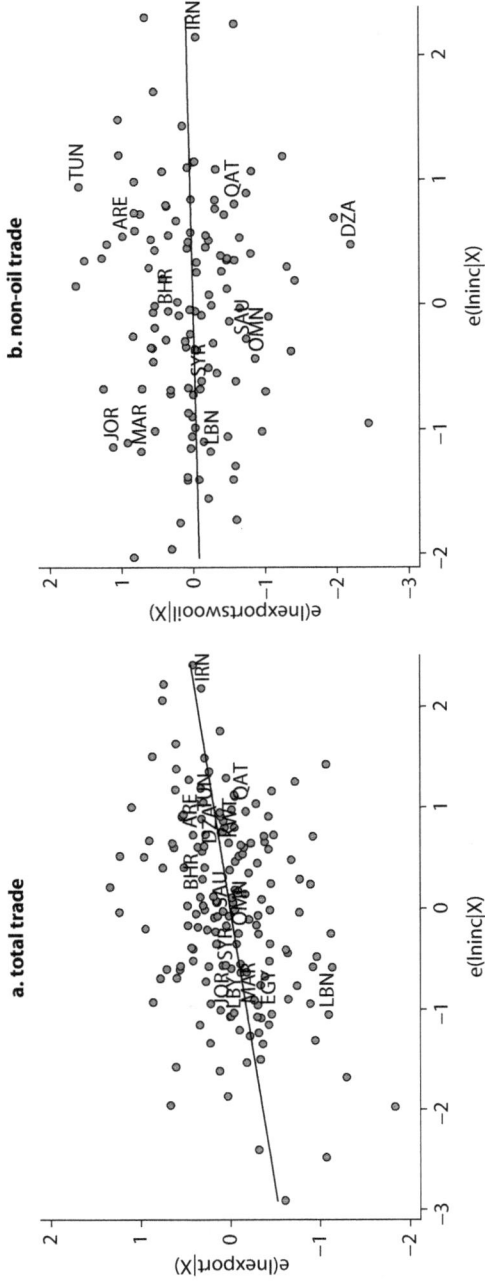

coef = 0.17904732, se = 0.04173083, t = 4.29

coef = 0.03895179, se = 0.07558655, t = 0.52

Source: Authors.

Notes: Partial plot of the share of total and non-oil exports in GDP (in logs) and GDP per capita at constant prices (in logs). Estimation is run on a cross-section of countries in 2005. For other control variables and estimates, refer to column 6 in table 2A.1.

Algeria's lagging manufacturing sector is mainly caused by the lack of connection between hydrocarbons and other sectors

The significance of the MENA dummy also holds when it is applied to each group one at a time. In conclusion, the three groups display different non-oil export patterns that are still in need of further exploration.

A Lagging Manufacturing Sector for the Resource-Rich Group

Next we look for a MENA specificity in the share of manufactures and services in GDP over the period. This gives a slightly different perspective and is more directly addressed to the de-industrialization effect associated with the Dutch Disease while at the same time changes in production are also a close indicator of changes in exports.[34] Evolution of these shares is also a measure of the speed of structural change.

The regressions in table 2A.2 are for a panel of 167 countries over the period 1980–2004. The top left panel reports the correlates for manufacturing shares and the right panel for services shares. Both have country fixed effects that absorb time-invariant factors specific to individual countries and time fixed effects for common changes in the external environment. Table 2A.3 displays the same regressions for the MENA region as a whole and for the MENA subgroups over the same periods, but without time fixed effects to preserve degrees of freedom.

Focusing on manufactures and services has its roots in the dual-economy vision of development. This view, largely accepted, calls for the movement of resources out of "traditional," relatively low-productivity activities into "modern," high-productivity activities where externalities help establish a virtuous circle of growth. The modern high-productivity goods are in manufacturing and more recently in the traded components of the services sectors (banking, transport, telecommunications, professional services). As Rodrik (2009, p. 4) put it, "Poor countries get rich by producing what rich countries produce." We comment first on the results for manufacturing, then for services.

Results for manufacturing for the whole sample are at the top left of the table. As expected, per capita income is significant, but so is the share of rents in GDP, which enters negatively as would be expected from the resource-curse literature. The negative coefficient on rents holds in table 2A.3, where the sample is restricted to MENA countries. Since per capita income is significant only for the resource-poor group, these results suggest resource-curse effects delaying the development of manufacturing in the resource-rich and GCC group.

Table 2A.2   Correlates of the Share of Manufactures and Services in GDP

	Share of manufacture (% GDP)			Share of services (% GDP)		
	(1)	(2)	(3)	(4)	(5)	(6)
Whole sample	All	All	All	All	All	All
Ln(GDPpc)	1.82***	1.69***	1.69***	0.78	0.74	0.74
	[0.39]	[0.38]	[0.38]	[0.77]	[0.78]	[0.78]
Ln(Rents)		−0.08*	−0.08*		−0.02	−0.02
		[0.05]	[0.05]		[0.06]	[0.06]
MENA Dummy			−14.15***			−19.15***
			[1.45]			[2.00]
Constant	16.19***	16.21***	16.21***	28.34***	28.34***	28.34***
	[0.78]	[0.78]	[0.78]	[0.90]	[0.90]	[0.90]
Country fixed effects	Yes	Yes	Yes	Yes	Yes	Yes
Year fixed effects	Yes	Yes	Yes	Yes	Yes	Yes
Observations	3,232	3,232	3,232	3,648	3,648	3,648
R-squared	0.838	0.839	0.839	0.828	0.828	0.828

Source: Authors.

Notes: GDP capita in thousands of $US at constant prices (2005). "Rents" is the share of total rents in GDP in percentage points. The sample is an unbalanced panel of 167 countries for the period 1980–2004. Robust standard errors in brackets. *** $p<0.01$, ** $p<0.05$, * <0.1.

Table 2A.3   Correlates of the Share of Manufactures and Services in GDP in MENA

MENA	Share of manufacture (% GDP)				Share of services (% GDP)			
	(1) All MENA	(2) Resource poor	(3) Resource rich	(4) GCC	(5) All MENA	(6) Resource poor	(7) Resource rich	(8) GCC
Ln(GDPpc)	−1.02	6.07***	−3.34	−2.22	−8.44***	3.71**	−12.45***	0.64
	[1.28]	[1.31]	[4.14]	[1.40]	[3.24]	[1.72]	[2.67]	[2.62]
Ln(Rents)	−0.33*	−0.14	−0.40	−3.67***	−0.82*	−0.04	−4.22***	−21.18***
	[0.18]	[0.08]	[1.17]	[0.86]	[0.42]	[0.08]	[0.77]	[1.84]
Constant	15.17***	9.63***	12.77***	31.30***	76.26***	43.04***	74.96***	109.85***
	[5.10]	[1.67]	[3.44]	[5.31]	[12.77]	[2.21]	[6.18]	[8.58]
Country fixed effects	Yes	Yes	Yes	Yes	Yes	Yes	Yes	Yes
Year fixed effects	No	No	No	No	No	No	No	No
Observations	304	111	83	110	312	111	91	110
R-squared	0.763	0.539	0.511	0.729	0.762	0.872	0.932	0.726

Source: Authors.

Notes: GDP capita in thousands of $US at constant prices (2005). Rents is the share of total rents in GDP in percentage points. The sample is an unbalanced panel of 16 countries for the period 1980–2004. Robust standard errors in brackets. *** p<0.01, ** p<0.05, * p<0.1.

Returning to the entire sample, there is also a strong MENA specificity after controlling for country and time fixed effects. Time-varying omitted country effects must then have been important in the development of manufactures. Many omitted factors, specific to countries, could account for the significance of this dummy variable, including different macroeconomic cycles, policy changes, country-specific external shocks, or measurement errors.

Figure 2A.2 takes the longest period of data available for trade and manufacturing shares in GDP for MENA countries and compares them with those predicted from a regression of the share on per capita GDP (PPP). It complements the cross-section results in figure 2A.1.

Two patterns stand out. From figure 2A.2a, one sees that, on average, MENA countries do not undertrade on an aggregate basis, but that the spread around the predicted relation is large. Consistently, for all estimated relations, the resource-poor group is closer to the predicted line. Figures 2A.2b and 2A.2c show that the share of manufacturing in GDP and the share of manufacturing exports in GDP are under the regression line, mostly for the resource-rich and GCC groups. Countries in the resource-poor group are either on or above the 95 percent confidence interval.

The bottom part of figure 2A.2 shows the evolution of the absolute deviation of country shares from the predicted relation over the four time periods. Across all shares, the resource-poor group is closest to the norm and is relatively stable. The resource-rich group gets closer to the predicted line for the overall trade share, but distances itself for the value added share of manufacturing in GDP and especially for the share of manufactured exports. On the other hand, the GCC group is either closer or getting closer to the predicted line for both the predicted share of manufacturing in value added or of the predicted share of manufactured exports.

A Lagging Services Sector in the Resource-Rich Countries

Services and services trade have taken a growing role as a source of growth around the world, even though this is not evidence that the services sector is an engine of growth. However, the dramatic changes in the 3Ts—technology, transportability, and tradability—of many services activities have contributed to the growing share of the services sectors in GDP growth (50 percent of South Asia's GDP's growth between 1980–85 and 2000–07; see Reis and Farole 2010).[35]

Figure 2A.2 Actual versus Predicted Shares of Manufactures and Manufacture Exports: MENA

a. predicted trade share (% of GDP)

b. trade share (% of GDP) on GDP per capita

c. predicted share of manufacture value-added (in production)

d. manufacture value-added (% of GDP) on GDP per capita

(continued next page)

Figure 2A.2 *(continued)*

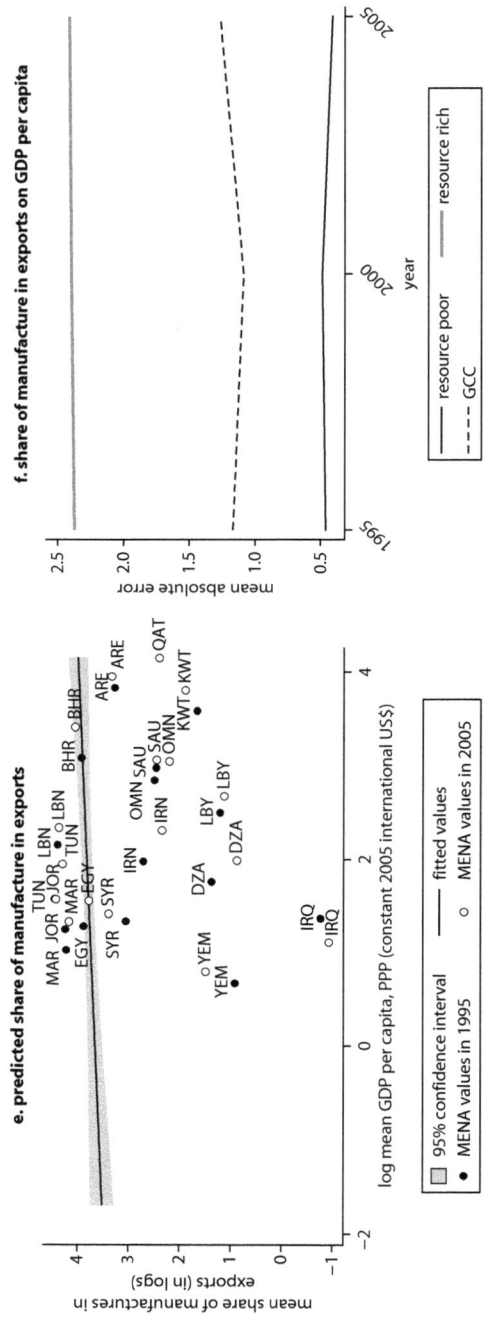

e. predicted share of manufacture in exports

mean share of manufactures in exports (in logs)

log mean GDP per capita, PPP (constant 2005 international US$)

- 95% confidence interval
- fitted values
- ● MENA values in 1995
- ○ MENA values in 2005

f. share of manufacture in exports on GDP per capita

mean absolute error

year

— resource poor
— resource rich
- - - GCC

Sources: Authors' calculations of the share of manufacture on total exports, based on WDI and BACI International Trade Database at the Product Level. Trade flows cover the period 1998–2007.

Notes: "Manufacture exports" is equal to total exports minus exports in HS 2-digit codes 01–28. The observed value of each variable in *t* is the average of the variable over the period (*t, t+4*). Fitted OLS line of variable on y-axis against log mean per capita income on x-axis.

However, it remains that the services sector is very heterogeneous, mingling very high- and very low-productivity activities, making services productivity difficult to capture with a single measure. Overall, one would expect a growing share of services in GDP as per capita income increases, capturing Engel effects, among others, in consumption and the development of human-capital-intensive professional services. In cross-section data, this should be reflected in a positive correlation between the share of services in GDP and per capita income (Hoekman and Mattoo 2008). But this is not the case for the MENA sample because the income per capita coefficient has a positive, but statistically insignificant sign (right-hand side of table 2A.3)—although the expected positive pattern between per capita income and the service share holds for the resource-poor group in the bottom of the table. Rents are also negatively associated with the share of services in GDP in the resource-rich and GCC groups in the right part of table 2A.3, a pattern again coherent with resource-curse effects.

Overall, the pattern across the three groupings is distinctive. As a region, MENA's openness to trade is close to predicted norms but, as expected, the share of non-oil manufactures in trade is below predicted patterns, and there is a MENA specificity in non-oil trade across all three groups. There is also evidence of a lagging manufacturing and services sector for the resource-poor group consistent with resource-curse effects.

Annex 2B Ten Observations on Successful Growth

General Principles

After four years of inquiry, acknowledging that there are "no recipes, just ingredients," the Commission on Growth and Development (2008) identified five common characteristics of successful growth—the fundamentals of competitiveness:[36]

1. Committed, credible, capable government: governments must have the capacity to devise and the institutions to implement a growth strategy.[37]
2. Macroeconomic stability: modest inflation and sustainable public finances.
3. High rates of savings and investment: high and sustained investment underpinned to a large extent by domestic savings. Countries that had

achieved high and sustained growth had impressive rates of public investment in infrastructure, education, and health.

4. Full exploitation of the world economy: knowledge acquired in the global economy and exploitation of global demand is the fundamental basis of economic catch up and sustained growth. Promoting foreign direct investment and foreign higher education can support knowledge transfer.
5. Letting markets allocate resources: policies need to ensure that product and labor markets are flexible enough to allow structural transformation of the economy from agriculture to manufacturing to take place and there is, at minimum, no bias against exports.

Correlates of Success

Evidence—economy-wide, sectoral, firm, and product level studies—has indicated some of the channels through which increases in productivity take place:

6. A substantial reduction in barriers to trade (tariffs, nontariff barriers) is associated with an increase in the growth rate (and in the investment share in GDP) (Wacziarg and Welch 2008).
7. A sustained real exchange rate depreciation, that is, a competitive currency (that is subsequently maintained) is a key ingredient to sustained export surges and to higher investments and growth (Freund and Pierola 2011).
8. A positive causal relationship flows from openness to income levels and from trade liberalization to medium-term growth.
9. Export spells are likely to last longer when carried out with physically closer partners and a preferential trading relation is associated with longer export spells (Brenton, Saborowski, and Von Uexkull 2010).
10. The linkages between a successful export strategy and the pattern of export expansion are still open to debate and are likely to be context specific and highly idiosyncratic as evidenced by recent case studies of firms' successes.

Annex 2C Applied Tariff Protection Is Still Relatively High

Controlling for per capita income, estimated applied tariffs around the world were about 10 percentage points lower in 2008 than they were around 1990 (figure 2C.1). The fit also became tighter, as the 95 percent

Figure 2C.1   Predicted Applied MFN Protection

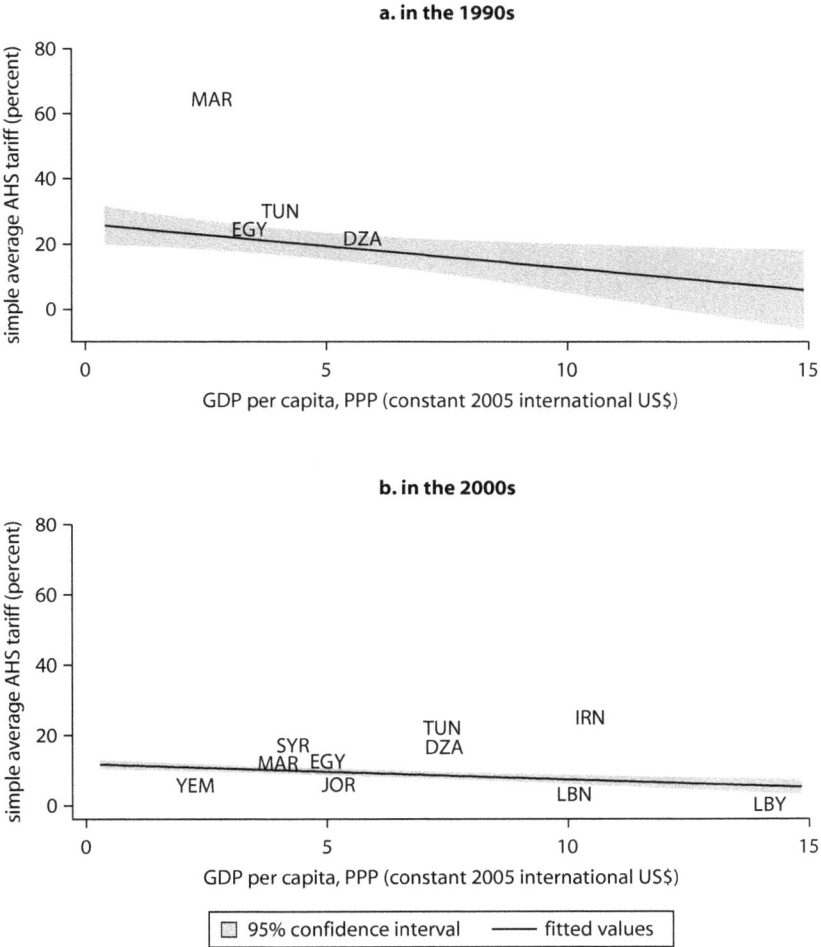

a. in the 1990s

b. in the 2000s

☐ 95% confidence interval   —— fitted values

Source: Authors' calculations from WITS data based on 1995 or closest available year for predicted protection in the 1990s and on 2008 or latest available year for the bottom figure.

Notes: Countries included have at least 0.5 million inhabitants and GDP per capita in PPP is less than US$15,000. In the 1990–95 period, only four MENA countries had tariffs. The estimated equations are: Tariff = 22.6 – 1.08 income + 0.04 pop for the 1990s based on 63 countries; and Tariff = 11.84 – 0.44 income + 0.00 pop for the 2000s based on 116 countries. The mean standard deviation of MENA countries has reduced from 44.57 to 15.57 over the period, calculated for Algeria (DZA), Egypt (EGY), Morocco (MAR) and Tunisia (TUN). For the mean absolute deviation, a reduction is also observed (from 14.91 to 6.28).

confidence interval bands narrowed. MENA countries improved their relative position and drew closer to the "norm" average protection level, even though Algeria, Tunisia, and the Islamic Republic of Iran still had high protection and their observations are still spread out of the confidence interval.

Annex 2D Ad-Valorem Equivalents Estimations

New estimates of the ad-valorem equivalents (AVEs) are computed for those countries that impose single nontariff measures (NTMs) on tariff lines (this gives a better estimate than the usual estimate where the AVE is computed over the four "core" NTMs).

To get a better idea of the importance of NTMs, the incidence of NTMs of MENA countries is compared with that of other countries in a large sample of countries.[38] Table 2D.1 shows the frequency distribution of core NTMs for the MENA countries in the NTM database. First, although not indicated in the table, the Arab Republic of Egypt had a core NTM in 4,941 tariff lines out of a potential of 4,961, that is, only 20 tariff lines at the HS-6 level did not have a core NTM in Egypt in 2002–04. On a comparative basis, this is an extremely high level of incidence for the core NTMs, even though prohibitions are important, and these are mostly on the basis of origin (such as ban on imports from Israel).[39] Second, whereas 74 percent of the tariff lines in the sample of 91 countries only had one core NTM, according to the table, only 31 percent of the tariff lines in the MENA sample had one core NTM. For the MENA countries, the multiple NTMs are usually a combination of a technical regulation and a prohibition at the HS-6 level either for the environment, a suspension of issuance of licenses, or a prohibition on the basis of origin (embargo).

Carrère and de Melo (2011) have calculated the average tariff equivalent for these single NTM lines (74 percent of the tariff lines in the Kee, Nicita, and Olarreaga 2009 sample). This has the advantage of estimating the tariff equivalent of each NTM separately so that one can distinguish between the AVE for, say, technical regulation and the one for nonautomatic licensing. These estimates are reported in table 2D.2 for the MENA countries that have single NTM lines.

Several patterns emerge. First, the distribution of AVEs is narrow with most NTMs having an AVE of around 40 percent, which is almost always greater than the corresponding tariff rate on that product line. Second, the simple tariff on the product line with the NTM

Table 2D.1 Frequency Distribution of the Number of NTMs

Number of NTMs per HS6 lines	Egypt, Arab Rep. of	Algeria	Morocco	Tunisia	Saudi Arabia	Oman	Lebanon	Jordan
1	0	0	4,641	1,510	685	642	1,298	2,073
2	9,774	7,354	590	276	106	36	322	764
3	162	2,418	15	30	0	0	3	21
4	0	1,760	0	0	0	0	0	0
5	0	90	0	0	0	0	0	0
Total lines	9,936	11,622	5,246	1,816	791	678	1,623	2,858

Source: Authors' calculations from Carrère and de Melo (2011).

Table 2D.2   Ad-Valorem Equivalents of NTMs

NTM codes	Frequency	AVE simple (%)	Tariff simple (%)	AVE weight (%)	Tariff weight (%)
31 Administrative pricing					
Saudi Arabia	8	42.90	11.69	12.35	15.77
61 Nonautomatic licensing					
Jordan	823	47.09	13.90	40.20	9.98
Lebanon	661	40.57	4.61	35.14	5.92
Oman	47	28.57	32.94	16.41	41.90
Saudi Arabia	540	35.50	10.96	16.35	5.45
Tunisia	226	33.21	26.39	15.69	20.59
63 Prohibitions					
Lebanon	9	63.65	2.18	4.67	0.05
Oman	27	47.63	6.92	28.95	8.23
Saudi Arabia	56	45.35	5.19	10.16	12.61
71 Single channels for imports					
Jordan	2	72.54	6.29	72.54	6.29
Lebanon	10	44.86	3.37	72.43	4.61
Saudi Arabia	3	74.09	5.20	35.99	5.77
Tunisia	34	24.55	19.10	16.83	15.00
81 Technical regulations					
Jordan	1,248	40.21	15.06	20.14	14.23
Lebanon	618	44.58	8.51	58.36	9.07
Morocco	4,641	13.99	27.08	7.36	22.50
Oman	568	49.43	8.73	55.97	3.23
Saudi Arabia	78	35.60	11.00	38.61	10.80
Tunisia	1,250	44.22	43.90	27.21	27.69

Source: Authors' calculations from Carrère and de Melo (2011). The 2-digit NTM classification level has the four NTMs listed here plus voluntary export price restraint (32), variable charges (33), and quotas (62).
Note: AVEs are calculated only for tariff lines that have a single NTMs.

is usually high, often above the average tariff for manufactures. Third, as can be seen from a comparison of the unweighted and import-weighted AVE, the estimates show that NTMs are associated with smaller import volumes.

As a final comparison, figure D2.1 plots the estimates of the AVEs for the sample of countries against per capita income for the two most important NTMs, nonautomatic licensing and technical regulations. Nonautomatic licensing is quite widespread, while technical regulations are more common in high-income countries.[40] For the other countries, they are spread around the estimated line, so one can confirm that the AVE of single-product-line NTMs are high for the MENA countries, but that the estimates are in line with those for other countries.

Figure 2D.1   Ad-Valorem Equivalent of NTMs and per Capita Income
(For HS lines with single NTM)

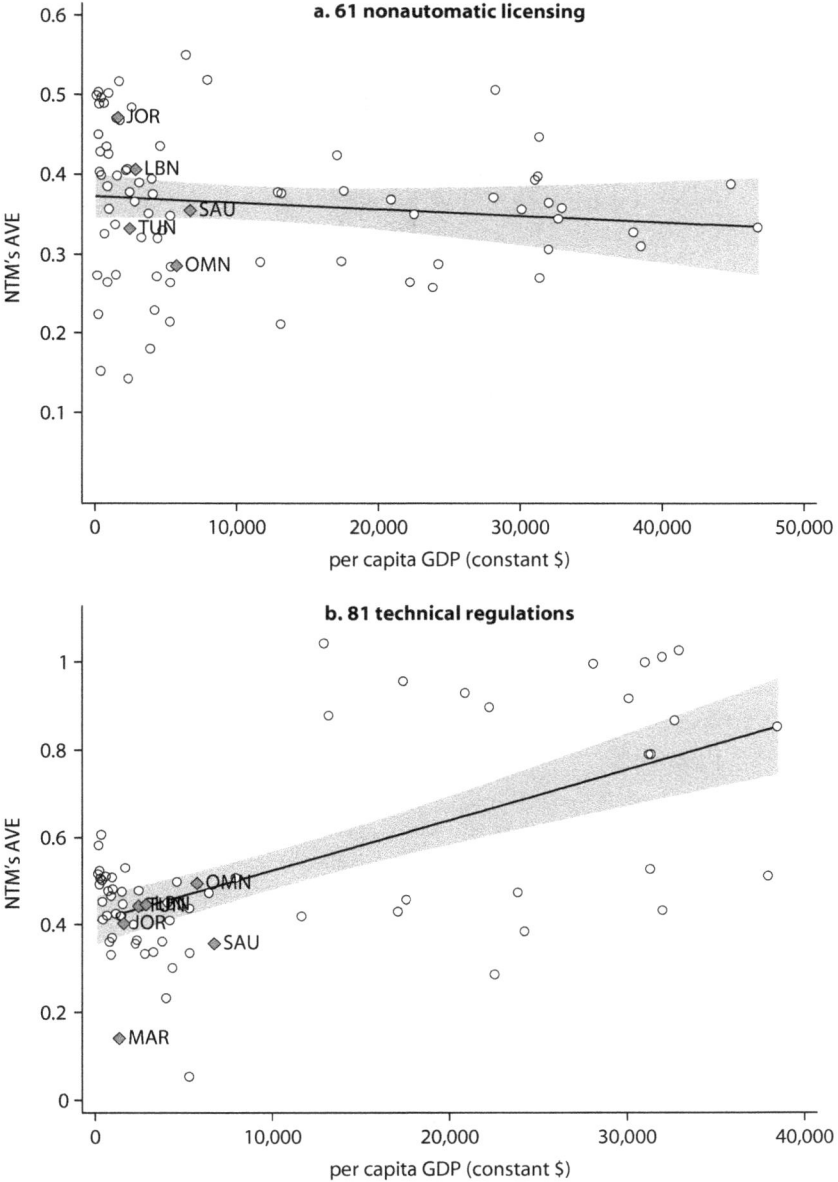

a. 61 nonautomatic licensing

b. 81 technical regulations

Notes

1. "Event analysis" refers to a situation when the data is reordered around an "event" that serves as the base year rather than the usual calendar year. In Hausmann, Pritchett, and Rodrik (2005), data are centered around the "event" of growth acceleration. Jerzmanowski (2006) also studies extreme growth events using a Markov-switching model that distinguishes four different growth regimes and finds that institutional quality helps determine the transition between these states. However, his study does not focus on regions, so it is not helpful in detecting a MENA specificity. See annex 2B for a list of factors considered essential for sustained growth.

2. Countries are benchmarked against per capita income level. The categories are OIL, LARGE and POINT (for more details see appendix A). LARGE countries are those with a population of at least 20 million in 2000; OIL exporters are the 15 major oil crude exporters listed by the U.S. Energy Information Administration (IEA 2005); and POINT countries are those with point source natural resources (classification taken from Isham et al. 2005).

3. Unfortunately over this period, more than one-third of the data for the two main groups of interest—resource-rich (6 countries) and resource-poor (5 countries)—are missing.

4. This sample includes 137 countries (22 countries, of which 5 are MENA countries, were excluded from the table because of incomplete data). It would have been desirable to evaluate the performance of nonmineral gross domestic product, but that would have reduced the sample to 80 countries, with only 4 MENA countries having complete data for the period 1982–2010.

5. Jordan regained its former UM status in 2010.

6. The REER is from the IMF's International Financial Statistics data, is computed as the relative price of a trade-weighted basket of foreign relative to domestic goods, and is an indicator of competiveness in world markets and of sustainability of the current account. It is different from the RER discussed later in the chapter.

7. See, for example, Koren and Tenreyro (2007), who show a statistically negative correlation between the volatility of growth and per capita income.

8. In the aggregate sample of Koren and Tenreyro (2010), there is no systematic correlation between sector and country-specific shocks, whereas there is a systematic positive covariance between the two in the GCC, indicating a procyclical fiscal policy that has persisted over the 30-year period they consider and contributed to greater growth volatility. Interestingly, high-performing Oman is the exception, displaying a negative covariance between sector-specific and country-specific shocks, suggesting the use of countercyclical fiscal policies.

9. Growth episodes are defined as an increase in GDP per capita growth of at least 2 percentage points for an eight-year period, with a post-acceleration growth of at least 3.5 percent a year.

10. With years of up breaks separated from years of down breaks by a semicolon, the following breaks were observed in the MENA region: Algeria (1981), Egypt (1975; 1970, 1980), Iran (1981; 1976), and Tunisia (1967;1972). Under this more stringent selection criterion, only three countries had an up break and the region had four down breaks.

11. As argued by Rodrik (2008), it also operates indirectly through two other channels: at the microlevel, market failures are likely to be more important in industrial production; and at the macrolevel, greater penalties from weak institutions that result in lower appropriability of returns to investment in tradables (because tradables depend more on property rights, contract enforcement, and hold-up problems). Thus undervaluation (an increase in the relative price of tradables) boosts tradables at the margin, contributing to higher growth.

12. And also of export surges—see below for microchannels through which an RER undervaluation could lead to export growth, especially of new products.

13. Before 1970, data for too many MENA countries were missing.

14. Country fixed effects control for omitted country-specific effects, such as the differences between resource-rich and resource-poor countries, and period fixed effects control for common shocks in a period. The five-year averages smooth fluctuations and attempt to capture the finding that undervaluation preceding and accompanying export surges typically lasts more than 10 years (see Freund and Rocha 2011).

15. The result is close to the one obtained by Rodrik (2008), although the RER appreciation associated with the Balassa-Samuelson effect (an increase in the productivity of tradables as income rises brings about an RER appreciation) is about half in value because the latest Penn World Tables have raised substantially their estimates of price levels for low-income countries.

16. Estimates for Lebanon and Iran reflect periods of conflict. We refrained from dismissing outlier observations according to a specific criterion (that is, all observations with an RER over- or undervaluation greater than 200 percent), not only because we would have lost MENA observations, but also because the extreme values in column 1 are an indicator of overall macroeconomic instability in the region. The only excluded observation from the full sample is Zimbabwe (2005).

17. Annex 2C to this chapter shows that, despite catching up, MENA tariffs are still high after controlling for per capita income and country size. The advalorem equivalents of nontariff measures in Annex 2D (computed from data for 2001) also show a high level of incidence of core nontariff barriers compared with other countries.

18. These indicators are averages of several subindicators, some subjective. There is overlap, and one could take an average across the indicators in columns 6 to 9.

19. Because we wish to estimate the model separately for MENA countries, estimation is over a panel of three years covering 2006 to 2008.

20. We thank Caroline Freund and Nadia Rocha for providing the data on time to export. Our specification is the same as theirs except that we deal only with exports of manufactures. All control variables in the vectors X and Z not reported here had expected signs and were usually significant.

21. As done by Freund and Rocha (2011) in their table 4.

22. Carrère, Gourdon, and Olarreaga (2011) detect an increase in intrapartner trade over the period 1990–2009 for MENA countries following the implementation of the Pan-Arab Free Trade Agreement and other regional agreements in MENA.

23. Drawing on interviews with 23 successful exporters across the region, Nassif (2010) concludes that successful export products in the region appear to depend most on information about new business opportunities and risk taking.

24. In their sample of 22 middle-income countries, 5 are from MENA (Algeria, Egypt, Lebanon, Morocco, and Saudi Arabia), and the firms are taken from 8 sectors (textiles, leather, garment, agroprocessing, metals and machinery, chemical and pharmaceuticals, wood and furniture, and plastics). The number of firms per industry per country is often small (no more than 1,600 in leather), calling for caution in interpreting the results.

25. Export concentration is associated with greater volatility of the real exchange rate, which in turn is associated with greater volatility in GDP growth. See Di Giovanni and Levchenko (2011) and Loayza and Raddatz (2007).

26. Easterly and Reshef (2010) document the extensive errors in the HS-6 level data for low-income countries and also opt for aggregation to the HS-4 level. As customary, we use reporter data. As in Brenton, Saborowski, and Von Uexkull (2010), we delete left-censored observations (right-censoring is not a problem).

27. Brenton, Saborowski, and Von Uexkull (2010) use a five-digit SITC product classification which gives 1,271 products for 82 exporting countries and 53 importing countries for 20 years (1985 to 2005). We only have data for the 10-year period covering 1998–2007 for HS-4 level (1,241 commodities). However the International Trade Dataset at the Product Level (BACI) from Centre d'Etudes et de Prospectives et d'Informations Internationales (CEPII) corrects for the reliability trade flow data. This gives us 142 countries, from which we exclude countries whose population is less than half a million.

28. Survival rates across the three MENA groups are very similar

29. The list of covariates is inspired by Brenton, Saborowski, and Von Uexkull (2010), but we have taken out those that are consistently insignificant. Estimates with the more general Prentice-Gloecker model often do not converge because of the large sample size, so we stick with estimates from the Cox model.

30. The expected effect of volatility on survival is ambiguous. On the one hand, higher volatility can cause more accidental deaths in trade relations. On the other, higher volatility means more hysteresis (that is, export spells last longer because of fixed costs in exporting). When volatility increases, the mean of the distribution moves up because of truncation of the distribution. A higher mean results in longer survival.

31. Oil is not necessarily a low-productivity sector with no positive externalities. Much of the successful experience of Norway, which moved from laggard to leader among the Nordic countries, has been ascribed to the positive externalities from the high-technology oil sector (Larsen 2004, 17, cited in Lederman and Maloney 2008). An example of low-productivity services are the 800,000 chauffeurs earning around $350 a month who are needed to drive Saudi women, who are not allowed to drive.

32. Work on patterns of growth and structural change over the long haul was initiated by Chenery and colleagues (Chenery and Syrquin 1975; Chenery, Robinson, and Syrquin 1986). That work established several stylized patterns: strong Engel effects in consumption associated with a diminishing share of agriculture in GDP at the expense of manufactures and services as a country develops; less trade in large countries; and a deepening of interindustry linkages as per capita income increases.

33. The data on rents are for a sample of 174 countries from the World Bank database on adjusted net savings (see Bolt, Matete, and Clemens 2002 for details). They include rents from 15 natural resources, which are calculated as the difference between the market value of extracted materials and the average extraction cost and expressed as a share of GDP. As discussed, rents are an outcome variable and hence not a good proxy for resource abundance.

34. Freund and Pierola (2011) report a correlation of 0.95 between production and exports in log levels for a sample of 113 countries over the period 1999–2008. In growth rates, the correlation is still 0.57.

35. Francois and Hoekman (2010) highlight some key characteristics of the services sector: "services facilitate transactions through space (transport, telecommunications) or time (financial services)" and "services are frequently direct inputs into economic activities, and thus determinants of the productivity of the 'fundamental' factors of production—labor and

capital—that generate knowledge, goods and other services. Education, R&D and health services are examples of inputs into the production of human capital."

36. The report identified 13 successes (that is, countries with an average growth rate of 7 percent over a 30-year period) and notes that pragmatism, skepticism, experimentalism, and persistence have high payoffs.

37. The commission stressed that policies need to be prioritized, reasonably well implemented, and, tolerantly administered, implying some minimum degree of probity and absence of the worst excesses of corruption.

38. Kee, Nicita, and Olarreaga (2009). This database covers 91 countries, of which 21 are OECD countries, for 4,961 HS-6 product categories. With 8 countries, MENA is sufficiently well represented to make comparisons.

39. For comparison, on average across countries, only 1,341 lines have at least one of the five core NTMs. The Republic of Korea is the country with the least incidence of core NTMs (two lines). Countries with the highest incidence (4,941 lines) are Algeria, Côte d'Ivoire, Egypt, Malaysia, Morocco, Nigeria, Philippines, Sudan, Senegal, and Tanzania. The median number of lines with at least one of the core NTMs is 799.

40. Because the AVE is computed as the estimated impact of the NTM on trade via the dummy variable (after controlling for other factors affecting trade including tariffs) divided by the corresponding estimated import demand elasticity, the positive correlation between the AVE and per capita income could reflect a lower elasticity coefficient (in absolute value) for high-income countries. However, this is not the case (see Carrère and de Melo 2011, figure 6). So the pattern reveals more restrictive technical regulations in high-income countries rather than differences in import demand elasticities. The scatter plot does not include Algeria and Egypt, the two countries with the most NTMs (only multiple NTMs per product line)

References

Acemoglu, D., S. Johnson, and J. Robinson. 2005. "Institutions as a Fundamental Cause of Long-Run Growth." In *Handbook of Economic Growth*, vol. 2, P. Aghion and S. Durlauf, eds., pp. 385–472. Amsterdam: North-Holland.

Amin, M., and S. Djankov. 2009. "Natural Resources and Reforms." CEPR Discussion Papers 7229, Center for Economic Policy Research, London.

Augier, P., O. Cadot, J. Gourdon, and M. Malouche. 2011. "Non-Tariff Measures in the MNA Region: Improving Governance for Competitiveness." World Bank, Washington, DC.

Besedes, T., and T. Prusa. 2006. "Ins, Outs and the Duration of Trade." *Canadian Journal of Economics* 104 (1): 635–54.

———. 2010. "The Role of Extensive and Intensive Margins and Export Growth." *Journal of Development Economics* 96 (2): 371–79.

Bhattacharya, S., and R. Hodler. 2010. "Natural Resources, Democracy and Corruption." *European Economic Review* 54 (4): 608–21.

Bolt, K., M. Matete, and M. Clemens. 2002. "Manual for Calculating Adjusted Net Savings." World Bank Environment Department, Washington, DC.

Brenton, P., M. Pierola, and E. Von Uexkull. 2009. "The Life and Death of Trade Flows: Understanding the Survival Rates of Developing Country Exporters." In *Breaking into New Markets: Emerging Lessons for Export Diversification*, ed. R. Newfarmer, W. Shaw, and P. Walkenhorst. Washington, DC: World Bank.

Brenton, P., C. Saborowski, and E. Von Uexkull. 2010. "What Explains the Low Survival Rate of Developing Country Export Flows." *World Bank Economic Review* 24 (3): 474–99.

Brunnschweiler, C., and E. Bulte. 2009. "Natural Resources and Violent Conflict: Resource Abundance, Dependence and the Onset of Civil Wars. " *Oxford Economic Papers* 61 (4): 651–74.

Cadot, O., C. Carrère, and V. Strauss-Kahn. 2011. "Export Diversification: What Is behind the Hump?" *Review of Economics and Statistics* 93 (2): 590–605.

Carrère, C., and J. de Melo. 2011. "Notes on Detecting the Effects of Non-Tariff Measures." *Journal of Economic Integration* (Center for Economic Integration, Sejong University) 26: 136–68.

Carrère, C., J. de Melo, and J. Wilson. 2010. "Distance and Rgionalization of Trade for Low-Income Countries." Policy Research Working Paper 5214, World Bank, Washington, DC.

Carrère, C., J. Gourdon, and M. Olarreaga. 2011. "Regional Integration in the Context of Diverse Resource Endowments." University of Geneva.

Chenery, H., S. Robinson, and M. Syrquin, eds. 1986. *Industrialization and Growth: A Comparative Study.* Oxford, U. K.: Oxford University Press for the World Bank.

Chenery, H., and M. Syrquin, eds. 1975. *Patterns of Development, 1950–70.* Oxford, U.K.: Oxford University Press for the World Bank.

Collier, P., and A. Hoeffler. 2004 "Greed and Grievance in Civil War." *Oxford Economic Papers* 56 (4): 563–95.

Comin, D., W. Easterly, and E. Gong. 2010. "Was the Wealth of Nations Determined in 1000 B.C.?" *American Economic Journal: Macroeconomics* 2 (3): 65–97.

Commission on Growth and Development. 2008. "The Growth Report: Strategies for Sustained Growth and Inclusive Development."

Corden, W. M., and J. P. Neary. 1982. "Booming Sector and De-Industrialization in a Small Open Economy." *Economic Journal* 92 (368): 825–48.

Di Giovanni, J., and A. Levchenko. 2011. "The Risk Content of Exports: A Portfolio View of International Trade." In *NBER International Seminar on Macroeconomics 2011*, 97–151. National Bureau of Economic Research, Cambridge, MA.

Easterly, W., and A. Reshef. 2010. "African Export Successes: Surprises, Stylized Facts and Explanations." NBER Working Papers 16597, National Bureau of Economic Research, Cambridge, MA.

Francois, J., and B. Hoekman. 2010. "Services Trade and Policy." *Journal of Economic Literature* 48 (3): 642–92.

Freund, C., and B. Bolaky. 2008. "Trade, Regulations and Income." *Journal of Development Economics* 87: 309–21.

Freund, C., and M. D. Pierola. 2011. "Global Patterns in Exporter Entry and Exit." World Bank, Washington, DC.

Freund, C., and N. Rocha. 2011. "What Constrains Africa's Exports?" *World Bank Economic Review* 25 (3): 361–86.

Gelb, A. H. 1988. "Oil Windfalls: Blessing or Curse?" World Bank, Washington, DC.

Gylafson, T. 2001. "Natural Resources, Education and Economic Development." *European Economic Review* 45 (6): 847–59.

Harrison, A., and A. Rodríguez-Clare. 2009. "Trade, Foreign Investment, and Industrial Policy for Developing Countries." NBER Working Paper 15261, National Bureau of Economic Research, Cambrige, MA.

Hausmann, R., J. Hwang and D. Rodrik. 2007. "What You Export Matters." *Journal of Economic Growth* 12 (1): 1–25.

Hausmann, R., B. Klinger and J. Lopez-Calix. 2010. "Export Diversification in Algeria." In *Trade Competitiveness of the Middle East and North Africa: Policies for Export Diversification*, ed. Lopez-Calix, Walkenhorst, and Diop. Washington, DC: World Bank.

Hausmann, R., L. Pritchett, and D. Rodrik. 2005. "Growth Accelerations Trade Competitiveness of the Middle East and North Africa: Policies for Export Diversification." *Journal of Economic Growth* 10 (4): 303–29.

Hausmann, R., and R. Rigobon. 2003. "An Alternative Interpretation of the Resource Curse: Theory and Policy Implications." NBER Working Papers 9424, National Bureau of Economic Research, Cambridge, MA.

Hausmann, R., and D. Rodrik. 2003. "Economic Development as Self-Discovery." *Journal of Development Economics,* 72 (2): 603–33.

Hidalgo, C., B. Klinger, A. Barabasi, and R. Hausmann. 2007. "The Product Space Conditions for the Development of Nations." *Science* 317 (5837): 482–87.

Hoekman, B., and A. Mattoo. 2008. "Services Trade and Growth." Policy Research Working Paper 4461, World Bank, Washington, DC.

Isham, J., M. Woolcock, L. Pritchett, and G. Busby. 2005. "The Varieties of Resource Experience: Natural Resource Export Structures and the Political Economy of Economic Growth." *World Bank Economic Review* 19 (2): 141–74.

Jerzmanowski, M. 2006. "Empirics of Hills, Plateaus, Mountains and Plains: A Markov-Switching Approach to Growth." *Journal of Development Economics* 81 (2): 357–85.

Jones, B., and B. Olken. 2008. "The Anatomy of Start-Stop Growth." *Review of Economics and Statistics* 90 (3): 582–87.

Kee, H., A. Nicita, and M. Olarreaga. 2009. "Estimating Trade Restrictiveness Indices." *Economic Journal* 119: 172–99.

Kinda, T., P. Plane, and M. A. Veganzones-Varoudakis. 2011. "Firm Productivity and Investment Climate in Developing Countries: How Does Middle East and North Africa Manufacturing Perform?" *The Developing Economies* 49 (4): 429–62.

Koren, M., and S. Tenreyro. 2007. "Volatility and Development." *Quarterly Journal of Economics* 112 (1): 243–87.

———. 2010. "Volatility, Diversification, and Development in the Gulf Cooperation Council Countries." Kuwait Program on Development, Governance, and Globalization in the Gulf States, no. 9.

———. 2012. "Volatility, Diversification and Development in the Gulf Cooperation Council Countries." In *The Transformation of the Gulf: Politics, Economics and the Global Order,* ed. David Held and Kristian Ulrichsen. London: Routledge.

Kuran, T. 2010. *The Long Divergence: How Islamic Law Held Back the Middle East.* Princeton, NJ: Princeton University Press.

Larsen, R. 2004. "Escaping the Resources and the Dutch Disease: When and Why Norway Caught up and Forged ahead of Its Neighbors." Discussion Paper 377, Statistics Norway Research Department, Oslo.

Lederman, D., and W. Maloney. 2008. "In Search of the Missing Resource Curse" *Economia* 9 (1): 1–57.

———, eds. 2007. *Natural Resources, Neither Curse nor Destiny.* Stanford, Calif.: Stanford University Press.

Leite, C., and J. Weidmann. 2002. "Does Mother Nature Corrupt? Natural Resources, Corruption, and Economic Growth." In *Governance, Corruption and Economic Perfomance,* ed. George T. Abed and Sanjeev Gupta. Washington, DC: International Monetary Fund.

Loayza, N. V., and C. Raddatz. 2007. "The Structural Determinants of External Vulnerability." *World Bank Economic Review* 21 (3): 359–87.

Mehlum, H., K. Moene, and R. Torvik. 2006. "Institutions and the Resource Curse." *Economic Journal* 116 (508): 1–20.

Nabli, M. K. 2007. "Breaking the Barriers to Higher Economic Growth." World Bank, Washington, DC.

Nassif, C. 2010. "Promoting New Exports: Experience from Industry Case Studies." In *Trade Competitiveness of the Middle East and North Africa: Policies for Export Diversification*, ed. Lopez-Calix, Walkenhorst, and Diop. Washington, DC: World Bank.

Rajan, R., and A. Subramanian. 2007. "Aid, Dutch Disease and Manufacturing Growth." International Monetary Fund, Washington, DC.

Reis, J. G., and T. Farole. 2010. "Exports and the Competitiveness Agenda: Policies to Support the Private Sector." World Bank, Washington, DC.

Rodrik, D. 2008. "The Real Exchange Rate and Economic Growth." *Brookings Papers on Economic Activity* 39 (2): 365–439.

———. 2009. "Growth after the Crisis." Discussion 65, Commission on Growth and Development, Washington, DC.

Shui, L., and P. Walkenhorst. 2010. "Regional Integration: Status, Developments and Challenges." In *Trade Competitiveness of the Middle East and North Africa: Policies for Export Diversification*, ed. Lopez-Calix, Walkenhorst, and Diop. Washington, DC: World Bank.

———. 2011. "Toward Open Regionalism in the Middle East and North Africa." In *Trade Competitiveness of the Middle East and North Africa: Policies for Export Diversification*, ed. Lopez-Calix, Walkenhorst, and Diop. Washington, DC: World Bank.

Wacziarg, R., and K. H. Welch. 2008. "Trade Liberalization and Growth: New Evidence." *World Bank Economic Review* 22 (2): 187–231.

Wood, A. 1997. "Openness and Wage Inequality in Developing Countries: The Latin American Challenge to East Asian Conventional Wisdom." *World Bank Economic Review* 11 (1): 33–57.

World Bank. 2004. "Trade, Investment, and Development in the Middle East and North Africa: Engaging with the World." World Bank, Washington, DC.

———. 2009. "From Privilege to Competition: Unlocking Private-Sector Led Growth." World Bank, Washington, DC.

CHAPTER 3

Rents, Regulatory Restrictions, and Diversification toward Services in Resource-Rich MENA

Ndiamé Diop and Jaime de Melo

For Middle East and North Africa (MENA) countries, especially the resource-rich ones, finding ways to develop services sectors is crucial for widening the scope of job creation. First, the public sector, the largest employer in the region, has reached a saturation point in almost every single country. Going forward, rapid job creation in the public sector is likely to hold down aggregate labor productivity and deprive the private sector of the skilled labor it needs to grow. Second, rents from natural resources have been an obstacle to the development of manufacturing industries because of currency overvaluation leading to a low profitability for tradable manufactures (Rodrik 2008; Havrylyshyn 2010; Lopez-Calix, Walkenhorst, and Diop 2010). Third, agriculture has become a minor source of labor absorption and is expected to continue declining as a share of GDP with income growth and technological advances. Thus, the services sector is the most promising source of job creation in resource-rich MENA countries.[1]

That vibrant local service sectors can be developed in resource-rich countries has been taken for granted for a long time. This belief was underpinned by at least two combined theoretical considerations. First, Engel's Law effects in consumption imply that demand for services tends to increase with income due to higher income elasticity of demand for services relative to agricultural products (Chenery and Syrquin 1975; Chenery, Robinson, and Syrquin 1986). At the same time, services sectors, implicitly assumed to be largely nontradable in earlier Dutch Disease models, would be positively affected by an appreciation of the real exchange rate subsequent to a natural resource boom (Corden and Neary 1982; Corden 1984).

While Engel's consumption effects are likely to operate, the "largely nontradable" status of services implicit in the earlier Dutch Disease literature is no longer valid. The revolutions in technology, transportability, and tradability of the past 20 years have significantly increased the tradability of services and have led to substantial cross-border "disembodied" trade in services (Francois and Hoekman 2010). A large number of services sectors are now able to be moved offshore, implying an imperative to be competitive to maintain domestic production. In addition to services enabled by information and communications technology (ICT) (back-office business process services, information technology services, software development, and so forth) that can be delivered from a distance, many professional services (engineering, legal, accounting, auditing, and the like) are now produced through temporary movement of professionals. In other words, firms located in a country such as Saudi Arabia are no longer dependent on domestic service providers and can import many of the services they need if local producers are not competitive.

This chapter investigates whether MENA has managed to diversify in services and, if not, why. The first section presents the stylized facts about the size and performance of services sectors in MENA. It shows that contrary to the global pattern, the share of services in gross domestic product (GDP) has been declining with income in the resource-rich MENA countries. Using econometric analysis, the second section shows the negative role of rents in explaining this observed structural change. The next section discusses the role of microeconomic regulations and shows that rather than alleviating the negative effect of rents on the relative contraction of services, regulatory restrictions compound the difficulty of developing competitive services sectors in MENA. The chapter concludes by highlighting the contrast between resource-rich and resource-poor MENA countries. While rents hinder the development of services sectors and encourage import of services in resource-rich countries, they can indirectly widen the scope for diversifying exports and increasing job creation in resource-poor countries of the region by demonstrating the potential benefits of regional integration in services.

Services in MENA: Stylized Facts

Recent Growth and Trade Performance

Although MENA's services sectors have grown faster than average GDP in the past decade, they remain much less dynamic than the same sectors in East Asia, South Asia, and, to a lesser degree, Europe and Central Asia. During the period 2000–10, services sectors grew at an average annual rate of 9.5 percent in East Asia, 8.3 percent in South Asia, and 5.4 percent in MENA. Within MENA, they grew by 1 percent of GDP more in the Gulf Cooperation Council (GCC) countries than in the rest of MENA.

Figure 3.1 illustrates the importance of services sectors to growth. It compares growth in the real GDP per capita to growth in services value added of MENA countries. The positive relationship between the two variables is by no means causality, but it is a correlation implying that MENA countries with high growth in services tend to have high GDP or, conversely, countries with high overall economic growth have high services growth. Ghani and Kharas (2010) have found this positive correlation for 136 countries. Finding ways to boost growth in services is thus an important instrument for increasing overall GDP growth in most countries, and MENA is no exception.

The relative underperformance of MENA on growth in services is mirrored by its poor performance in services trade. In 2000–08, trade in services grew 23 percent annually in South Asia, 16 percent in East Asia, and 14 percent in Europe and Central Asia compared with 12.4 percent annually in MENA in the same period. Along with Latin America and Sub-Saharan Africa, MENA is a minor exporter in the global market for ICT, finance, and other business services—a market that has exploded over the past decade. MENA's share in global services trade stagnated at around 2.8 percent between 2000 and 2008 (Borchert, Gootiiz, and Mattoo 2011).

Figure 3.1   Services Value-Added Growth and GDP Growth in MENA

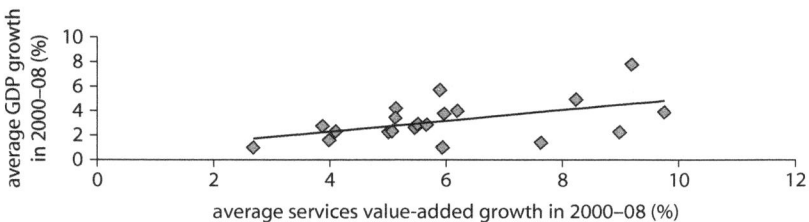

Source: World Development Indicators, World Bank.

The lack of dynamism of MENA's services exports reflects its low value added orientation. Exports of services remain largely dominated by travel services (tourism-related). In 2008, this category accounted for 53 percent of total services exports. Travel and transport together made up 78 percent of total exports. This is in sharp contrast with South Asia (driven by India), where ICT and finance are the leading export services, making up 55 percent of exports. Transport and travel services account for a mere 24 percent of total exports in that region (figure 3.2). Although resource-poor MENA (Jordan, Lebanon, Morocco, and Tunisia) has shown strong potential for growth in exporting nontraditional services (such as ICT-enabled and business services) in recent years, they are still minor players in the global market.

Has MENA Diversified toward Services?

One of the key objectives that MENA countries set for themselves in the early 1990s was to diversify away from natural resources toward services and manufacturing (see chapter 1). Typically, as countries become richer, the share of agriculture declines, giving way to a rise in the share of manufacturing and services. This often happens because of technological advances in agriculture, which increase agricultural productivity and drive resources out of agriculture toward manufacturing and services (Baumol 1967; Chenery and Syrquin 1975). At the same time, Engel's

Figure 3.2   Composition of Exports in MENA and South Asia, 2008

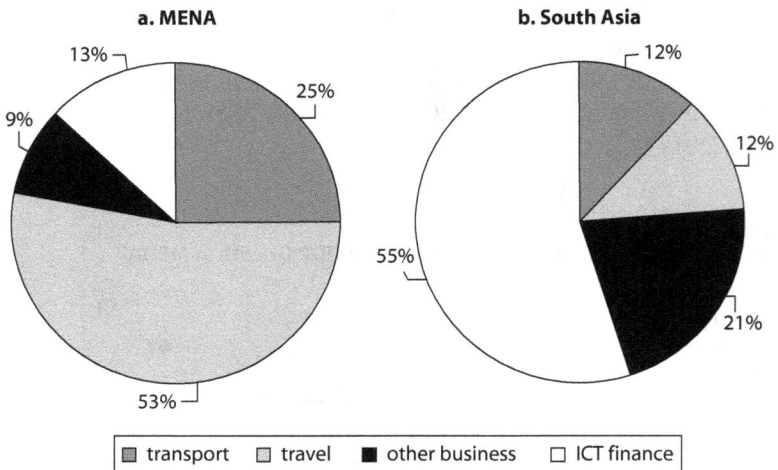

a. MENA

13%
25%
9%
55%
53%

b. South Asia

12%
12%
55%
21%

□ transport   □ travel   ■ other business   □ ICT finance

Source: International Monetary Fund.

Law stipulates that as household income increases, the percentage of income spent on food decreases, while the proportion spent on other goods and services increases. Thus both supply and demand forces suggest a decline in the share of agriculture in overall GDP and an increase in nonagricultural GDP as income increases.

Consistent with theoretical predictions, agriculture has shrunk over the past 30 years, to varying degrees, in all regions of the world. The share of agriculture in GDP contracted by more than 60 percent in East Asia, 58 percent in Europe and Central Asia, 46 percent in South Asia, 38 percent in Latin America and the Caribbean, 36 percent in MENA, and 23 percent in Sub-Saharan Africa. Figure 3.3 shows how the economic structures of the different regions of the world have changed following the relative contraction of agriculture. In Asia and Europe and Central Asia, the contraction of agriculture has given way to a large services sector. In contrast with the rest of the world, the services sector has shrunk overall in MENA, but the share of industry (dominated by mining and oil) in GDP has increased. While this aggregate result certainly conceals large variations across MENA, it indicates that services have contracted in a least some countries of the region.

It is important to distinguish different groups of countries within MENA, given the region's heterogeneity and the abundance of natural resources in

Figure 3.3   Changes in the Composition of GDP: 1980–83 to 2007–10

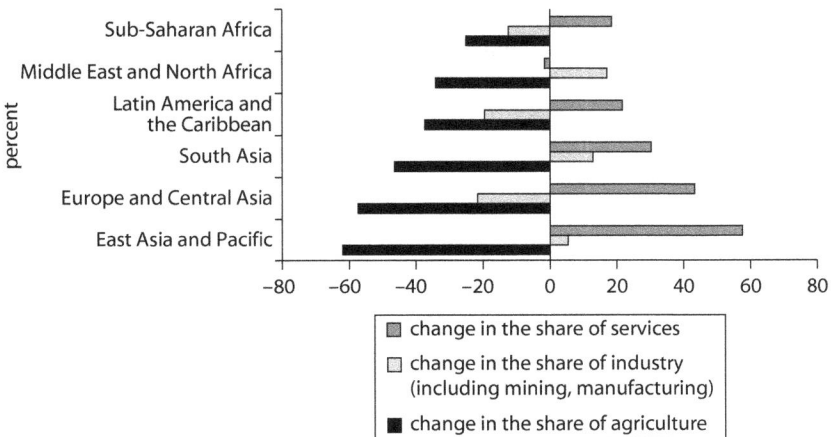

Source: World Development Indicators.

many of them. Figure 3.4 shows a pooling (five-year averages for each observation) of the pattern of services in GDP for each of three MENA groups: resource-poor labor-abundant countries (RPLA), resource-rich labor-abundant countries (RRLA), and resource-rich labor-importing countries (RRLI). The figure shows a clear positive correlation between services shares in GDP and per capita GDP for the resource-poor group, implying that resource-poor countries—the Arab Republic of Egypt, Jordan, Lebanon, Morocco, and Tunisia—conform to theoretical expectations. In contrast, for the two resource-rich country groups, the curve fitting consistently shows that the share of services in GDP is a decreasing function of per capita GDP. In other words, the decline in the share of services in GDP in the region is driven by both the resource-rich labor-importing countries (Bahrain, Kuwait, Oman, Qatar, Saudi Arabia, and United Arab Emirates) and the resource-rich labor-abundant countries (Algeria, Islamic Republic of Iran, Iraq, Syrian Arab Republic, and Republic of Yemen).

As figure 3.5 shows, the contraction of services sectors in resource-rich MENA is at odds with global trends. There is indeed evidence of a

Figure 3.4   Services Share in GDP by Level of Income

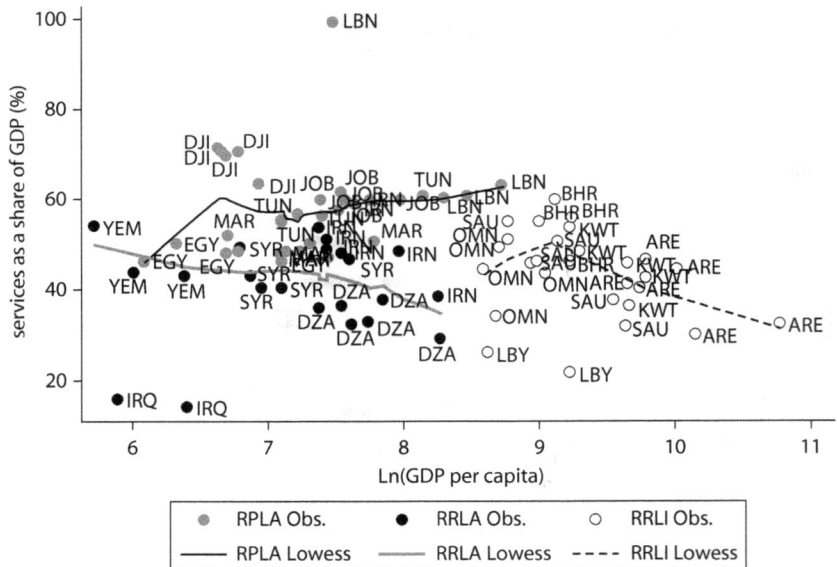

Source: Authors.
Note: The figure is showing averages over five-year periods. RPLA = resource-poor labor-abundant; RRLA = resource-rich labor-abundant; RRLI = resource-rich labor-importing; Obs = observations; Lowess = locally weighted scatterplot smoothing = fitting trend. Lowess (band width = 0.8) excludes Iraq, Libya, and Qatar.

Figure 3.5 Services Share in GDP, MENA versus Rest of the World

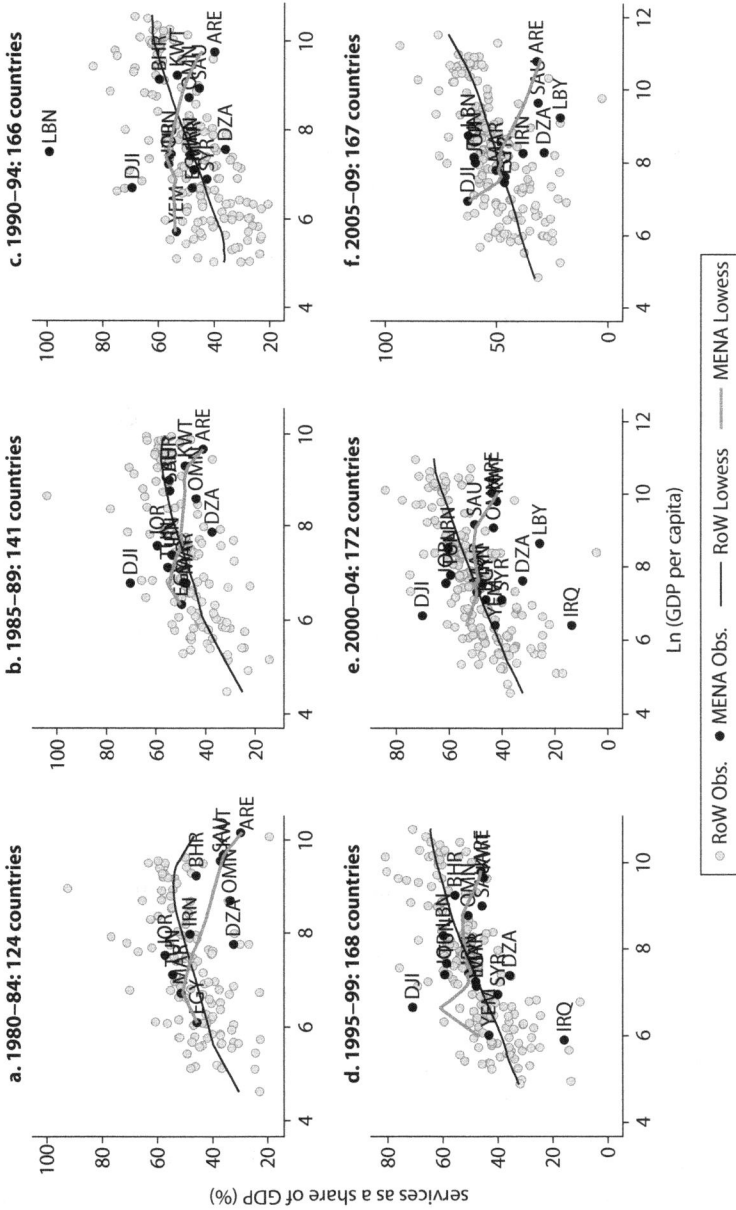

Source: Authors.

Note: The figure shows averages over five-year periods. RoW = rest of world; Obs = observations; Lowess = locally weighted scatterplot smoothing = fitting trend. Lowess (band width = 0.8) excludes Iraq, Libya, and Qatar.

positive correlation between the share of services in GDP and income per capita as shown by Hoekman and Mattoo (2008), who use a large cross-section sample of countries from around the world.

Before examining the correlates of the apparent relative shrinking of services in resource-rich MENA in the next section, it is important to examine whether the above result is a statistical artifact, reflecting a rapid increase in the share of the mining sector (dominated by oil) in these economies. In other words, we need to control for the role of oil. One way to do this is to examine the changes in the composition of nonmining GDP over time and see how the share of services in nonmining GDP evolves.[2] Unfortunately, we do not have a complete series of nonmining value added for many MENA countries. For the countries for which data are available, however, the observation of a shrinking share of services over time is confirmed. This observation contrasts with resource-poor countries, where the share of services in nonmining GDP is either increasing or stagnant. Figure 3.6, which shows the share of services in nonmining GDP declining in resource-rich Kuwait and Saudi Arabia and Kuwait while increasing in resource-poor Jordan and Tunisia and Jordan, illustrates this point.

Relative Roles of Engel's Effects in Consumption and Rents

There are two traditional explanations for the positive correlation between the share of services and income. First is Engel's effects in consumption: as incomes rise, demand for services tends to rise owing to higher income elasticity of demand for services relative to agricultural products (Chenery and Syrquin 1975; Chenery, Robinson, and Syrquin 1986). The second explanation is Baumol's cost "disease" effect: fast productivity growth in agriculture as a result of mechanization frees up resources allocated to manufacturing and services (Baumol 1967).

In addition to these effects, under the assumption that services are (largely) nontradable, an appreciation of the real exchange rate subsequent to a natural resource boom would increase the relative profitability of the services sectors and promote their development. As noted, however, the revolutions in technology, transportability, and tradability have made a large number of the services sectors tradable, weakening this argument. In any case, empirically, the positive correlation between the share of services in GDP and per capita income is well established for most countries in the world (Hoekman and Mattoo 2008).

Figure 3.6   Share of Services in Nonmining GDP

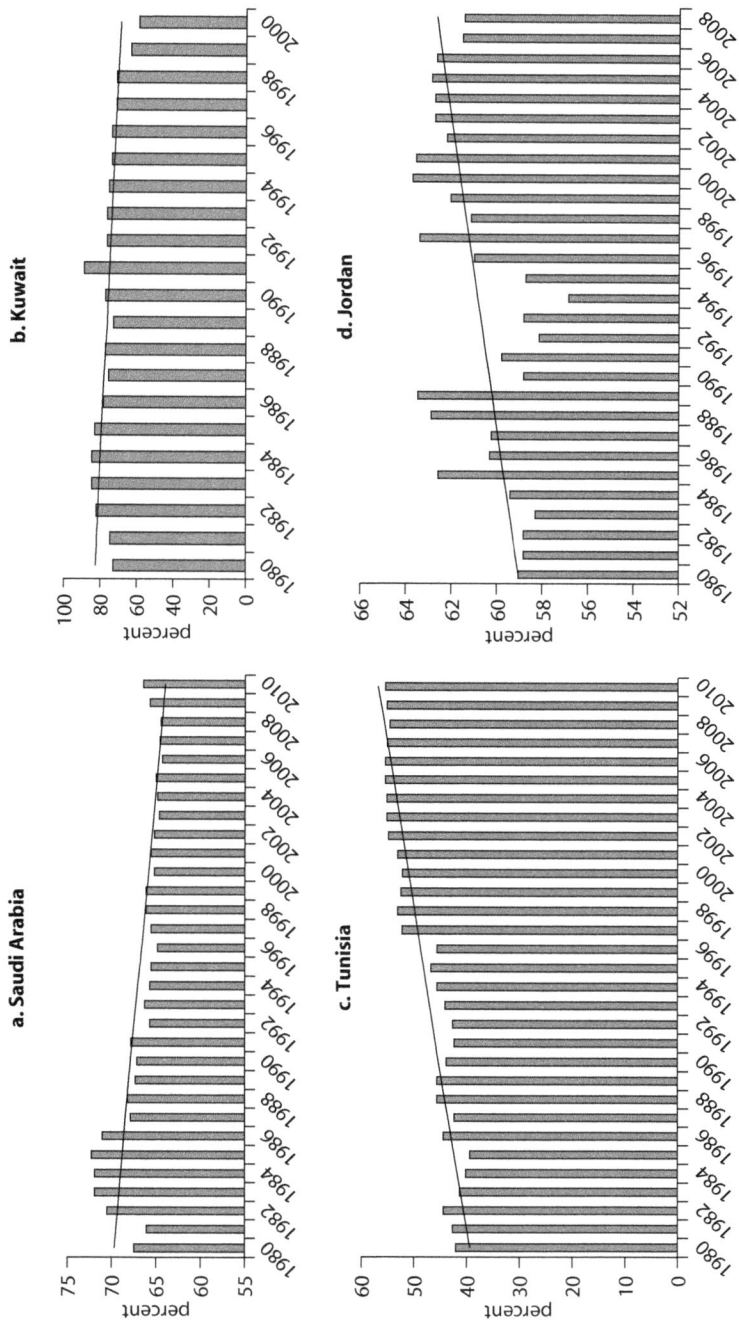

a. Saudi Arabia

b. Kuwait

c. Tunisia

d. Jordan

Source: World Development Indicators, World Bank.
Note: Data for Kuwait are not available after 2000.

Engel's Effects

We start by examining whether Engel's effects operate for services in MENA. Figure 3.7 confirms a rising share of consumption of services in GDP as GDP per capita rises. Thus, Engel's effects in consumption operate for services in MENA. However, a large and growing share of this consumption of services is satisfied by imports in MENA in sharp contrast with the rest of the world. Figure 3.8 shows that imports of services have been growing in MENA, thereby compensating for the low domestic production of services in resource-rich countries and supplying the local consumption market.

The Role of Resource Rents

The pattern of production and imports of services observed above may be associated with a real exchange appreciation that accompanies the rents from exports of natural resources in the region. With an increasing share of services becoming tradable as transaction costs have fallen, rather than observing a general expansion of the services sector when the real exchange rate appreciates for the resource-rich group, one observes an increase in the imports of services that cannot be produced competitively domestically because of the depressed relative profitability of production in these activities. We turn to the possible effects of rents and appreciation of the real exchange rate below.

To explore the role of natural resources in the development of services sectors, we draw on data on rents from natural resources for a sample of 174 countries. This data is obtained from the World Bank database on adjusted net savings (see details in Bolt, Matete, and Clemens 2002). More specifically, rents are calculated as the difference between the market value of extracted materials and the average extraction cost and are expressed as a share of GDP. Rents from 150 natural resource-rich countries are compiled in this way from 1970 to 2004 (services data are available only since 1980). Table 3.1 shows clearly that resource-rich labor-abundant (RRLA) and especially resource-rich labor-importing (RRLI) countries in MENA have, by far, the largest share of rents in GDP in the world. Although data on rents in the period 2005–10 are not available, one can safely assume that they have only grown larger as a result of the dramatic increase in oil price during that period.

To explore further the correlates of the share of services in GDP, table 3.2 reports the results of the regressions of the share of value-added in services over GDP on country and year fixed effects, the

Figure 3.7   Share of Consumption of Services in GDP

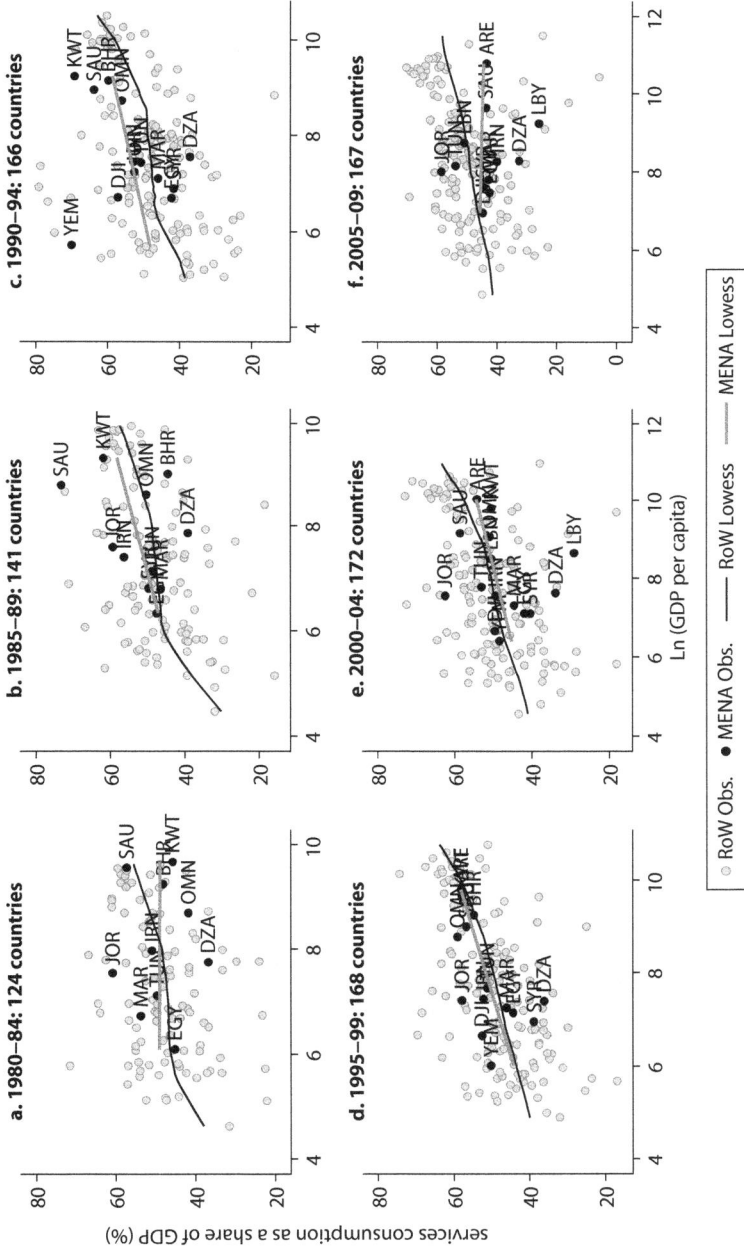

Source: Authors.

Note: The figure shows averages over five-year periods. RoW = rest of world; Obs. = observations; Lowess = locally weighted scatterplot smoothing = fitting trend. Lowess (band width = 0.8) excludes Iraq, Libya, and Qatar.

Figure 3.8 Share of Imported Services in GDP

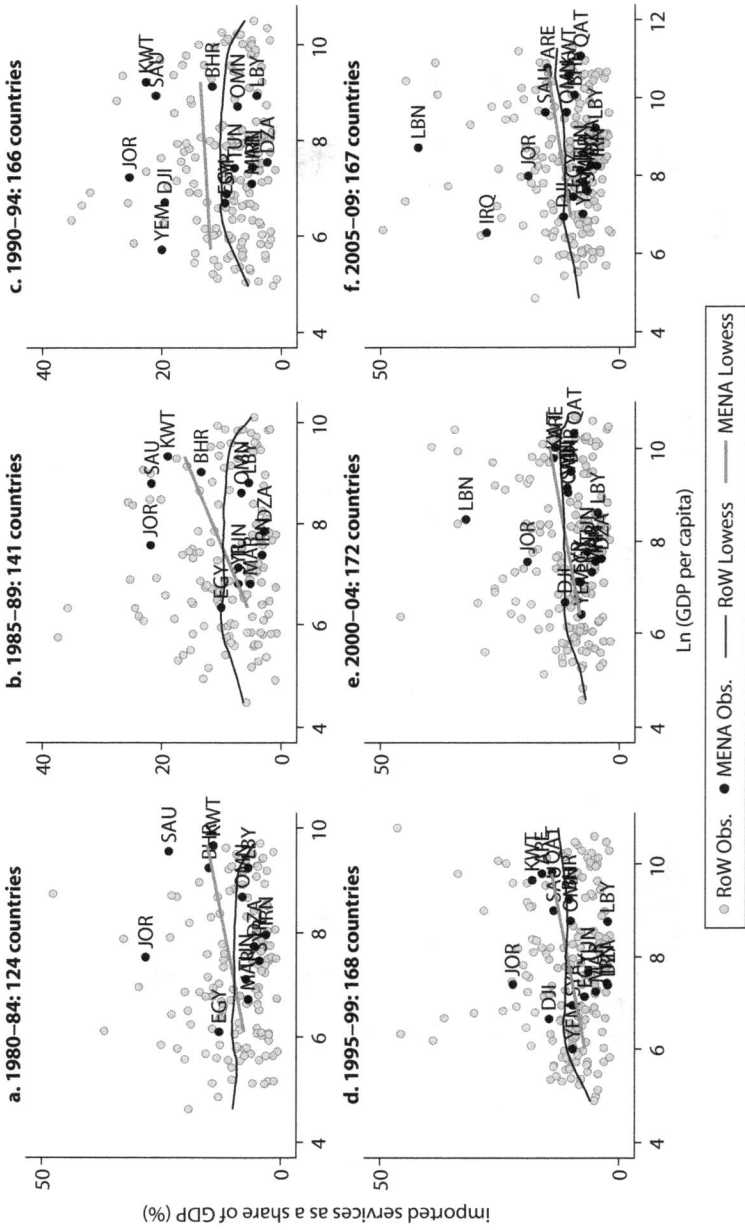

a. 1980–84: 124 countries

b. 1985–89: 141 countries

c. 1990–94: 166 countries

d. 1995–99: 168 countries

e. 2000–04: 172 countries

f. 2005–09: 167 countries

imported services as a share of GDP (%)

Ln (GDP per capita)

○ RoW Obs.   ● MENA Obs.   —— RoW Lowess   —— MENA Lowess

Source: Authors.

Note: The figure shows averages over five-year periods. RoW = rest of world; Obs = observations; Lowess = locally weighted scatterplot smoothing = fitting trend. Lowess (band width = 0.8) excludes Iraq, Libya, and Qatar.

Table 3.1   Share of Rents from Natural Resources in GDP
percentage

Region	1980–84	1985–89	1990–94	1995–99	2000–04
MENA RPLA	13	5	2	1	2
MENA RRLA	19	16	23	22	32
MENA RRLI	55	35	34	30	41
East Asia and Pacific	4	4	3	3	4
Europe and Central Asia	3	1	1	3	3
Latin America and Caribbean	7	4	3	3	4
North America	6	3	2	2	3
South Asia	5	3	3	2	3
Sub-Saharan Africa	6	4	4	4	6

Source: Authors' computation from UNCTAD data.

country fixed effects controlling for time invariant omitted variables, and the time fixed effects for time-dependent common shocks. The regressions are run for a large number of countries including those in MENA (first three columns of table 3.2), then for all countries except MENA, for MENA only, and for the three subgroups within MENA, namely resource-poor, resource-rich labor-abundant, and resource-rich labor-importing. The first three columns confirm the positive correlation between the share of services in GDP and per capita GDP. A 10 percent increase in GDP per capita is associated with an increase of 0.2 to 0.5 percent in the share of services in GDP. Column 5 shows that this correlation turns negative for MENA, mostly because of the resource-rich countries (columns 8 and 9).

As documented in table 3.1, a large share of the GDP of resource-rich countries is composed of rents generated by their natural resources. To control for the association between rents and the share of services in GDP, table 3.3 introduces the logarithm of the rents among the correlates. In all the specifications, the share of rents in GDP is significantly negatively correlated with the share of services in GDP. Moreover, the relationship between the share of services in GDP and GDP per capita becomes positive for resource-rich labor-importing countries in regression 7. For resource-rich labor-abundant countries (regression 6), the relationship is still negative, but much less significant. While these are only correlations because they do not account for the potential endogeneity of rents, nor does the inclusion of fixed effects only control for time-invariant omitted variables, it would appear that rents associated with natural resource abundance in MENA countries partially account for the

Table 3.2 Correlates of the Share of Services in GDP

Services/GDP	(1) All	(2) All	(3) All	(4) All but MENA	(5) MENA	(6) MENA	(7) RPLA	(8) RRLA	(9) RRLI
Ln(GDP Cap)	0.02***	0.02***	0.05***	0.03***	−0.07***	−0.02***	−0.01	−0.08***	−0.14**
	(0.00)	(0.00)	(0.00)	(0.00)	(0.02)	(0.01)	(0.01)	(0.02)	(0.06)
MENA Dummy		−0.13***	−0.02***						
		(0.03)	(0.01)						
Constant	0.19***	0.19***	0.12***	0.16***	0.97***	0.61***	0.73***	0.93***	1.66***
	(0.02)	(0.02)	(0.01)	(0.02)	(0.10)	(0.04)	(0.07)	(0.14)	(0.60)
Country fixed effects	Yes	Yes	No	Yes	Yes	No	Yes	Yes	Yes
Time fixed effects	Yes	Yes	No	Yes	Yes	No	Yes	Yes	Yes
Observations	3,644	3,644	3,644	3,311	333	333	127	88	118
R-squared	0.84	0.84	0.35	0.85	0.85	0.03	0.94	0.95	0.78

Source: Authors.

Notes: Robust standard errors in brackets. *** p<0.01, ** p<0.05, * p<0.1.

Table 3.3 Determinants of the Services Share in GDP

Services/GDP	(1) All	(2) All	(3) All	(4) All but MENA	(5) MENA	(6) MENA	(7) RPLA	(8) RRLA	(9) RRLI
Ln(GDP Cap)	0.02***	0.02***	0.05***	0.03***	-0.07***	0	-0.01	-0.04**	0.08*
	(0.00)	(0.00)	(0.00)	(0.00)	(0.02)	(0.01)	(0.01)	(0.02)	(0.04)
Ln(Rents)	-0.002***	-0.002***	-0.005***	-0.005**	-0.01*	-0.01***	0	-0.07***	-0.17***
	(0.001)	(0.001)	(0.000)	(0.001)	(0.003)	(0.001)	(0.001)	(0.017)	(0.02)
MENA Dummy		-0.12***	0						
		(0.03)	(0.01)						
Constant	0.22***	0.22***	0.18***	0.19***	1.05***	0.72***	0.50***	2.13***	3.71***
	(0.02)	(0.02)	(0.01)	(0.03)	(0.11)	(0.03)	(0.08)	(0.35)	(0.40)
Country fixed effects	Yes	Yes	No	Yes	Yes	No	Yes	Yes	Yes
Time fixed effects	Yes	Yes	No	Yes	Yes	No	Yes	Yes	Yes
Observations	3,644	3,644	3,644	3,311	333	333	127	88	118
R-squared	0.84	0.84	0.43	0.85	0.85	0.40	0.94	0.96	0.85

Source: Authors.
Notes: Robust standard errors in brackets. *** p<0.01, ** p<0.05, * p<0.1.

negative correlation between services' production and per capita income.

The Role of Microeconomic Regulations

The preceding section shows that rents associated with natural resource abundance for MENA countries partially account for the negative correlation between services production and per capita income. Here we examine the role that policy and regulations may have played in the relative underperformance of MENA's services sectors. Restrictions on entry and business conduct either create rents within the services sectors that are captured by "protected incumbents," or increase the real cost of producing services. In both cases, these restrictions inflate the price of services (Dee 2005). Opening up the services sectors to competition would therefore reduce the behind-the-border "tax equivalent" or the "productivity loss equivalent" of the restrictions, thereby enhancing the competitiveness of services.

The underdevelopment of the services sectors in resource-rich MENA countries has deep policy roots in addition to the effects of rents. Indeed, regulatory barriers to market entry, licensing, and business conduct remain significant in MENA. The World Bank has compiled a database of restrictions to trade in services in five services sectors of 11 countries of the Pan Arab Free Trade Agreement (PAFTA), consisting of five GCC countries—Bahrain, Kuwait, Oman, Qatar, and Saudi Arabia—as well as Egypt, Jordan, Lebanon, Morocco, Tunisia, and the Republic of Yemen. Using this database, Borchert, Gootiiz, and Mattoo (2011) shed light on the degree of restrictiveness in five key services sectors in MENA compared with the rest of the world.

Figure 3.9 shows the services trade restrictiveness average indexes (STRI) calculated by Borchert, Gootiiz, and Mattoo (2011) using the World Bank database compiled from 102 countries. The GCC stands out as the region that is consistently more restrictive than the rest of the world in the five sectors surveyed.[3] When the share of services in GDP is overlaid on the same graph, there appears to be a net negative correlation between the magnitude of restrictions to trade in services and the share of services in GDP. Countries that have the most open services sectors are also those in which services make the largest contribution to overall GDP.

Furthermore, Borchert, Gootiiz, and Mattoo (2011) identified the "desire on the part of government authorities to retain a considerable

Figure 3.9   Restrictiveness of Services Trade Policies and Share of Services in GDP, MENA-GCC, GCC, and Other Regions

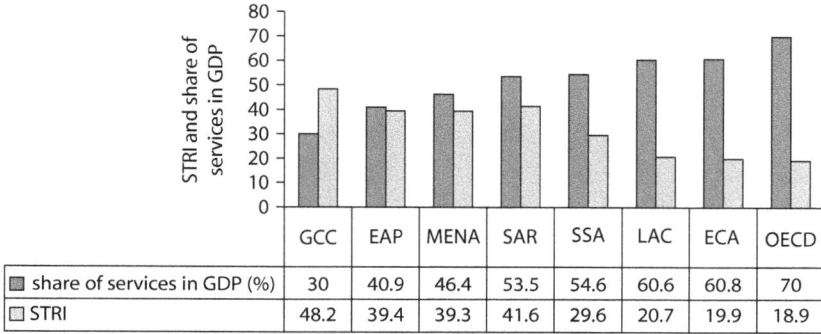

	GCC	EAP	MENA	SAR	SSA	LAC	ECA	OECD
share of services in GDP (%)	30	40.9	46.4	53.5	54.6	60.6	60.8	70
STRI	48.2	39.4	39.3	41.6	29.6	20.7	19.9	18.9

Source: Borchert, Gootiiz, and Mattoo 2011.
Note: STRI = services trade restrictiveness index.

degree of regulatory discretion" as a distinctive feature of PAFTA countries' applied policies. As a result, even in areas free of explicit restrictions, de jure openness may not always imply a commensurate degree of de facto openness, and vice versa. In many instances, the restriction is on business conduct or related to foreign equity limits. Across different sectors, the granting of new licenses remains opaque and highly discretionary in many countries. This discretion creates uncertainty about the rules of the game and may discourage domestic and foreign investors in the services sectors.

The high restrictions found by Borchert, Gootiiz, and Mattoo (2011) are consistent with those found by other studies or specific countries and service sectors in the region (box 3.1). They are also consistent with recent evidence pointing to a negative relationship between natural resources and the likelihood of undertaking microeconomic reforms. Drawing on the Doing Business data in a large sample of 133 countries, Amin and Djankov (2009) find that the proclivity to undertake microeconomic reforms that reduce regulation is much less in countries whose exports are concentrated in abundant natural resources. In the same vein, Freund and Bolaky (2008) find that the 12 MENA countries sampled have among the 50 percent most regulated economies among a large sample of 126 countries. Here, too, there may be a correlation with the presence of natural resources, given the multiple possibilities for regulatory capture in high-rent environments.

Box 3.1

Regulatory Restrictions in MENA: Findings from Other Case Studies

Case studies conducted in the Arab Republic of Egypt, Jordan, Lebanon (Marouani and Munro 2009); Morocco (World Bank 2007); and Tunisia (Dee and Diop 2010) show that services sectors in the region are liberalized but only to a limited extent. Governments tend to retain control, which leads to lack of transparency and discretion in how restrictions are applied:

- Foreign equity limits, for example, have been relaxed in most MENA countries in recent years, yet many service markets remain dominated by state-owned or domestic enterprises. High levels of state control persist in such cases through conflicting regulations that protect current market structures.
- In banking Morocco and Tunisia display many restrictions. In particular, these countries' capital accounts are only partially open, leading to constraints for cross-border and consumption abroad trade in services; Egypt has an intermediate level of openness driven by mode 2 (domestic consumption) whereas restrictions span modes 1, 3, and 4, Jordan's banking sector is relatively open, with restrictions only in modes 1 and 4, whereas Lebanon's banking sector is the most open in the region, with very few restrictions across modes 1, 2, and 3.
- In insurance, Egypt is among the least restrictive countries in non-GCC MENA, reflecting the liberalization of the sector in recent years. However, specific restrictions on commercial presence and economic needs tests are noted. On the other end of the spectrum, Morocco and Tunisia have among the most restrictive regulatory environment mainly because of restrictions on cross-border and consumption abroad. For Morocco, important nondiscriminatory concessions have been made as part of its free trade agreement with the United States (signed in 2004); once effective, the provisions in that agreement will significantly open the sector.
- In telecom, Dihel and Shepherd (2007) note that Middle East countries rank among the most restrictive for entry in fixed telecom services (relative to Asian and transition economies). However, in line with recent reforms, the sector is increasingly open, especially for mobile devices. Morocco and Jordan have the most open telecom sectors in the region.
- In maritime transport, major restrictions exist in Morocco and, to a lesser degree, Egypt. In contrast, Tunisia and Jordan have fairly open maritime sectors. Across the MENA countries, it is common to award preferential treatment to

(continued next page)

Box 3.1 *(continued)*

> ships flying the national flag. Jordanian and Egyptian flag carriers, for instance, are given discounts on prices such as port services. Egypt also gives flag carrier priority access to the cabotage market. In Morocco, regular shipping line services established in the country must fly the national flag. While open to foreign carriers, nonliner shipping is also restricted. Foreign shippers need to contract Moroccan liner intermediaries who have the exclusivity of chartering foreign vessels.
>
> • Finally, in air transport, Egypt displays high restriction levels in modes 1 and 2. On the other hand, Morocco, the most open in modes 1 and 4, has recently introduced many air service reforms in an effort to promote growth in the tourism industry, but it remains more closed than Jordan, which overall has the most open sector.

Export Diversification Opportunities for Resource-Poor MENA

If the increased tradability of services makes it challenging for resource-rich MENA countries to maintain domestic production of services, it offers formidable opportunities to resource-poor countries of the region. Indeed, given their cultural proximity and common language, these countries are well placed to capture a share of the large and growing market of tradable services in resource-rich MENA. To take advantage of these opportunities, however, resource-poor countries will need to undertake autonomous reforms to improve their competitiveness and work with resource-rich countries to reduce barriers to labor mobility within the region.[4] The competition with "enclaves" within the resource-rich countries where strategies are put in place to "force" diversification will remain stiff. Dubai, of the seven monarchies of the United Arab Emirates, is a good example (box 3.2).

Resource-poor countries will need to reduce the regulatory restrictions on business entry, licensing, and business conduct in their own services sectors to foster competition. As noted, the restrictions are significant, including in sectors that have a high potential for capturing a growing market in the region's resource-rich countries (such as professional services). In addition, improvements of the so-called backbone services (such as air transport and telecom) will be needed. These services are core inputs into most economic activities in all sectors, including

Box 3.2

Dubai's Successful Approach to Diversification

The United Arab Emirates (UAE) is a federation of seven monarchies: Abu Dhabi, Ajman, Dubai, Fujairah, Ras Al-Khaimah, Sharjah, and Umm al-Qaiwain. Abu Dhabi is the real "oil-rich" monarchy of the UAE, accounting for about 90 percent of national oil production. Capitalizing on the financial support of Abu Dhabi, Dubai has positioned itself as a world center of finance, commerce, transportation, and tourism. Dubai's model was based on attracting foreign direct investment; free movement of labor, capital, and goods across borders; an efficient bureaucracy with no hassle to private firms; and state-of-the-art infrastructures and backbone services. A key instrument was creation of free trade zones, which offer 100 percent foreign ownership with no taxation.

Dubai's market-oriented policies have led to significant diversification of the economy. New sectors have emerged, such as high-class tourism and international finance. The Dubai International Financial Centre offers 55.5 percent foreign ownership, no withholding tax, freehold land and office space, and a tailor-made financial regulatory system with laws similar to those governing leading financial centers in New York, London, Singapore, and Zürich. Dubai has also developed Internet and media free zones, offering 100 percent foreign ownership and untaxed office space for the world's leading ICT and media companies, along with the latest communications infrastructure to service them. Recent liberalization of the property market allowing noncitizens to buy freehold land has resulted in a major boom in the construction and real estate sectors.

While Dubai illustrates that diversification is possible in resource-rich countries, whether the Dubai model is sustainable is not clear. In 2008–09, the UAE was hit hard by the global banking crisis and a collapse of a real estate bubble. The economy has slowly rebounded since then. Furthermore, the diversification of the economy did not fully solve the Emirates' employment problem. Despite the establishment of an "Emiratization" program in the early 2000s to boost employment of nationals in the public and private sectors, UAE citizens account for less than 1 percent of the labor force in the private sector.

A very positive aspect of the UAE's strategy for long-term diversification is its massive investments in education. In 2010, investments in education accounted for 22.5 percent ($2.6 billion) of the overall budget. Multiple governmental initiatives actively promote training of high school dropouts and graduates in a multitude of skills needed in the private sector. Beyond directly sponsoring

(continued next page)

exporting service industries. To enhance their competitiveness, ICT-
enabled and professional services firms will need good quality and low-
cost services.[5]

Resource-poor governments also need to facilitate business-to-business
contacts and work with their resource-rich partners to reduce barriers to
mobility and promote "contract-based" movement of service suppliers.[6]
The main impediments to the movement of people arise from labor market laws in resource-rich countries, which rarely distinguish between
temporary and permanent labor mobility. Restrictions in this category in
the GCC (the main resource-rich services market) include burdensome
and costly procedures for work permits, limitations on the length of stay,
quantitative limits on work permits and sectoral bans, job nationalization,
educational conditions, and restrictions on foreign investment.[7]

Although a number of regulated professions feature nationality restrictions in both resource-poor and resource-rich countries, large niches exist.
In Libya, for example, jobs such as accountants are reserved for Libyan
nationals. In the United Arab Emirates, regulated professions in the areas
of accounting, engineering, law, and medicine, as well as agricultural, economic, fishing, industrial, and managerial and technical consultants, are
open to practitioners and employees from any GCC member state and
are accessible to non-GCC suppliers under certain conditions.

Bilateral agreements are a key vehicle for fostering trade in services
among neighboring countries. For instance, Iraq and Lebanon have concluded an agreement aimed at increasing the economic cooperation
between them, including exchange of expertise, specialists, and trainers
(Article 3). A similar agreement was concluded between Kuwait and
Lebanon, stipulating that the two parties shall facilitate the procedures for
granting entry visas to businessmen in both countries (Article 6). Other
agreements have been signed by Lebanon and Syria that promote labor
mobility between the two countries. Yet even though these agreements
mention some provisions related to exchanging expertise or facilitating

visa procedures, they do not include direct provisions organizing the temporary movement of people. Resource-poor countries interested in exporting services to the GCC and other resource-rich countries of MENA should aim at signing comprehensive bilateral agreements that address the specific barriers their firms are facing in these markets.

In brief, the services sectors of MENA present interesting complementarities and a huge potential for trade but all countries need to implement relevant policies to exploit these potential benefits.

Concluding Remarks

This chapter has shown that despite recent good growth performance, services sectors in resource-rich MENA countries have been declining as a share of GDP (and as a share of nonmining GDP) over time even as income per capita has increased. This negative relationship between the share of services in GDP and income per capita is opposite to observed global patterns. The analysis here suggests that this result is linked to the large rents generated by natural resources in these MENA countries. A large number of services sectors can now be stationed offshore or produced by temporary movement of service providers, implying that countries need to be competitive to maintain local production. Rents from natural resources tend to inflate wages and nontradable prices in resource-rich countries, thereby appreciating the real exchange rate and discouraging domestic production of tradable goods and services. This explains why resource-rich countries of MENA have become large importers of tradable services and why only domestic production of nontradable services (such as real estate, retail trade, hotels, and restaurants) has really developed.[8]

Microeconomic regulations on business have tended to compound the problem, rather than compensating for it. Restrictions on business entry, licensing, and business conduct are indeed significant and correlate negatively with the share of services in GDP. The MENA region, in particular resource-rich countries, stands out for heavy and discretionary restrictions of services sectors compared with the rest of the world. These restrictions either create rents within the services sector that are captured by "protected incumbents" or increase the real cost of producing services—in both cases inflating the price of services and further reducing competitiveness of tradable services sectors.

Regardless of the relative weight of different explanatory factors, the underdevelopment of tradable services in MENA resource-rich countries creates a big challenge for these countries. Indeed, manufacturing is difficult to develop competitively in these countries for similar reasons (rents and Dutch Disease)—oil-related industries are capital-intensive rather than labor-intensive, and public sectors are bloated. The scope for creating jobs for nationals in the productive sectors of these countries is limited. This situation is particularly problematic for resource-rich countries with abundant labor supply, such as Algeria, Saudi Arabia, Syria, and the Republic of Yemen. It is crucial for these countries to reduce regulatory restrictions in services sectors and invest heavily in education to compensate for the negative effect of rent on competitiveness.

Resource-rich economies should thus strive to reduce production costs thus offsetting the negative effect of rents on production in the nonresource tradable sectors. This can be done by reducing regulatory restrictions on entry and competition in these sectors. Experience from resource-rich countries around the world also shows the importance of investing in human capital and strengthening institutions (see Gelb 2011 for a summary). Finland, the Republic of Korea, and Norway are examples of countries that have invested to build a high-quality human capital base and have successfully diversified into high-tech manufacturing and services. Similarly, there is strong evidence that institutions matter for diversification. Gelb (2011, 67) argues that manufacturing sectors are "heavily dependent on strong contract enforcement, a rule of law and generally strong business environment." These arguments equally apply to services, if not more strongly so. Institutions that prevent or reduce rent-seeking are also important, as the example of Botswana shows (see Acemoglu, Johnson, and Robinson 2005).

If the increased tradability of services makes it challenging for resource-rich MENA to maintain domestic production of services, it offers formidable opportunities to resource-poor countries of the region. Indeed, given their cultural proximity and common language, these countries are well placed to capture a share of the large and growing market for tradable services in resource-rich MENA. To capture these opportunities, however, resource-poor countries will need to undertake autonomous reforms to improve their competitiveness, and work with resource-rich countries to reduce barriers to labor mobility within the region. More specifically, they will need to reduce their own restrictions to entry and competition in professional services, improve their backbone services (such as telecom and transport), and proactively engage resource-rich countries in reducing barriers to trade and mobility through specific bilateral agreements.

Notes

1. Resource-rich countries are net receivers of migrant workers, and outmigration is generally not a source of employment for nationals of these countries.
2. The mining sector in MENA is dominated by oil industries in resource-rich countries. Jordan, Morocco, and Tunisia, all considered "resource-poor countries" in this volume, do have a sizable phosphates sector. Rents from phosphates, however, are limited compared with those from oil.
3. Note that the United Arab Emirates is not included in the sample. This country's economy is the most open one in the GCC.
4. See Marouani and Zaki (2011) for a comprehensive discussion of barriers to mode 4 trade in MENA.
5. For empirical evidence on the impact of backbone services on productivity and competitiveness, see, for instance, Arnold, Javorcik, and Mattoo (2011) and Arnold, Mattoo, and Narciso (2008).
6. See Hoekman and Ozden (2009) for details on the distinction between "contract-based" movement of services providers and employment-based movements of persons.
7. An elaborate administrative mechanism exists to regulate the inflow and residence of non-GCC migrant workers to GCC countries. All foreign workers and their dependents entering a GCC country are issued a resident visa for the number of years stipulated in the work contract. All such visas are issued under the authority of a sponsor that wishes to hire the foreign worker.
8. The rapid development of a nontradable service, namely, the real estate sector, in conjunction with the underdevelopment of tradable services is an illustration of this point.

References

Acemoglu, D., S. Johnson, and J. Robinson. 2005. "Institutions as a Fundamental Cause of Long-Run Growth." In *Handbook of Economic Growth*, vol. 2, P. Aghion and S. Durlauf, eds., pp. 385–472. Amsterdam: North-Holland.

Amin, M., and S. Djankov. 2009. "Democracy and Reforms." Policy Research Working Paper 4835, World Bank, Washington, DC.

Arnold, J. M., B. S. Javorcik, and A. Mattoo. 2011. "Does Services Liberalization Benefit Manufacturing Firms? Evidence from the Czech Republic." *Journal of International Economics* 85 (1): 136–46.

Arnold, J. M., A. Mattoo, and G. Narciso. 2008. "Services Inputs and Firm Productivity in Sub-Saharan Africa: Evidence from Firm-Level Data." *Journal of African Economics* 17 (4): 578–99.

Baumol, W. J. 1967. "Macroeconomics of Unbalanced Growth: The Anatomy of Urban Crisis." *American Economic Review* 62 (June): 415–26.

Bolt, K., M. Matete, and M. Clemens. 2002. "Manual for Calculating Adjusted Net Savings." Environment Department, World Bank, Washington DC.

Borchert, I., B. Gootiiz, and A. Mattoo. 2011. "Policy Barriers to International Trade in Services: New Empirical Evidence." World Bank, Washington, DC.

Chenery, H., S. Robinson, and M. Syrquin, eds. 1986. *Industrialization and Growth: A Comparative Study.* Oxford, U.K.: Oxford University Press for the World Bank.

Chenery, H., and M. Syrquin. 1975. *Patterns of Development, 1950–1970.* Oxford, U.K.: Oxford University Press for the World Bank.

Corden, W. M. 1984. "Booming Sector and Dutch Disease Economics: Consolidation and Survey." *Oxford Economic Papers* 36: 359–80.

Corden, W. M., and J. P. Neary. 1982. "Booming Sector and De-Industrialisation in a Small Open Economy." *Economic Journal* 92 (368, December): 825–48.

Dee, P. 2005. "A Compendium of Barriers to Services Trade." Paper prepared for the World Bank, http://www.crawford.anu.edu.au/pdf/Combined_report.pdf.

Dee, P., and N. Diop. 2010. "The Economy-Wide Effects of Further Trade Reforms in Tunisia's Services Sectors." Policy Research Working Paper 5341, World Bank, Washington, DC.

Dihel, N., and B. Shepherd. 2007. "Modal Estimates of Services Barriers." OECD Trade Policy Working Papers 51, Organisation for Economic Co-operation and Development, Paris.

Francois. J., and B. Hoekman. 2010. "Services Trade and Policy." *Journal of Economic Literature* 48 (3): 642–92.

Freund, C., and B. Bolaky. 2008. "Trade, Regulations, and Income." *Journal of Development Economics* 87 (2): 309–21.

Gelb, A. 2011. "Economic Diversification in Resource Rich Countries." Center for Global Development, Washington, DC, www.imf.org/external/np/seminars/eng/2010/afrfin/pdf/Gelb2.pdf.

Ghani, E., and H. Kharas. 2010. "Service-Led Growth in South Asia: An Overview." In *The Service Revolution in South Asia*, ed. E. Ghani. New York: Oxford University Press.

Havrylyshyn, O. 2010. "Does the Global Crisis Mean the End of Export-Led Open-Economy Strategies?" Paper prepared for World Bank, Washington, DC.

Hoekman, B., and A. Mattoo. 2008. "Services Trade and Growth." Policy Research Working Paper 4461, World Bank, Washington, DC.

Hoekman, B., and C. Ozden. 2009. "The Euro-Mediterranean Partnership: Trade in Services as an Alternative to Migration?" Policy Research Working Paper Series 5049, World Bank. Washington, DC.

Lopez-Calix, J., P. Walkenhorst, and N. Diop. 2010. *Trade Competitiveness of the Middle East and North Africa*. Washington, DC: World Bank.

Marouani, M. A., and L. Munro. 2009. "Assessing Barriers to Trade in Services in the MENA Region." Trade Policy Working Papers 84, OECD, Paris.

Marouani, M. A., and Zaki. 2011. "Trade in Mode 4 in MENA and Barriers to Labor Mobility." Draft.

Rodrik, D. 2008. "The Real Exchange Rate and Economic Growth." *Brookings Papers on Economic Activity* 2008 (2).

World Bank. 2007. "Morocco's Backbone Services Sectors: Reforms for Higher Productivity and Deeper Integration with Europe." Draft Report 39755–MA, World Bank, Washington, DC.

CHAPTER 4

Patterns of Diversification in MENA: Explaining MENA's Specificity

Marcelo Olarreaga and Cristian Ugarte

Early stages of development are often accompanied by diversification of the production bundle as more economic opportunities become available. There is evidence, however, that the relationship between diversification and development is nonmonotonic. Imbs and Wacziarg (2003) and Koren and Tenreyro (2007) show that if the two are positively correlated at low levels of development, once countries reach a certain income-per-capita threshold, the concentration of production increases with income levels. Cadot, Carrère, and Strauss-Kahn (2011) show that the U-shaped relationship between economic concentration and income holds not only for production but also for export diversification.

A potential explanation for this empirical regularity is the need to diversify production (or investment opportunities) in the presence of incomplete financial markets at very low levels of development. Moreover, as financial markets develop, the forces of comparative advantage push toward specialization (Saint-Paul 1992; Acemoglu and Zilibotti 1997). Faini (2004) suggests an alternative explanation: at early stages of development, when income rises, the opportunities for risk diversification through sectorally diversified investment become stronger, leading initially to diversification. As economies become richer, however, they also become economically and institutionally more stable, which mitigates business risks and diminishes the incentives to diversify. An alternative explanation in a Ricardian model with a continuum of goods is the tension that may exist between productivity increases that could lead to a larger number of products being produced in the home country and falling trade costs that could lead to a decline in the number of goods that are cheaper to produce domestically. If productivity increases tend to be followed by declines in trade policy barriers, then a U-shaped relationship between concentration and income per capita is likely.

This empirical regularity, however, seems to be at odds with the patterns of diversification in the Middle East and North Africa (MENA) region.[1] The objective of this chapter is twofold: to search for the existence of a systematic difference in the patterns of development and diversification between MENA and the rest of the world; and to attempt to explain these systematic differences beyond the obvious observation that MENA is relatively more abundant in natural resources than the rest of the world. The two alternative explanations explored are Dutch Disease–type phenomena that lead to a strong appreciation of the exchange rate and the presence of weak links.

The Dutch Disease phenomenon takes its name from the experience of the Netherlands in the 1960s with the discovery of large reserves of natural gas. As income from gas increased, the guilder appreciated quickly, making the rest of the economy less competitive. Moreover, the booming sector increased its demand for factors of production, making the rest of the economy even less competitive (see Corden and Neary 1982 for a full economic model of Dutch Disease). This type of phenomenon will naturally lead to a decline in the share of the manufacturing sector, but it may also affect the extent of industrial concentration, because some sectors will see stronger increases in their production costs associated with the exchange rate appreciation. Whether manufacturing concentration increases with Dutch Disease is therefore an empirical question.

The weak links alternative explanation is based in the ideas of a recent paper by Jones (2011). It builds on earlier work by Hirschman (1958) and Kremer (1993) that emphasizes the important role played by linkages and complementarities in economic development. Low productivity in one nontradable input sector for which there is little substitutability will act as a weak link in the production chain, hurting all the sectors downstream and the overall development prospects of the country. Ugarte (2012) formally shows how the presence of weak links results in a less diversified production bundle as downstream sectors are hurt by higher nontradable input prices and factor prices. Examples of sectors that can be considered weak links are the energy production or oil refining industries, whose products are broadly used by others sectors as intermediate inputs, and which have a nonnegligible, nontradable component. Energy is required by almost every sector, and while oil is highly tradable, energy production can be highly nontradable. Low levels of productivity in energy production will imply higher costs for users of energy and might constrain diversification into new sectors as their expected profitability falls. Thus, the presence of weak links may lead to higher levels of concentration.

The empirical results suggest that MENA's pattern of development and diversification is indeed different from the rest of the world. MENA countries tend to concentrate rather than diversify at early stages of development, and they seem to start diversifying only at relatively high levels of income. The evidence also suggests that weak links seem to be a better explanation than Dutch Disease for this different pattern of development and diversification in MENA; the appreciation of the real exchange rate seems to have no impact.

Empirical Methodology

The empirical methodology of this work closely follows Imbs and Wacziarg (2003). The following relationship is estimated both parametrically and nonparametrically:

$$\text{Concentration} = f(\text{income}) + \varepsilon \qquad (4.1)$$

where *Concentration* measures the lack of sectoral diversification using different indexes and along different dimensions (output, employment, or value added); *income* is gross domestic product (GDP) per capita at constant prices, noted as GDPpc hereafter; and ε is an error term. The f relationship is estimated across countries and time, and therefore country and year fixed effects are generally included. Imbs and Wacziarg (2003) found a quadratic relationship between sectoral concentration and income per capita. This is the starting point of our empirical study, but higher orders of the f function will also be checked.[2] The potential heterogeneity that may exist in the relationship between MENA and the rest of the world will also be explored by estimating equation 4.1 for different samples.[3]

Economic concentration is measured by Gini coefficients, and Herfindhal indexes are also used to check for the robustness of the results. Each of them will be calculated along three different dimensions: output (Giniout, Herfout), employment (Giniempl, Herfempl), and value added (Ginivadd, Herfvadd) for each country and year, using the 28-sector disaggregation provided at the 3-digit level of the International Standard Industrial Classification.[4]

The Gini coefficient is calculated as follows. After ordering the shares of output, employment, or value added in increasing order, we calculate

$$\text{Gini} = 1 - \frac{1}{n_{c,t}} \sum_{i=1}^{n_{c,t}} \left(S_{i-1}^c + S_i^c \right) \tag{4.2}$$

where S_i^c is the cumulated share of output/employment/value added of sector i in country c, $n_{c,t}$ is the number of active sectors in country c at period t, and $S_0 = 0$. The Gini index ranges between zero and one, where zero represents a fully diversified economy (where all sectors have an equal share of total production, employment, or value added) and one a fully concentrated economy (where all production, employment, or value added are generated in one sector).

The Herfindhal indexes are presented below:

$$\text{Herf} = \sum_{i=1}^{n_{c,t}} (S_i)^2 \tag{4.3}$$

This index ranges between $1/n_{c,t}$ and 1 and it also increases with the degree of concentration. Unlike the Gini index, this index is not affected by the absence of production, employment, or value added in a sector.[5] On the other hand, the Herfindhal is very sensitive to large sectors, whereas the Gini is more sensitive to what happens in the middle of the distribution and will better capture changes toward diversification.

Measuring Weak Links and Dutch Disease Effects

This section explores the impact of Dutch Disease phenomena and weak links on the patterns of development and diversification by testing the equation below:

$$\text{Concentration} = f(\text{income}) + \alpha \, \text{WeakLinks} + \beta \, \text{DutchDisease} + \varepsilon \tag{4.4}$$

Dutch Disease phenomena are proxied here by percentage changes of the real exchange rate. By considering the change of the real exchange rate instead of the exchange rate in levels, the variable is more likely to have an impact on concentration through a Dutch Disease–type phenomenon because it will give more weight to observations where the appreciation of the exchange rate has been accelerating. Note that a fall in the exchange rate signals an appreciation of the exchange rate and implies that a negative correlation between changes in the exchange rate and concentration is commonly expected (beta < 0).[6]

As argued above, the presence of weak links is expected to lead to a more concentrated manufacturing sector (that is, alpha > 0). Weak links can be measured in different ways. One is to measure differences between the mean (or median) productivity and the productivity in the least productive sector. Another is simply to use the minimum level of productivity in the economy as a potential indicator of weak links. Whatever the measure, it must capture the underlying distribution of productivity across sectors in a given country: the difference between two points, or the minimum level of productivity, does not capture the probability of observing this difference of productivity level. The same minimum level of productivity or productivity differences may be very likely in one country but almost never observed in another. This will be missed by the simple use of a ratio or a difference. Therefore, the measure of weak links chosen here will be the probability of observing a productivity lower than a certain threshold in a given country and year. To arrive at this measure, the kernel density of labor productivity for each country in each year is estimated.[7] The kernel density is weighted as the share of output by sector in total output, to consider the economic importance of each sector in every year and every country.[8] Thus, this procedure estimates a distribution for each observation in the sample and allows us to independently calculate moments of the distribution for a given country in a given year. The proxy for weak links is calculated as a probability of observing productivity lower than the mean productivity minus two,[9] times the standard deviation of the distribution:

$$P(\text{low}) = Prob(\text{productivity} < \text{meanproductivity} - 2 \times \text{stddev}) \quad (4.5)$$

An important caveat with this measure of weak links is that it does not take into account the extent to which sectors are used as inputs by other sectors, or the degree of tradability of input sectors. This is important when measuring weak links, because they are by definition nontradable input sectors. To construct a measure of weak links that takes these two characteristics into account, however, one would need input-output tables. This is the path followed in Ugarte (2012) in a cross-section of developed and developing countries, where the author weights the productivity of each sector in estimated density function by its importance as an input in other sectors as well as by its degree of tradability.[10] Unfortunately, this measure cannot be used for MENA because of the lack of input-output data.

Data Description

Table 4.1 lists the names of the countries, including MENA countries, in the sample, as well as the number of observations available for the period 1963–2003. The unbalanced nature of the panel suggests that after controlling for country fixed effects, the coefficients will mainly capture the country variability with a large number of observations.[11] Tables 4.2 and 4.3 present summary statistics of the different measures of diversification. Concentration indexes for MENA tend to be slightly higher, but the differences from the general mean values are statistically insignificant. The variation of concentration indexes is less important in the MENA region than in the rest of the world. The Gini index of diversification based on output information tends to show more concentration than other Gini indexes. Even though they are not statistically significant, the Herfindhal indexes show the same tendency. The correlation between measures is highly significant and positive in all cases. It is worth pointing out that output measures are highly correlated with value added measures. The structure of output and value added is very similar within countries. Even if different measures of concentration are highly correlated, we can reject perfect co-linearity among measures, so it is important to provide results for different measures as robustness checks.

Table 4.4 provides descriptive statistics of the probability of observing a weak link in the world and the MENA samples. A test on mean values suggests no statistically significant difference between MENA and the rest of the world. Weak links are as likely in both.

Empirical Results

The parametric results in Imbs and Wacziarg (2003) are reproduced in table 4.5. The estimates reported in the table are slightly different from those in their paper because we use GDP per capita at constant dollars rather than purchasing power parity (PPP) prices; moreover, we no longer

Table 4.1   Sample Coverage and Number of Observations

Middle East and North Africa

Algeria (31), Bahrain (1), Arab Republic of Egypt (36), Islamic Republic of Iran (38), Iraq (27), Israel (39), Jordan (38), Kuwait (36), Lebanon (1), Libya (17), Morocco (28), Oman (11), Qatar (11), Saudi Arabia (8), Syrian Arab Republic (36), Tunisia (33), United Arab Emirates (11), Republic of Yemen (13).

Others in Asia

Afghanistan (18), Armenia (17), Azerbaijan (13), Bangladesh (28), Bhutan (1), Cambodia (7), China (26), Hong Kong SAR, China (40), India (39), Indonesia (33), Japan (39), Kazakhstan (10), Republic of Korea (39), Kyrgyz Republic (16), Lao PDR (1), Macao SAR, China (25), Malaysia (33), Mongolia (6), Myanmar (14), Nepal (10), Pakistan (30), Philippines (35), Russian Federation (12), Singapore (40), Sri Lanka (35), Tajikistan (14), Thailand (19), Turkey (38), Vietnam (3).

Others in Africa

Angola (7), Benin (17), Botswana (22), Burkina Faso (15), Burundi (19),Cameroon (25), Cape Verde (14), Central African Republic (19), Chad (1), Côte d'Ivoire (31), Democratic Republic of Congo (5), Eritrea (10), Ethiopia (38), Gabon (20), The Gambia (13), Ghana (28), Equatorial Guinea (3), Kenya (40), Lesotho (12), Liberia (14), Madagascar (22), Malawi (35), Mauritania (6), Mauritius (32), Mozambique (25), Namibia (1), Niger (9), Nigeria (28), Republic of Congo (18), Rwanda (16), Senegal (30), Seychelles (12), Sierra Leone (5), Somalia (14), South Africa (36), Sudan (11), Swaziland (26), Tanzania (30), Togo (16), Uganda (14), Zambia (18), Zimbabwe (34).

Americas

Argentina (30), Bahamas (20), Barbados (28), Belize (4), Bermuda(12), Bolivia 31), Brazil (28), Canada (39), Chile (38), Colombia (38), Costa Rica (40), Cuba (15), Dominican Republic (23), Ecuador (40), El Salvador (31), Grenada (8), Guatemala (26), Guyana (14), Haiti (27), Honduras (33), Jamaica (34), Mexico (31), Netherlands Antilles (22), Nicaragua (23), Panama (37), Paraguay (20), Peru (22), Puerto Rico (36), St. Lucia (7), St. Vincent and the Grenadines (9), Surinam (20), United States (38), Uruguay (33), Trinidad and Tobago (33), RB Venezuela (34).

Europe

Albania (11), Austria (37), Belgium (38), Bosnia and Herzegovina (5), Bulgaria (40), Croatia (17), Cyprus (40), Czech Republic (16), Denmark (36), Estonia (10), Finland (38), France (38), Germany (10), Greece (36), Hungary (38), Ireland (38), Italy (34), Latvia (17), Lithuania (11), Luxembourg (38), FYR Macedonia (10), Malta (39), Moldova (17), Netherlands (38), Norway (39), Poland (38), Portugal (38), Romania (38), Slovak Republic (7), Slovenia (16), Spain (38), Sweden (38), Switzerland (12), Ukraine (10), United Kingdom (34).

Others

Australia (39), Iceland (30), Fiji (29), New Zealand (38), Papua New Guinea (27), Solomon Islands (7), Tonga (19), Western Samoa (2).

Source: Authors.

have access to data for some former Soviet countries.[12] The bottom panel shows that the U-shaped relationship between concentration indexes and income per capita is robust to the inclusion of country fixed effects, as in Imbs and Wacziarg (2003). The turning points of the U-shaped curve

Table 4.2   Summary Statistics of Measures of Diversification

Variable	Mean	Standard deviation	Minimum	Maximum	Number
World					
Gini_{out}	0.5935	0.0984	0.1499	0.9043	3,438
Herf_{out}	0.1598	0.1090	0.0583	0.9104	3,438
Gini_{empl}	0.5622	0.0980	0.0122	0.8792	3,695
Herf_{empl}	0.1403	0.0981	0.0598	0.8772	3,695
Gini_{vadd}	0.5638	0.0999	0.2030	0.8682	3,264
Herf_{vadd}	0.1384	0.1016	0.0509	0.8878	3,264
MENA countries					
Gini_{out}	0.6124	0.0970	0.4158	0.8802	389
Herf_{out}	0.1767	0.1295	0.0673	0.6342	389
Gini_{empl}	0.5649	0.0687	0.3387	0.7396	402
Herf_{empl}	0.1252	0.0488	0.0711	0.2879	402
Gini_{vadd}	0.5874	0.0993	0.3780	0.8682	379
Herf_{vadd}	0.1501	0.1043	0.0584	0.6523	379

Source: Authors.

Table 4.3   Correlation between Measures of Diversification

Variables	Gini_{out}	Herf_{out}	Gini_{empl}	Herf_{empl}	Gini_{vadd}	Herf_{vadd}
Gini_{out}	1.000					
Herf_{out}	0.627	1.000				
Gini_{empl}	0.650	0.279	1.000			
Herf_{empl}	0.467	0.625	0.547	1.000		
Gini_{vadd}	0.907	0.584	0.716	0.528	1.000	
Herf_{vadd}	0.525	0.897	0.288	0.642	0.625	1.000

Source: Authors.
Note: All correlations are statistically significant at the 99 percent level.

Table 4.4   Descriptive Statistics of *P*(low)

Statistic	World	MENA
Average	0.0021	0.0017
Standard deviation	0.0087	0.0067
Maximum	0.1040	0.0611
% of *P*(low) > 0.01	6.17	5.56

Source: Authors.

Table 4.5 Imbs and Wacziarg's Results (2003)

Variables	$Gini_{empl}$ (I)	$Herf_{empl}$ (II)	$Gini_{vadd}$ (III)	$Herf_{vadd}$ (IV)	$Gini_{empl}$ (V)	$Herf_{empl}$ (VI)	$Gini_{vadd}$ (VII)	$Herf_{vadd}$ (VIII)
GDP_{pc}	−0.0245***	−0.0195***	−0.0288***	−0.0162***	−0.0058***	−0.0099***	−0.0085***	−0.0040*
	(0.0013)	(0.0016)	(0.0014)	(0.0012)	(0.0022)	(0.0020)	(0.0028)	(0.0022)
$[GDP_{pc}]^2$	0.0011***	0.0008***	0.0013***	0.0007***	0.0003***	0.0004***	0.0005***	0.0002**
	(0.0001)	(0.0001)	(0.0001)	(0.0001)	(0.0001)	(0.0001)	(0.0001)	(0.0001)
Constant	0.6209***	0.1748***	0.6262***	0.1555***	0.5727***	0.1520***	0.5739***	0.1264***
	(0.0034)	(0.0041)	(0.0035)	(0.0030)	(0.0068)	(0.0062)	(0.0081)	(0.0064)
R^2	0.273	0.155	0.320	0.174	0.835	0.892	0.776	0.763
Observations					1,433		1,349	

Source: Authors.

Notes: Estimates in columns V-VIII include country fixed effects. GDP_{pc} stands for GDP per capita at constant prices (thousands US$). Standard errors in parentheses. Statistically significant: *** p<0.01, ** p<0.05, * p<0.1.

can be calculated by equalizing the first derivative to zero. It occurs around $10,000.

Table 4.6 presents the estimates obtained using the full 1963–2003 sample provided in table 4.1. The estimated U-shaped relationship between concentration and level of development is now inverted. All the results suggest that at lower levels of development, economies tend to become more concentrated as income rises, and at later stages to diversify as income grows.[13] This is quite surprising and warrants further investigation using nonparametric techniques, as in Imbs and Wacziarg (2003).[14] The nonparametric estimates are shown in figures 4.1–4.3 for the three Gini coefficients on output, employment, and value added. The relationship between concentration and income levels does not appear to be U-shaped, as indicated by the parametric estimates; it appears to be of a higher order than quadratic. At low levels of income per capita, however, the relationship indeed appears U-shaped, as found by Imbs and Wacziarg (2003) in their sample.

Higher orders of income per capita are therefore included in the parametric estimations: the number of higher-order terms to include is chosen by checking their statistical significance and changes in adjusted R-squares (which stopped at the fourth-order terms). The estimates obtained with GDP per capita at powers three and four are presented in table 4.7. As with the nonparametric estimates, economic concentration falls with GDP per capita at very low levels of development for all concentration indexes (with the exception of the Gini on employment in the second column), but then increases.[15]

At the bottom of table 4.7, the saddle points (minimum and maximum) of each of these functions are provided.[16] There is no analytical solution, but the numerical solutions suggest that at levels of income per capita between $2,000 and $6,000, countries tend to diversify (become less concentrated) as income rises, after which they tend to concentrate their production bundle at least until they reach levels of income per capita around $18,000 to $25,000.

Thus the U-shaped relationship between concentration and income per capita found by Imbs and Wacziarg (2003) is validated in our sample for levels of income per capita below $20,000 to $25,000. After that threshold, the relationship changes, but not many countries in MENA are at that level of development and therefore this different pattern may not be relevant for them.

To explore the potential heterogeneity of the relationship in equation 4.4 between MENA and the rest of the world, the samples are divided

Table 4.6 Basic Regressions of Concentration on a Quadratic Function of GDP$_{pc}$

Variables	Gini$_{out}$	Gini$_{empl}$	Gini$_{vadd}$	Herf$_{out}$	Herf$_{empl}$	Herf$_{vadd}$
GDP$_{pc}$	0.0090***	0.0080***	0.0128***	0.0056***	0.0028***	0.0049***
	(0.0011)	(0.0010)	(0.0012)	(0.0010)	(0.0008)	(0.0010)
[GDP$_{pc}$]^2	−0.0002***	−0.0002***	−0.0003***	−0.0002***	−0.0001***	−0.0001***
	(0.0000)	(0.0000)	(0.0000)	(0.0000)	(0.0000)	(0.0000)
Constant	0.6035***	0.5205***	0.6446***	0.2238***	0.1408***	0.3477***
	(0.0359)	(0.0358)	(0.0544)	(0.0330)	(0.0294)	(0.0482)
R^2	0.776	0.775	0.747	0.838	0.853	0.798
Observations	3,182	3,357	3,027	3,182	3,357	3,027

Source: Authors.

Notes: GDP$_{pc}$ stands for GDP per capita at constant prices (thousands US$). Standard errors in parentheses. Statistically significant: *** $p<0.01$, ** $p<0.05$, * $p<0.1$. All regressions include time and country fixed effects.

Figure 4.1   Diversification of Output (Gini$_{out}$) on GDP per Capita

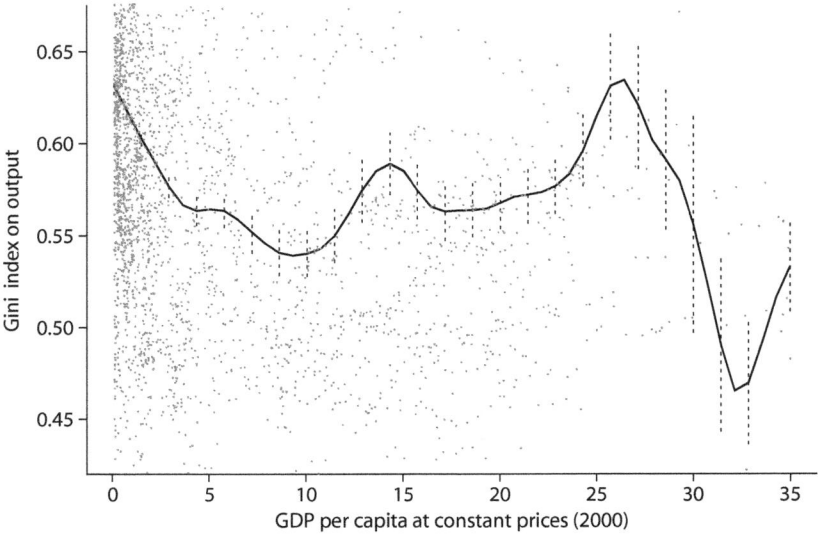

Source: Authors.

Figure 4.2   Diversification of Output (Gini$_{empl}$) on GDP per Capita

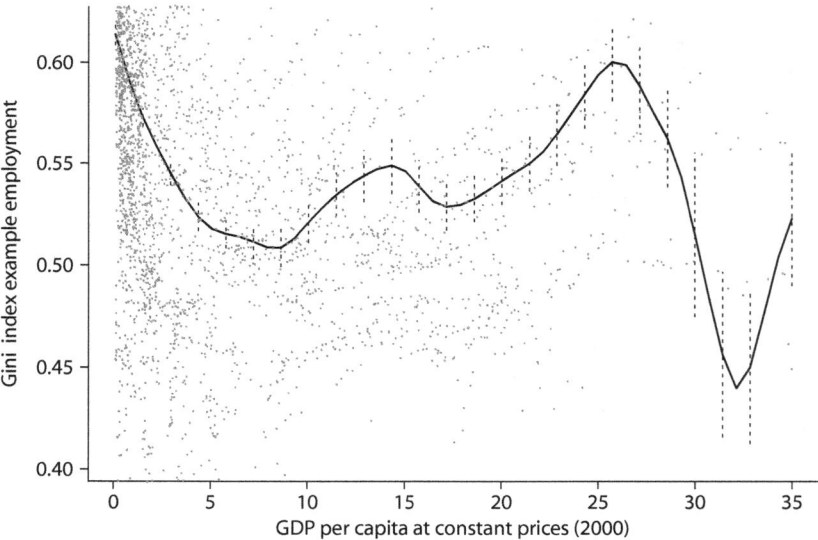

Source: Authors.

Figure 4.3   Diversification of Output (Gini$_{vadd}$) on GDP per Capita

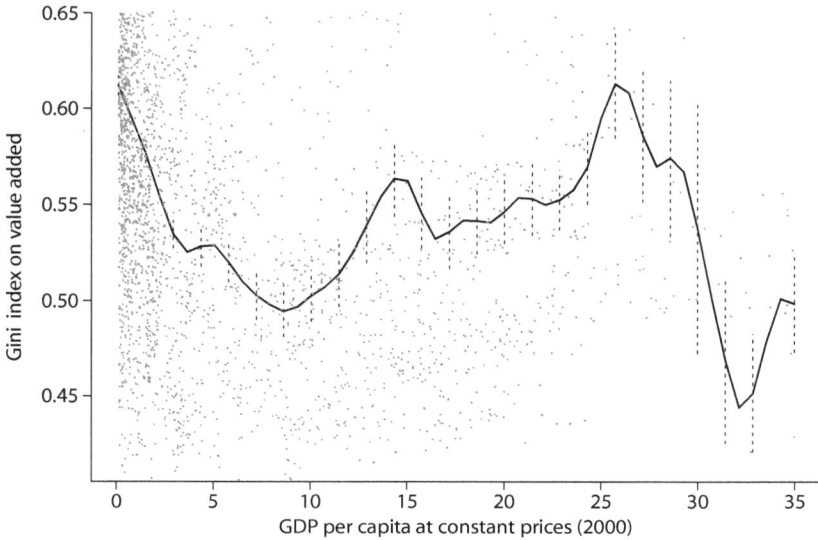

Source: Authors.

accordingly. The results, displayed in table 4.8, show some important differences between MENA and the rest of the world. In the latter sample, we observe the same pattern as in table 4.7. But in the MENA sample, the pattern observed in the rest of the world is actually reversed. MENA countries have a tendency to become more concentrated as income grows at low and intermediate levels of development, and they start to diversify only when GDP per capita reaches $17,000 to $22,000. Given that most MENA countries are below this threshold, this finding suggests that concentration is the most common pattern of development in the region. The statistical relation between concentration and income per capita is thus not convex but concave.[17]

Figures 4.4, 4.5, and 4.6 plot the derivative of the concentration index with respect to income per capita using the estimates for the MENA countries (solid line) and the rest of the world (dashed line). A positive value of the derivative suggests that concentration increases with income per capita, whereas a negative value suggests that concentration declines with income per capita at that level of development. At low and intermediate levels of development, the derivative is positive for MENA countries, suggesting that an increase in income tends to be associated with a more

Table 4.7 Regressions of Concentration Including [GDP$_{pc}$]^3 and [GDP$_{pc}$]^4

Variables	Gini$_{out}$ (I)	Gini$_{empl}$ (II)	Gini$_{vadd}$ (III)	Herf$_{out}$ (IV)	Herf$_{empl}$ (V)	Herf$_{vadd}$ (VI)
GDP$_{pc}$	−0.00946494***	0.00126482	−0.0092499***	−0.00186707	−0.00441353**	−0.00379962
	(0.00307744)	(0.00255713)	(0.00339791)	(0.00284778)	(0.00209783)	(0.00301235)
[GDP$_{pc}$]^2	0.00131129***	0.00044252**	0.00167939***	0.00052016**	0.00052041***	0.00101347***
	(0.00025496)	(0.00018029)	(0.00028863)	(0.00023593)	(0.00014791)	(0.00025588)
[GDP$_{pc}$]^3	−0.00004638***	−0.00001879***	−0.00006470***	−0.00002269***	−0.00001788***	−0.00004835***
	(0.00000878)	(0.00000517)	(0.00001018)	(0.00000813)	(0.00000424)	(0.00000903)
[GDP$_{pc}$]^4	0.00000047***	0.00000019***	0.00000071***	0.00000025***	0.00000017***	0.00000064***
	(0.00000010)	(0.00000005)	(0.00000012)	(0.00000009)	(0.00000004)	(0.00000011)
Constant	0.64605132***	0.53397540***	0.69463459***	0.23962964***	0.15631615***	0.35924320***
	(0.03624372)	(0.03620361)	(0.05450849)	(0.03353905)	(0.02970082)	(0.04832346)
Minimum (US$)	4,711	—	3,398	2,065	5,900	2,211
Maximum (US$)	23,155	25,068	22,851	19,395	21,273	18,871
R^2	0.779	0.776	0.751	0.838	0.854	0.801
Observations	3,182	3,357	3,027	3,182	3,357	3,027

Source: Authors.

Notes: All regressions include time and country fixed effects. GDP$_{pc}$ stands for GDP per capita at constant prices (thousands US$). Standard errors in parentheses. — = nonexistent.

Statistically significant: *** p<0.01, ** p<0.05, * p<0.1.

Table 4.8   Splitting Samples between Middle East and North Africa and the Rest of the World

Variables	Rest of the world			Middle East and North Africa		
	$Gini_{out}$	$Gini_{empl}$	$Gini_{vadd}$	$Gini_{out}$	$Gini_{empl}$	$Gini_{vadd}$
GDP_{pc}	−0.00810690**	−0.00408470	−0.00909016***	0.01862887	0.08287829***	0.03597924*
	(0.00322383)	(0.00265546)	(0.00340832)	(0.01684508)	(0.01719385)	(0.02149334)
$[GDP_{pc}]^2$	0.000090447***	0.00082254***	0.00121907***	0.00039008	−0.00495654***	0.00046735
	(0.00028012)	(0.000019007)	(0.00029570)	(0.00109583)	(0.00108921)	(0.00145475)
$[GDP_{pc}]^3$	−0.00002705***	−0.00003039***	−0.00004003***	−0.00004226	0.00012329***	−0.00007064*
	(0.00001012)	(0.00000550)	(0.00001067)	(0.00003012)	(0.00002848)	(0.00004218)
$[GDP_{pc}]^4$	0.00000019	0.00000029***	0.00000032**	0.00000058*	−0.00000110***	0.00000108**
	(0.00000012)	(0.00000005)	(0.00000013)	(0.00000030)	(0.00000026)	(0.00000044)
Constant	0.62302618***	0.58085743***	0.59270500***	0.57998615***	0.30586937***	0.51914496***
	(0.04989810)	(0.04966570)	(0.01635957)	(0.06459647)	(0.06918234)	(0.08069581)
Minimum (US$)	6,011	2,838	4,809	—	31,192	—
Maximum (US$)	22,743	23,069	22,055	21,400	16,692	21,987
R^2	0.781	0.794	0.767	0.848	0.595	0.762
Observations	2,856	3,028	2,711	326	329	316

Source: Authors.

Notes: All regressions include time and country fixed effects. GDP_{pc} stands for GDP per capita at constant prices (thousands US$). Standard errors in parentheses. — = nonexistent.
Statistically significant: *** $p<0.01$, ** $p<0.05$, * $p<0.1$.

Figure 4.4   Marginal Effect of GDP$_{pc}$ on Output Concentration [Gini$_{out}$]

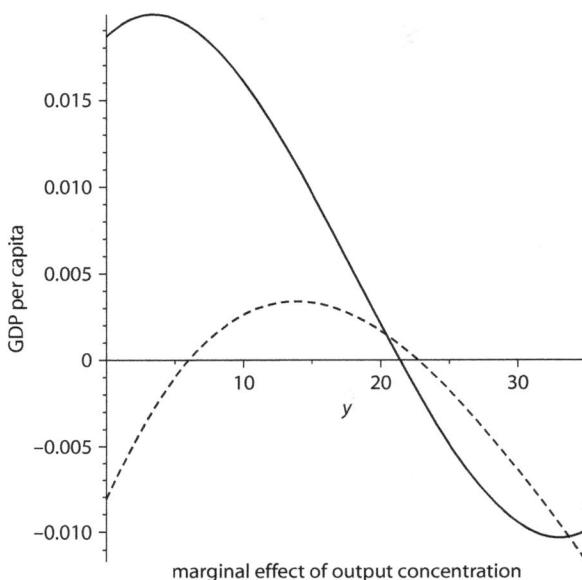

Source: Authors.
Notes: The solid line shows the marginal effect of GDP per capita on output concentration in MENA countries (column 4 of table 4.8), above. The dashed line shows the marginal effect of GDP per capita on output concentration in the rest of the world (column 1 of table 4.8).

concentrated production bundle. In the rest of the world, on the other hand, at low levels of development the derivative tends to be negative, whereas at intermediate levels it is positive, which corresponds to the U-shaped curve. At very high levels of development both in MENA and in the rest of the world, a negative derivative is observed, suggesting that countries in both samples diversify as income rises.[18]

To investigate the potential explanation of these differences in the pattern of diversification and development between MENA and the rest of the world, the explanatory variables for weak links (measured as the probability of observing a sector with a labor productivity below two times the average labor productivity in the country in that year), and a proxy for Dutch Disease–type phenomena (that is, the change in the exchange rate) are included.[19] Table 4.9 presents the results for the full sample and MENA subsample. In the full sample (the first three columns), the U-shaped relationship at low levels of income per capita is still

Figure 4.5   Marginal Effect of GDP$_{pc}$ on Employment Concentration [Gini$_{empl}$]

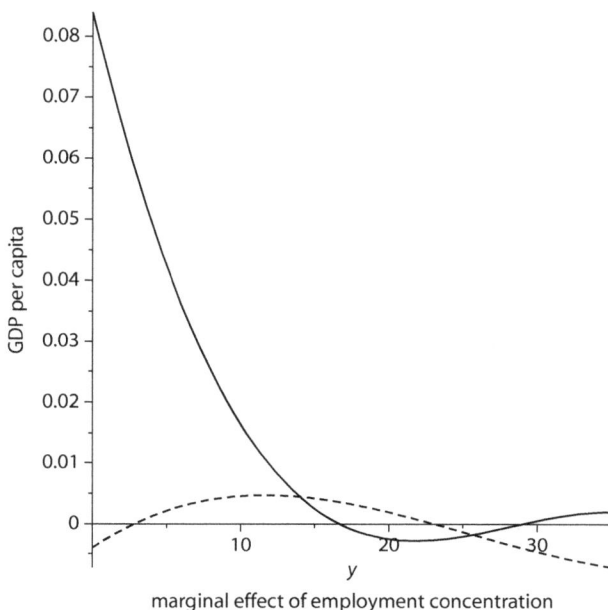

marginal effect of employment concentration

Source: Authors.
Notes: The solid line shows the marginal effect of GDP per capita on employment concentration in MENA countries (column 5 of table 4.8), above. The dashed line shows the marginal effect of GDP per capita on employment concentration in the rest of the world (column 2 of table 4.8).

present after controlling for weak links and changes in the exchange rate. Interestingly, the presence of weak links tends to make economies more concentrated. On the other hand, exchange rate acceleration (that is, a decrease in our explanatory variable) has no impact on manufacturing concentration. When turning to the MENA subsample, neither weak links nor changes in the exchange rate level have a statistically significant impact on concentration indexes.

As a further check of the relative explanatory power of weak links and exchange rate accelerations in the U-shaped relationship reversal, these specifications are run separately for countries with a higher and lower than average probability to observe weak links, as well as for countries with exchange rate appreciation or depreciation. The idea is to see whether the presence of significant weak links or opposite exchange rate patterns are consistent with a reversal of the U-shaped relationship. Results are reported in tables 4.10 and 4.11.

Figure 4.6   Marginal Effect of GDP$_{pc}$ on Value-Added Concentration [Gini$_{vadd}$]

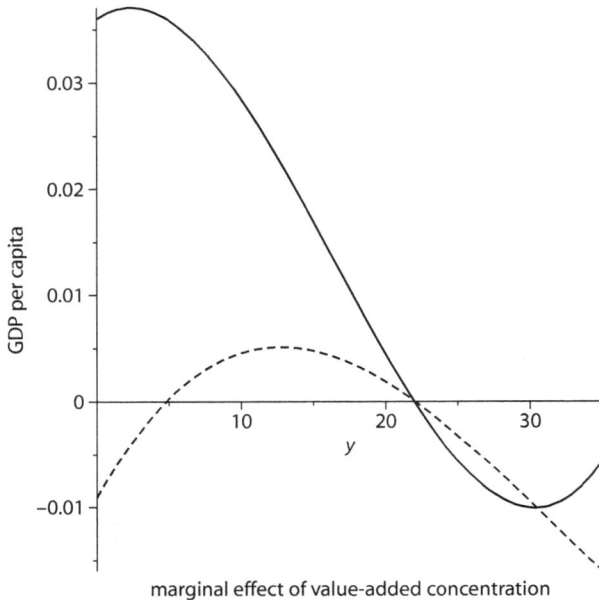

marginal effect of value-added concentration

Source: Authors.
Note: The solid line shows the marginal effect of GDP per capita on value-added concentration in MENA countries (column 6 of table 4.8). The dashed line shows the marginal effect of GDP per capita on value-added concentration in the rest of the world (column 3 of table 4.8).

In table 4.10, it appears that the presence of significant weak links can explain a reversal in the U-shaped relationship. For countries with mildly (below average) weak links, the relationship is the classic U shape. For countries with very weak links, however, the U-shaped relationship is inverted, with a maximum at around $14,000. On the other hand, table 4.11 suggests that no real difference exists in the relationship between concentration and income per capita for countries with appreciation or depreciation of their exchange rate. This suggests that the main explanation behind MENA's inverted U-shaped relationship between concentration and income per capita lies with weak links in their production chain, rather than with Dutch Disease.

Concluding Remarks

An influential paper by Imbs and Wacziarg (2003) suggests that there is a U-shaped relationship between economic development and

Table 4.9 Stages of Diversification and Weak Links versus Exchange Rate Appreciation

Variables	World			Middle East and North Africa		
	$Gini_{out}$	$Gini_{empl}$	$Gini_{vadd}$	$Gini_{out}$	$Gini_{empl}$	$Gini_{vadd}$
GDP_{pc}	−0.00514478	−0.00529379	−0.02084442***	0.03213498	0.06411107*	0.04358153
	(0.000431789)	(0.00457301)	(0.00531031)	(0.02510432)	(0.03342117)	(0.03702011)
$[GDP_{pc}]^2$	0.000068925**	0.00044620	0.00200579***	0.00349863	−0.00286479	0.00254568
	(0.000032853)	(0.00034794)	(0.00040268)	(0.00298112)	(0.00396874)	(0.00438068)
$[GDP_{pc}]^3$	−0.00002267**	−0.00001390	−0.00006319***	−0.000028460**	−0.000000595	−0.000023179
	(0.00001063)	(0.00001126)	(0.00001300)	(0.00013954)	(0.000018577)	(0.00020444)
$[GDP_{pc}]^4$	0.00000019	0.000000011	0.00000060***	0.00000424**	0.00000082	0.00000349
	(0.00000012)	(0.00000013)	(0.00000015)	(0.00000183)	(0.00000243)	(0.00000267)
P(low)	0.77385947***	0.00175064	1.00649919***	−0.40209100	−0.28687306	−0.20878525
	(0.15979803)	(0.16923974)	(0.22608409)	(0.60802414)	(0.80945744)	(0.88844989)
Δ (exch.rate)	−0.00113460	−0.000051930	−0.00304585	−0.01917969	0.03129908	−0.02867972
	(0.00710858)	(0.00752859)	(0.00963133)	(0.02655145)	(0.03534772)	(0.03934538)
Constant	0.64004582***	0.57093807***	0.74197483***	0.47702340***	0.38066509***	0.45261880***
	(0.02915177)	(0.03087421)	(0.04731559)	(0.07879516)	(0.10489934)	(0.11622175)
Minimum (US$)	4,814	1,0573	7,766	—	—	—
Maximum (US$)	22,685	16,912	23,374	15,310	11,676	16,653
R^2	0.882	0.844	0.819	0.928	0.587	0.802
Observations	1,770	1,770	1,651	167	167	162

Source: Authors.

Notes: All regressions include time and country fixed effects. GDP_{pc} stands for GDP per capita at constant prices (thousands US$). Standard errors in parentheses. — = nonexistent.
Statistically significant: *** $p<0.01$, ** $p<0.05$, * $p<0.1$.

131

Table 4.10 Splitting the Sample after Lower Tails of Productivity

Variables	P(low) < mean probability			P(low) > mean probability		
	$Gini_{out}$	$Gini_{empl}$	$Gini_{vadd}$	$Gini_{out}$	$Gini_{empl}$	$Gini_{vadd}$
GDP_{pc}	-0.00192358	0.00557568**	-0.00548106*	0.04680312**	0.00707754	0.08016101***
	(0.00261861)	(0.00258135)	(0.00301095)	(0.02276563)	(0.02705268)	(0.02816104)
$[GDP_{pc}]^2$	0.00052438**	-0.00008797	0.00117795***	-0.00259070	0.00040708	-0.00451626**
	(0.00022416)	(0.00022097)	(0.00025689)	(0.00180861)	(0.00214919)	(0.00223159)
$[GDP_{pc}]^3$	-0.000001572**	0.00000493	-0.00004291***	0.00005035	-0.00004163	0.00009270
	(0.00000795)	(0.00000784)	(0.00000910)	(0.00006449)	(0.00007663)	(0.00007953)
$[GDP_{pc}]^4$	0.00000010	-0.00000012	0.000000044***	-0.00000042	0.00000056	-0.00000076
	(0.00000009)	(0.00000009)	(0.00000011)	(0.00000081)	(0.00000096)	(0.00000100)
P(low)	7.20139983	11.47958274**	6.97866028	0.64945983***	0.01800120	0.89740199***
	(5.38486269)	(5.30824491)	(6.27875255)	(0.22165798)	(0.26339893)	(0.29356710)
Constant	0.65789379***	0.48981432***	0.67919801***	0.54584944***	0.59815816***	0.38127892***
	(0.04065571)	(0.04007725)	(0.04622884)	(0.07817760)	(0.09289942)	(0.10297652)
Minimum (US$)	2,013	—	2,714	—	—	—
Maximum (US$)	26,817	(31,054)	25,591	13,624	14,105	13,958 US$
R^2	0.837	0.826	0.801	0.948	0.920	0.927
Observations	2,625	2,625	2,477	294	294	275

Source: Authors.

Notes: All regressions include time and country fixed effects. GDP_{pc} stands for GDP per capita at constant prices (thousands US$). Standard errors in parentheses. — = Nonexistent. Statistically significant: *** p<0.01, ** p<0.05, * p<0.1.

Table 4.11 Splitting the Sample after Changes in the Real Exchange Rate

Variables	Δ (exch.rate) < 0			Δ (exch.rate) > 0		
	$Gini_{out}$	$Gini_{empl}$	$Gini_{vadd}$	$Gini_{out}$	$Gini_{empl}$	$Gini_{vadd}$
GDP_{pc}	-0.00398480	-0.00441760	-0.01613240**	-0.00667477	-0.00141009	-0.03041253***
	(0.00624957)	(0.00644974)	(0.00742766)	(0.00707383)	(0.00747091)	(0.00890573)
$[GDP_{pc}]^2$	0.00066400	0.00025944	0.00170760***	0.00087846	0.00029640	0.00299197***
	(0.00046775)	(0.00048273)	(0.00055392)	(0.00056430)	(0.00059598)	(0.00070774)
$[GDP_{pc}]^3$	-0.00002153	-0.00000512	-0.00005199***	-0.00003230*	-0.00001455	-0.00010429***
	(0.00001500)	(0.00001548)	(0.00001773)	(0.00001900)	(0.00002007)	(0.00002377)
$[GDP_{pc}]^4$	0.00000016	-0.00000001	0.00000044**	0.00000035	0.00000019	0.00000116***
	(0.00000017)	(0.00000017)	(0.00000020)	(0.00000022)	(0.00000023)	(0.00000028)
P(low)	0.59904842**	-0.28359026	1.04717963***	1.00820494***	0.33614873	1.13410210***
	(0.25001225)	(0.25801991)	(0.36050322)	(0.22722656)	(0.23998159)	(0.31250446)
Constant	0.62661865***	0.57258443***	0.72226081***	0.58501060***	0.54826477***	0.60627680***
	(0.03384095)	(0.03492484)	(0.05118088)	(0.04079015)	(0.04307985)	(0.05129346)
R^2	0.889	0.859	0.839	0.893	0.861	0.831
Observations	855	855	796	914	914	854

Source: Authors.

Notes: All regressions include time and country fixed effects. GDP_{pc} stands for GDP per capita at constant prices (thousands US$). Standard errors in parentheses.
Statistically significant: *** $p<0.01$, ** $p<0.05$, * $p<0.1$.

economic concentration: at early stages of development, economic concentration falls with income per capita, but starts increasing with income per capita after a certain threshold. This U-shaped relationship is confirmed by recent evidence in Cadot, Carrère, and Strauss-Kahn (2011) of export diversification. This empirical regularity contradicts casual observation of the development process in the MENA region, where the production seems to become more concentrated as income rises.

This chapter empirically confirms, for MENA, this inverted U-shaped relationship between income per capita and concentration: at early stages of development, economic concentration increases with income per capita and starts falling with income per capita only at relatively high levels of economic development. This contrasts with what is observed, on average, in the rest of the world.

To explain these differences in the development process, two alternatives have been tested. MENA is a resource-rich region and subject to Dutch Disease–type phenomena (à la Corden and Neary 1982). It is also a region where some sectors have notoriously low levels of productivity, and these weak links (Jones 2011) can lead not only to lower levels of growth but also to a higher concentration of production. It was found that weak links contribute to a more concentrated production bundle than Dutch Disease. Moreover, after controlling for these two variables, the differences in development patterns between MENA and the rest of the world become smaller.

This result has some interesting policy implications, at least in terms of the timing of industrial policy reforms. Policies aimed at diversifying the production process should first try to address the region's weak links. Otherwise resources may be wasted in trying to diversify into sectors that are not economically viable. Although more research is needed in this area, this chapter suggests that if governments first address the existing weak links in their economies, diversification may naturally follow. If addressing weak links may sometimes seem like a daunting task requiring large infrastructure investments with a long-term objective, it is important to note that one characteristic of weak links is that they are nontraded goods. If there is an easily imported substitute, then the low productivity of the domestic input sector is no longer a drag on growth. Thus, when restrictive trade policies limit the tradability of input sectors, liberalization may be sufficient to address those weak links.

Annex Table 4A.1   Expanding Imbs and Wacziarg's Samples

Variable	$Gini_{empl}$ (I)	$Herf_{empl}$ (II)	$Gini_{vadd}$ (III)	$Herf_{vadd}$ (IV)	$Gini_{empl}$ (V)	$Herf_{empl}$ (VI)	$Gini_{vadd}$ (VII)	$Herf_{vadd}$ (VIII)
Sample Extended on Time dimension								
GDP_{pc}	-0.0235***	-0.0187***	-0.0275***	-0.0162***	-0.0017	-0.0057***	-0.0027	-0.0021
	(0.0012)	(0.0015)	(0.0014)	(0.0012)	(0.0020)	(0.0017)	(0.0024)	(0.0019)
$[GDP_{pc}]^2$	0.0010***	0.0008***	0.0013***	0.0008***	0.0001	0.0002***	0.0003***	0.0002**
	(0.0001)	(0.0001)	(0.0001)	(0.0001)	(0.0001)	(0.0001)	(0.0001)	(0.0001)
Constant	0.6180***	0.1727***	0.6217***	0.1546***	0.5601***	0.1381***	0.5547***	0.1198***
	(0.0033)	(0.0038)	(0.0035)	(0.0030)	(0.0061)	(0.0053)	(0.0070)	(0.0055)
R^2	0.259	0.153	0.266	0.138	0.813	0.882	0.765	0.764
Observations	1,605	1,605	1,502	1,502	1,605	1,605	1,502	1,502
Sample Extended on Country dimension								
GDP_{pc}	-0.0176***	-0.0183***	-0.0206***	-0.0143***	-0.0020	-0.0044***	-0.0044**	-0.0019
	(0.0012)	(0.0012)	(0.0012)	(0.0012)	(0.0019)	(0.0015)	(0.0021)	(0.0018)
$[GDP_{pc}]^2$	0.0008***	0.0008***	0.0010***	0.0006***	0.0002**	0.0002***	0.0003***	0.0001*
	(0.0001)	(0.0001)	(0.0001)	(0.0001)	(0.0001)	(0.0001)	(0.0001)	(0.0001)
Constant	0.6025***	0.1859***	0.6079***	0.1694***	0.5619***	0.1506***	0.5642***	0.1365***
	(0.0029)	(0.0031)	(0.0030)	(0.0031)	(0.0053)	(0.0043)	(0.0061)	(0.0052)
R^2	0.106	0.120	0.145	0.079	0.787	0.877	0.761	0.826
Observations	2,649	2,649	2,435	2,435	2,649	2,649	2,435	2,435

Source: Authors.

Notes: Estimates (V–VIII) include country fixed effects. GDP_{pc} stands for GDP per capita at constant prices (thousands US$). Standard errors in parentheses. Statistically significant: *** p<0.01, ** p<0.05, * p<0.1.

Annex Table 4A.2   Regressions of Diversification on Income Level for OPEC Countries

Variables	OPEC members in the world			and in Middle East and North Africa		
	$Gini_{out}$	$Herf_{empl}$	$Gini_{vadd}$	$Gini_{out}$	$Herf_{empl}$	$Gini_{vadd}$
GDP_{pc}	−0.02553112	−0.04145684***	−0.06333541**	−0.00256212	0.04676321	0.06587556*
	(0.01670605)	(0.01527436)	(0.02456196)	(0.03072678)	(0.02817441)	(0.03747950)
$[GDP_{pc}]^2$	0.00157978	0.00301565***	0.00438903***	0.00039342	−0.00141172	−0.00297038
	(0.00109037)	(0.00099693)	(0.00160311)	(0.00175157)	(0.00160607)	(0.00213651)
$[GDP_{pc}]^3$	−0.00004292	−0.00008484***	−0.00012361**	−0.00001440	0.00001161	0.00005499
	(0.00003218)	(0.00002942)	(0.00004731)	(0.00004561)	(0.00004182)	(0.00005563)
$[GDP_{pc}]^4$	0.00000040	0.00000081***	0.00000122**	0.00000013	0.00000003	−0.00000035
	(0.00000034)	(0.00000031)	(0.00000050)	(0.00000044)	(0.00000041)	(0.00000054)
P(low)	2.37809157**	0.76363598	3.75498455**	1.84114404	−0.80956578	7.55797790***
	(1.12525591)	(1.02882283)	(1.65439997)	(1.43137131)	(1.31247224)	(1.74593921)
Constant	0.71045758***	0.61610932***	0.83534762***	0.68692604***	0.50784998***	0.43498098***
	(0.06119162)	(0.05594757)	(0.08996657)	(0.11866039)	(0.09178294)	(0.14473801)
R^2	0.942	0.907	0.860	0.970	0.897	0.948
Observations	169	169	169	88	88	88

Source: Authors.

Notes: All regressions include time and country fixed effects. GDP_{pc} stands for GDP per capita at constant prices (thousands US$). Standard errors in parentheses.
Statistically significant: *** p<0.01, ** p<0.05, * p<0.1.

Annex Table 4A.3 Regressions of Concentration for Subsamples of MENA Countries

GCC countries

Variables	$Gini_{out}$	$Herf_{empl}$	$Gini_{vadd}$
GDP_{pc}	0.14142876*	-0.05326200	0.46837357**
	(0.07450386)	(0.03156220)	(0.16984645)
$[GDP_{pc}]^2$	-0.00855715	0.00392086**	-0.02546998**
	(0.00463079)	(0.00179743)	(0.01055682)
$[GDP_{pc}]^3$	0.00023041	-0.00009918***	0.00058363*
	(0.00013230)	(0.00004314)	(0.00030159)
$[GDP_{pc}]^4$	-0.00000221	0.00000083***	-0.00000477
	(0.00000137)	(0.00000037)	(0.00000313)
Constant	-0.02294480	0.73102625***	-2.12637846*
	(0.45108237)	(0.20472003)	(1.02934527)
Observations	51	57	49
R^2	0.993	0.947	0.969

Resource-rich countries in MENA

Variables	$Gini_{out}$	$Herf_{empl}$	$Gini_{vadd}$
GDP_{pc}	0.43601900	1.68026933**	1.85225279
	(0.09625068)	(0.73139736)	(1.40517389)
$[GDP_{pc}]^2$	-0.71423004	-1.91413946**	-2.40558891
	(1.20373896)	(0.91469358)	(1.74205785)
$[GDP_{pc}]^3$	0.38979807	0.89289429*	1.23280251
	(0.62385671)	(0.47405438)	(0.89416658)
$[GDP_{pc}]^4$	-0.07141563	-0.14865827*	-0.22136144
	(0.11474395)	(0.08719129)	(0.16293497)
Constant	0.60297395**	0.07049948	0.19973671
	(0.26330246)	(0.20007749)	(0.38623254)
Observations	147	147	143
R^2	0.788	0.881	0.672

Resource-poor countries in MENA

Variables	$Gini_{out}$	$Herf_{empl}$	$Gini_{vadd}$
GDP_{pc}	12.38241006	-12.50140040**	-1.53006248
	(8.76513390)	(6.01454027)	(7.84293129)
$[GDP_{pc}]^2$	-11.66214385	13.82743647**	2.65724461
	(8.96555270)	(6.14512808)	(7.96496817)
$[GDP_{pc}]^3$	4.64694100	-6.58550407**	-1.70714867
	(3.98852226)	(2.72895854)	(3.52736893)
$[GDP_{pc}]^4$	-0.66305553	1.14630129**	0.36705754
	(0.65165408)	(0.44490378)	(0.57453171)
Constant	-4.16860225	3.25204578*	0.90636716
	(3.14625478)	(1.63004036)	(2.66930229)
Observations	89	86	85
R^2	0.688	0.869	0.682

Middle East and North Africa excluding Israel

Variables	$Gini_{out}$	$Herf_{empl}$	$Gini_{vadd}$
GDP_{pc}	-0.00882500	0.06455250***	0.01852906
	(0.01821666)	(0.01766061)	(0.02290436)
$[GDP_{pc}]^2$	0.00096733	-0.00359912***	0.00038176
	(0.00113941)	(0.00108819)	(0.00154124)
$[GDP_{pc}]^3$	-0.00003510	0.00008686***	-0.00000394
	(0.00003208)	(0.00002866)	(0.00004741)
$[GDP_{pc}]^4$	0.00000037	-0.00000077***	0.00000066
	(0.00000032)	(0.00000027)	(0.00000051)
Constant	0.70665730***	0.39152287***	0.64078851***
	(0.06362725)	(0.06430421)	(0.07929306)
Observations	287	290	277
R^2	0.860	0.656	0.775

Source: Authors.

Notes: All regressions include time and country fixed effects. GDP_{pc} stands for GDP per capita at constant prices (thousands US$). Standard errors in parentheses. Statistically significant: *** $p<0.01$, ** $p<0.05$, * $p<0.1$.

Notes

1. The lack of diversification is often seen as a problem faced by the region, because a relatively concentrated economy may be heavily exposed to a few very volatile sectors. Moreover, if only a few sectors are growing fast in the world economy, a concentrated production bundle minimizes the chances of benefiting from those high-growth sectors.

2. In fact, the nonparametric analysis suggests that the relationship should be extended beyond the quadratic specification.

3. The lack of data does not allow for a complete analysis of the heterogeneity within the MENA region. We also explore the heterogeneity that might be related to the natural resources endowments of oil producers.

4. The source of the data is the United Nations Industrial Development Organization's Industrial Statistics (INDSTAT), rev. 2.

5. If data for some small sectors are missing but are considered instead as a zero, the value of the Gini index will increase, while the Herfindhal will be unaffected. Given that sometimes the data for small sectors are missing in the dataset used for this work, these sectors are considered inactive (that is, not producing) rather than missing when they represented, on average over the entire 1963–2003 period, less than 2 percent of total manufacturing output, employment, or value added. Thus, the number of active sectors varies by country and year in our sample. The Herfindhal index is not significantly affected by this rule, but the Gini can be downward biased.

6. Besides the variable used here as a proxy for Dutch Disease, we check the robustness of the results using other proxies, that is, exchange rate in levels and the dependence of countries on oil exports and oil prices. Our conclusions are unaffected when using these alternative proxies; results are available upon request.

7. Labor productivity is used instead of total factor productivity (TFP) mainly because data to estimate TFP are available only for a much smaller number of countries. Many countries do not have the sufficiently long investment series that is necessary to build capital stocks. We measure labor productivity as the ratio of output to the number of employees. An alternative would be to use value added instead of output, but that would leave us with a smaller sample. A shortcoming associated with the use of labor productivity is that it is affected by the capital intensity of the sector. An alternative measure controlling for relative factor endowments of countries, the degree of tradability in each sector, and use as an intermediate input is provided in Ugarte (2012). This measure corrects for the fact that labor productivity may be affected by relative factor endowments, and that for a weak link to exist the low productivity sector needs to be nontradable and intensively used as an intermediate input by other sectors. The correlation between our simple measure here and

the one in Ugarte (2012) is positive and significant, suggesting that the simple measure is an adequate proxy for weak links.

8. Otherwise, the estimated productivity distribution will give the same weight to sectors with very different economic importance. After discarding the negative values of the estimated density, the mean and the standard deviation of the distribution are obtained using the estimated density function evaluated over 1,000 points.

9. We try several other thresholds and also calculate deviations with respect to median instead of mean productivity. We decided to report this version using the cutoff at two standard deviations, which is close to a usual cutoff for the normal distribution. Concerning the sensitivity of the proxy with respect to factor endowments, fixed effects included in the regression analysis control for this characteristic. The measure is based on manufacturing data, so it is less subject to productivity shocks than data on oil production. Moreover, we did not detect a statistical correlation between the estimated likelihood and the dispersion of the distribution.

10. Input-output tables used there are from Organisation for Economic Co-operation and Development (OECD) and cover around 40 countries, none of them from the MENA region. Using this information would imply imposing an average structure of economy to these countries.

11. The data on production, employment, and value added come from UNIDO's INDSTAT 3 (3 digit of the ISIC rev. 2); GDP per capita in constant prices is from the 2009 World Development Indicators; and the real exchange rate index is from International Financial Statistics/IMF. Although trade data are more detailed and generally of better quality, we prefer to use production data to measure concentration so that our results are comparable to Imbs and Wacziarg (2003).

12. Measuring GDP per capita at constant dollars rather than PPP allows us to have a much larger expanded sample later on, and there is no strong reason to use one rather than the other when looking at the relationship between production diversification and level of development.

13. Only when we expand the sample along one of the two dimensions (time or countries) are results robust to the ones obtained in Imbs and Wacziarg (2003). Along the time dimension, we extend the sample for the period 1993–2003, but we keep the same countries as in the original paper. Along the country dimension, we keep the same time span as in the original paper, 1963–93, but allow for more countries for which we have data. The U-shaped relationship between concentration and income per capita is maintained (results are available from the authors upon request). However, when we add the two dimensions simultaneously the relationship seems to reverse.

14. Our estimation procedure uses the package *np* from Hayfield and Racine (2008) in *R*. It includes optimal bandwidth selection and cross validation of estimates, as suggested by Racine and Li (2004).

15. The different pattern observed for the Gini coefficient on employment may be because employment is stickier than production or value added. One can increase production and value added without changing employment by buying more of other factors or in by being in the presence of technological progress. The fact that the Gini coefficient is more sensitive to what is happening in the middle of the employment distribution suggests that another potential explanation lies in different changes in concentration at the top and bottom of the distribution.

16. Note that in these high-order functions, even if different orders have different signs, the first derivative may never be equal to zero (in real number space).

17. Annex table 4A.2 suggests that this difference in the pattern of diversification and development is also valid for Organization of the Petroleum Exporting Countries members inside and outside MENA, although the statistical significance of the results is not as strong as for the full MENA and RoW samples. Table 4A.3 explores the heterogeneity that may exist within MENA countries. A first subsample is defined by the members of the Gulf Cooperation Council (GCC), and nonmembers are split into resource-rich and resource-poor countries. Given the reduced number of observations in each subsample and the fixed effects included, estimates are not highly significant. However, results in annex table 4A.3 do not differ substantially from the results in table 4.8. Results for resource-poor countries differ from those in table 4.8 (size and sign), but their interpretation can be misleading, since only three countries (Jordan, Morocco, Tunisia) are represented in this subsample. The exclusion of Israel from MENA does not have a significant impact on the pattern described by the results in table 4.8.

18. In MENA, income per capita measured in 2000 constant U.S. dollars ranges from \$434 in the Republic of Yemen to \$49,329 in the United Arab Emirates. The mean income per capita in MENA is \$6,308 and the median is \$1,528.

19. We also include an interaction term between Dutch Disease and weak links to explore the idea that weak links may be less harmful in countries with a rapidly appreciating exchange rate, as imported goods become cheaper. The interaction is never statistically significant.

References

Acemoglu, D., and F. Zilibotti. 1997. "Was Prometheus Unbound by Chance? Risk, Diversification, and Growth." *Journal of Political Economy* 105 (4): 709–51.

Cadot O., C. Carrère, and V. Strauss-Khan. 2011. "Export Diversification: What's Behind the Hump?" *Review of Economics and Statistics* 93 (2): 590–605.

Corden, M., and P. Neary. 1982. "Booming Sector and De-Industrialisation in a Small Open Economy." *Economic Journal* 92 (December): 825–48.

Faini, R. 2004. "Trade Liberalization in a Globalizing World." Discussion Paper 4665, Centre for Economic Policy Research, London.

Hayfield, T., and J. S. Racine. 2008. "Nonparametric Econometrics: The np Package." *Journal of Statistical Software* 27 (5): 1–32.

Hirschman, A. 1958. *The Strategy of Economic Development.* New Haven, CT: Yale University Press.

Imbs, J., and R. Wacziarg. 2003. "Stages of Diversification." *American Economic Review* 93 (1): 63–86.

Jones, C. 2011. "Intermediate Goods and Weak Links in the Theory of Economic Development." *American Economic Journal: Macroeconomics* 3 (2): 1–28.

Koren, M., and S. Tenreyro. 2007. "Volatility and Development." *Quarterly Journal of Economics* 122 (1): 243–87.

Kremer, M. 1993. "The O-Ring Theory of Economic Development." *Quarterly Journal of Economics* 108 (3): 551–75.

Racine, J., and Q. Li. 2004. "Nonparametric Estimation of Regression Functions with Both Categorical and Continuous Data." *Journal of Econometrics* 119 (1): 99–130.

Saint-Paul, G. 1992. "Technological Choice, Financial Markets and Economic Development." *European Economic Review* 36 (4): 763–81.

Ugarte, C. 2012. "Weak Links and Diversification." University of Geneva.

CHAPTER 5

Fiscal Policy and Diversification in MENA

Ali Zafar

One of the central policy instruments that governments have to influence economic activity is fiscal policy. Over the years, both developed- and developing-country governments have used fiscal policy to stabilize economic activity, promote growth, develop trade, and manage terms-of-trade shocks. In the Middle East and North Africa (MENA), governments have traditionally played a dominant role in the economies and have had high expenditures by international standards. Economic diversification, particularly in the Gulf Cooperation Council (GCC) countries, has depended on fiscal policy to help lay the foundation for successful growth. In MENA, governments have traditionally been forced to allocate budgets between consumption subsidies and longer-term investment. Fiscal policy in the region has tried to insulate the economy from shocks while safeguarding long-term development. Fiscal policy (mainly expenditure policy) has two roles to play in the region—as a stabilizer for terms-of-trade shocks and as a tool for longer-term growth and development.

Fiscal policy was very prominent during the recent financial crisis in 2008, which partially reversed the gains from the unprecedented oil boom that led to significant wealth accumulation in some of the MENA economies.[1] However, the resource-rich countries of MENA have been less affected by the global recession than most other developing regions, especially since oil prices have rebounded and reserves have been strengthened. The impact of the crisis has depended on the nature of the economy. The GCC economies, such as Bahrain and Saudi Arabia, with their large oil exports and reserves, have been the least affected, whereas oil exporters with larger populations relative to their oil wealth—Algeria, the Islamic Republic of Iran, Iraq, Libya, and the Syrian Arab Republic— have had a deterioration in their fiscal and current account positions. The oil importers, such as the Arab Republic of Egypt, Jordan, and Lebanon, with tight links to the GCC economies, have been hurt by high oil prices and reduced foreign direct investment (FDI) and remittances from the resource-rich countries of the region.

This chapter assesses the relationship between fiscal policy, growth, and diversification in the MENA region. The chapter begins by briefly describing the contemporary fiscal dynamics in MENA countries in the aftermath of the Arab Spring. Stylized facts are then analyzed to assess the historic behavior of fiscal policy in terms of consumption versus investment. The goal is to understand the use of fiscal instruments for diversification. The countries are disaggregated into three groups: the GCC, the Mashreq (Arab-speaking countries to the east of the Arab Republic of Egypt and north of the Arabian Peninsula) and the Maghreb (Arab-speaking countries of North Africa). The impact of the global crisis on fiscal policy is examined and the behavior of fiscal policies over a 30-year horizon is investigated in relation to previous commodity booms and busts. Case studies of Algeria, Jordan, and Saudi Arabia provide a closer analysis of the links between fiscal policy and diversification in countries representing different parts of the MENA region.

Role of Fiscal Policy in the Aftermath of the Arab Spring

In the first half of 2011, a series of revolts happened spontaneously in the Arab world, with strong repercussions for economic stability, fiscal management, and long-term growth in the affected countries. Motivated by a combination of authoritarian rule, government corruption, police intimidation, and lack of economic opportunities, the uprisings gathered momentum and succeeded in toppling regimes in Egypt, Libya, and Tunisia. The demands centered on greater political enfranchisement and economic opportunity, and to a large extent were motivated by rising expectations. While the full impact of these revolts is still to be borne out, some preliminary estimates can be made of their potential impacts on the region based on historical, anecdotal, and available empirical evidence. Figure 5.1 provides a background chart to show the economic condition of the different regions before the Arab Spring.

By the spring of 2012, the MENA region had settled into an unstable equilibrium, with some regime change coupled with uncertainty on many fronts. In addition to the governments that were overthrown in Egypt, Libya, and Tunisia, the people of Bahrain, Syria, and the Republic of Yemen have experienced strong discontent and rebellion, while citizen demands for political liberalization have been growing in Jordan and Morocco. Across the board, there has been discontent, regardless of whether a country is an oil importer, Sunni- or Shia-dominated, or located in the Maghreb or Mashreq. Governments have tried to react to the rising tide of popular discontent on the economic front by increasing subsidies, wages, and pensions and by offering large stimulus programs. Currently, the macroeconomic horizon is uncertain, although there are strong downside risks.

One of the major challenges for policy makers over the medium and long term is the need to maintain fiscal stability while actively trying to ramp up public investment and help shield the poor from exogenous food and oil shocks. The recent crises, both international and domestic, have led to greater demands for government expenditure and service delivery. The political revolts caught almost all MENA governments by surprise, and many have reacted with strong fiscal stimulus packages or expansion of subsidies. Because the Middle East depends on large inflows

Figure 5.1   Fiscal Dynamics in the Middle East on the Eve of the Arab Spring, 2010

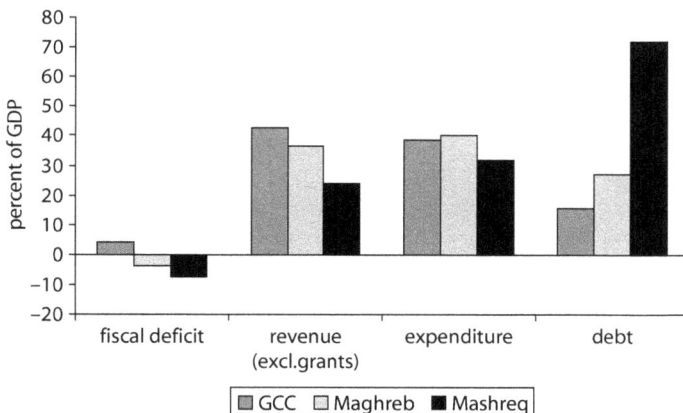

Source: IMF 2011.

of imported foods, an extensive subsidy system has been set up to shield local populations from food price inflation. In the wake of the recent international financial crisis, however, recognition is growing that large public deficits are not sustainable throughout the world and that fiscal instability can have bad effects on longer-term growth. The biggest danger for MENA countries in the postrevolutionary era is to overspend on improperly targeted subsidies and underspend on vital physical and social infrastructure. Given the overall history of the region, governments have to maintain a careful balance between the various expansions in expenditures and the quest for fiscal stability.

The countries with perhaps the greatest risk of fiscal slippages in the medium term are oil-importing countries such as Egypt, Jordan, and Tunisia, which have a multiplicity of risk factors. There has been increasing pressure on government expenditures for subsidies, public investment, and employment generation. In these countries, where consumption subsidies absorb a large share of government resources and have dwarfed public investment spending—frequently reaching 8 percent of gross domestic product (GDP) in Egypt and more than 4 percent of GDP in the others—fiscal pressures will be strong in the years ahead.[2] A combination of fuel subsidies to reduce the impact of higher oil prices on the population and food subsidies to help cushion price shocks has hurt the countries' fiscal positions. In addition, strong stimulus packages in the wake of the political crisis may have deleterious fiscal implications down the road. Egypt has reversed its decision to scale back food subsidies in the aftermath of the crisis, and Tunisia's interim government announced in April 2011 that it would adopt a fiscal stimulus package, focusing on a series of fiscal and financial measures designed to encourage investment, especially in regional development zones; ease the burden on taxpayers; and simplify tax obligations (table 5.1). In February 2011, to prevent unrest, the Moroccan authorities announced an additional $2 billion in subsidies to reduce costs of consumer staples, such as bread and cooking oils.

The oil-exporting countries have also been affected by the political crisis, but they have more fiscal space to maneuver (figure 5.2). The oil-exporting countries of the Gulf and the other oil exporters of the region, such as Algeria, Iraq, and Libya, can benefit from the recent oil price boom, and their ample reserves allow them to undertake postcrisis expansionary fiscal policy without jeopardizing macroeconomic stability. The availability of sovereign wealth funds for many of the oil exporters gives an ample fiscal cushion. After responding to the 2008 financial crisis

TABLE 5.1   Selected MENA Economics: Real GDP Projections and Fiscal Assessment

	Real GDP Projections %			Fiscal changes after Arab Spring
	2010	2011	2012	
Oil exporters	3.5	4.9	4.1	
Iran, Islamic Rep.	1.0	0.0	3.0	No measures announced
Saudi Arabia	3.7	7.5	3.0	$100 billion stimulus program including public works; 15% pay increases for civil servants
Algeria	3.3	3.6	3.2	Close to $160 billion in new infrastructure projects; main focus, road and rail
United Arab Emirates	3.2	3.3	3.8	No major shift in policy
Qatar	16.3	20.0	7.1	Continued subsidies on petrol and diesel
Kuwait	2.0	5.3	5.1	Free daily meals to population for a year; cash allocations of $5,000 per citizen
Iraq	0.8	9.6	12.6	No policy articulated
Sudan	5.1	4.7	5.6	No policy articulated
Oil importers	4.5	1.9	4.5	
Egypt, Arab Rep.	5.0	1.0	4.0	Increase in some state wages and pensions by 15% maintenance of all subsidies in full, costing close to $18 billion; exemptions of late loan and tax payments from fines
Morocco	3.2	3.9	4.6	Doubling of funds allocated to state subsidies; compensation system for wheat importers
Syria, Arab Republic	3.2	3.0	5.1	Significant financial benefits on public-sector employees and on low-wage earners in general; public sector wages will be increased by S£1,500 ($32) a month and basic state pension will be increased by S£1,500 a month: some lowering of tax rates
Tunisia	3.7	1.3	5.6	Massive stimulus package combining public investment in special development zones; tax exemptions for investors in these areas; plans to reduce the value added tax (VAT); 6% rate imposed on imported equipment; some projected increases in subsidies
Lebanon	7.5	2.5	5.0	No key policy departures announced
Jordan	3.1	3.3	3.9	$225 million cuts in fuel, sugar, and rice prices; pay increase for civil servants and retirement pensions

Source: Real GDP figures form IMF; other information from government authorities and World Bank staff.

Figure 5.2   Fiscal Balances in MENA, 2000–10

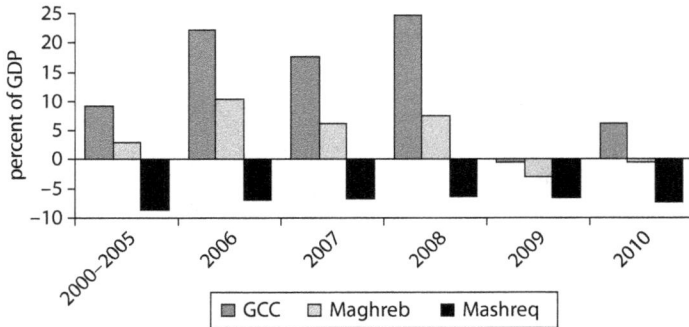

Source: IMF 2010.

with the largest stimulus of any country in the Group of 20, Saudi Arabia announced in February 2011 about $36 billion in bailouts and $67 billion in spending plans to combat social unrest.[3] Other countries have announced similar measures, although on a much smaller scale. Overall, the evidence is fairly clear that any future fiscal shocks to the oil exporters, especially the GCC countries, will be mild, especially given the high projected international prices of oil until 2015.

Fiscal Policy in MENA: Stylized Facts

The global commodity boom since 2003 has positively affected growth in MENA, although the region has been strongly impacted by the 2008 economic crisis. Overall GDP growth in the region averaged more than 5 percent during the 2000s. Growth reached more than 4 percent in 2008, fell to 2.3 percent in 2009, and rebounded to more than 4 percent in 2010. The GDP growth rates of oil importers and exporters followed similar trends, although volatility was greater among the GCC countries (figure 5.3). Average per capita income surpassed $10,000 by 2005 for the oil exporters, and oil importers also made significant progress. Total oil and gas exports increased significantly from 2000 to 2009, although the crisis reduced their overall value, in large part, because oil prices fell to less than $50 a barrel. Fiscal and current account surpluses had reached record levels before the crisis, with the combined current account topping $350 billion. Inflation, as measured by the consumer price index (CPI), was in the low single digits for most countries in the 2000s, partly

Figure 5.3   Real GDP Growth Rates in MENA, 2000–10

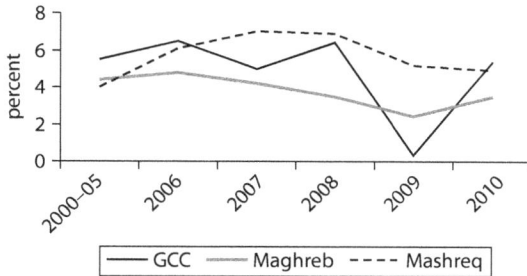

Source: IMF 2011.

helped by prudent exchange rates and monetary management. Debt dynamics on the whole have been quite favorable, but the degree of overhang has been much lower in the oil-exporting economies than in the oil importers. In parallel, life expectancy increased in the GCC by almost 12 years, to 75 years, between 1980 and 2010.

Oil-exporting countries, particularly the GCC countries, maintained a reasonable fiscal stance over the past decade. During the early boom years of the 1970s and 1980s, governments recycled the windfall gains through a welfare system and public investment program, but there also was a surplus of hastily planned infrastructure projects that did not have the projected impact on economic growth, coupled with weakening fiscal positions and growing debt. Fiscal policy expansion strongly tended to be correlated with revenue increases. By the 2000s, MENA countries made a strong attempt to build up substantial international reserves through carefully managed fiscal policy.[4]

The GCC countries were much more careful than other MENA countries in their spending and ensured that the commodity booms resulted in reserve accumulation (figure 5.4a). In the current era, hydrocarbon revenues are being used more carefully to catalyze stronger private sector investment in infrastructure, with a focus on road and rail projects. In the wake of the crisis, the GCC countries had strong reserves to tap for stimulus capital. As a result of stimulus measures during the crisis and a general countercyclical fiscal policy, the GCC countries have maintained non-oil GDP growth, averaging more than 3 percent a year. Imports were contained, and the drop in oil prices led current account surpluses to fall from just under $380 billion in 2008 to about $50 billion in 2009. The subsequent return of high oil prices led to a current account surplus of $400 billion in 2011 for

Figure 5.4   Revenue and Expenditures in MENA, 2000–10

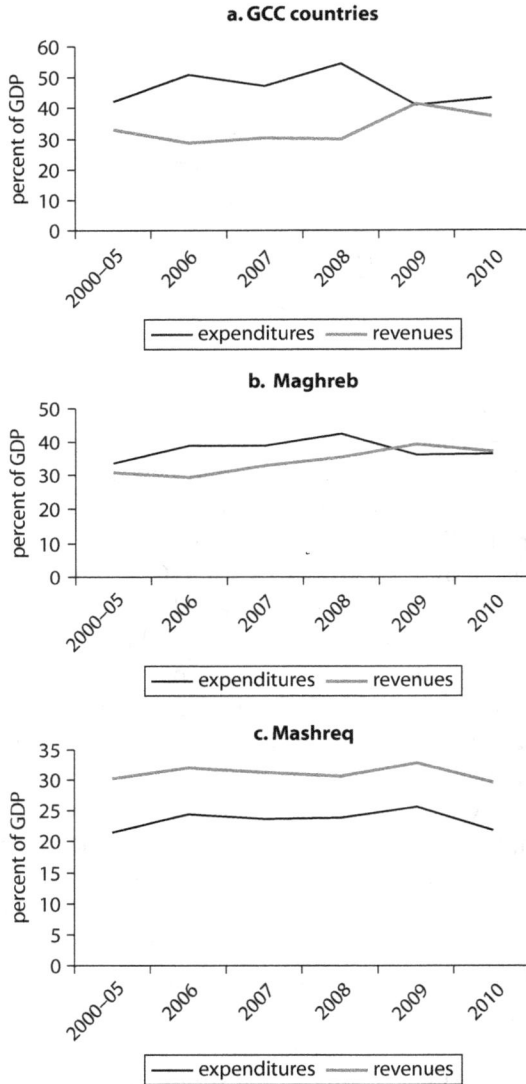

a. GCC countries

b. Maghreb

c. Mashreq

Source: IMF 2011.

the GCC economies. Overall, the hydrocarbon sector remains dominant in the GCC economies, accounting for more than 50 percent of GDP and two-thirds of fiscal revenue over the last ten years.

Macroeconomic and fiscal management in the non-GCC economies has been mixed (figure 5.4b and figure 5.4c). For most of the 2000s, the countries managed their fiscal houses to preserve underlying macroeconomic stability. However, in countries such as Jordan and Lebanon the primary deficit has remained high even during these high-growth years. Following the global crisis, Egypt and Jordan temporarily increased capital expenditures to help stimulate the economy, and quickly thereafter, with the advent of the Arab Spring, food and energy subsidies were raised significantly. The Maghreb has fared better than the Mashreq in keeping its expenditures more closely aligned to revenues. Resource-rich labor importers like Algeria have had an easier time than resource-poor oil importers like Jordan and Egypt. In a number of oil-importing countries, particularly Egypt, Jordan, and Lebanon, economic activity has slowed and unemployment increased in the wake of the Arab Spring. However, all oil-importing countries of MENA have seen a sharp deterioration of their fiscal positions and more limited economic policy options because of reductions in foreign exchange buffers. This translates into a decrease in public resources for key infrastructure investments that could propel diversification.

The big concern for the medium term is the fiscal situation in the marginal oil exporters and oil importers. The stimulus may have an adverse long-run fiscal impact, especially on public investment, wages, and subsidies. The strong pre-crisis fiscal positions may evaporate over the medium term. Evidence suggests that the overall fiscal balance in MENA fell from a surplus of 13 percent of GDP in 2008 to a deficit of about 1.2 percent of GDP in 2009 before rising to a small surplus in 2010. A decomposition of fiscal numbers shows considerable diversity within the region, with the GCC countries in a strong fiscal position, while the Mashreq and, to a lesser extent, the Maghreb, ran deficits.

The Complementary Role of Monetary Policy in the MENA Countries

Complementary to fiscal policy, monetary policy also plays a role in the MENA region, although its role varies significantly depending on the exchange rate regime in each country. In the GCC countries, monetary policy has been used to maintain the peg to the dollar. All six countries of the GCC union, with the exception of Kuwait, have pegged their currencies to the dollar to stabilize exports and government revenues, as well as to maintain price stability (Khan et al. 2008). The monetary union was established because of several commonalities among the nations: dependence on oil exports, low tax and tariff regimes, traditionally low inflation, free capital convertibility, and similar economic structures. This regime has served to strengthen the credibility of the monetary authorities. The main goal of monetary policy is to support the fixed regime. Because the central banks of the GCC countries do not use interest rates as a monetary tool to control inflation, fiscal policy has been the primary tool to influence economic performance. Fiscal policy, via subsidies, has also been an important dampening force on inflation in MENA countries. Inflation has historically averaged in the single digits, although it has been higher in oil-importing than in oil-exporting countries and has been managed by tight monetary policy at the central banks.

In the GCC, the U.S. dollar peg has served as the external anchor for monetary policy and has been used to help maintain overall macroeconomic stability. The policy has served the region well over the years and has helped shield the economies from excessive volatility. Given that the currency is pegged to the dollar, monetary policy in the Gulf has closely followed the American monetary policy. Since the economies are heavily dependent on oil (priced in U.S. dollars), the monetary arrangement has helped support that structure. In effect, fiscal and external current account balances have largely followed movements in the price of oil. However, some costs are associated with this policy. In light of the weakening dollar in 2009, dollar depreciation reignited inflation in the GCC through higher import prices, although the degree of exchange rate pass-through has varied by country. Furthermore, while nominal exchange rates have not appreciated in respect to other currencies, the trade-weighted real effective exchange rate has increased.[5] The GCC countries are not expected to alter their current exchange rate policy given that nominal effective exchange rates have not shown a high degree of appreciation vis-à-vis other currencies.

The oil importers have used monetary policy to keep inflation stable and to prevent it from undermining export competitiveness. Most oil importers in the Middle East have had relatively conservative monetary policies and exchange rate–based stabilization programs to prevent strong credit expansion and avoid double-digit inflation. While practices differ depending on the country, monetary policy has acted to safeguard macroeconomic stability. For countries such as Egypt and Syria, where the exchange rate is not pegged to any currency, monetary policy has been carefully used as a countercyclical tool to control inflation. Over the years, stable inflation rates in most of the MENA countries have led central banks to be relatively accommodative. When inflationary surges have occurred, as in the food price shocks of 2008, monetary policy has been constrained in these countries to dampen inflationary pressures. For countries in MENA linked to the euro, such as Morocco, there has been some overvaluation of currencies but no major inflationary surges.[6] In Jordan, which has a fixed peg to the dollar, monetary policy has been accommodative and has supported the exchange rate. Overall, oil importers have a strong degree of prudent monetary policy that has helped complement their fiscal management.

Fiscal Policy Cyclicality in Oil Exporters and Oil Importers: A Long-Term View

To understand recent fiscal policy, it is important to understand the historical fiscal dynamics in the MENA region. This section examines the historical response to trade shocks and assesses the degree of pro- or countercyclicality in the past. By definition, cyclicality means the response of fiscal policy to shocks. Ideally, fiscal policy should contract during booms and expand during recessions to ensure a smooth output. The differences between the conduct of fiscal policy before and after the financial crisis are assessed. The effect of fiscal policy on output volatility is also considered. Given the strong linkages among the MENA countries, the fiscal analysis sheds light on the interrelationships between the oil exporters and the oil importers.

An understanding of the GCC's economic structure is vital to understanding the evolution of the members' fiscal policy over several decades. The GCC economies, particularly Oman, Saudi Arabia, and the United Arab Emirates (UAE), represent the founding structure of the Organization of the Petroleum Exporting Countries (OPEC) and have been the leading oil producers. Oil has been the foundation of the GCC economies over the last four decades, contributing to more than half of their GDP, and more than three-fourths of government revenue and exports. Accounting for close to half of proven world oil reserves, GCC countries have been important beneficiaries of the oil booms and shocks of the last decade, particularly the two oil shocks of the 1970s and the recent commodity boom of the 2000s.

A historical analysis of the stylized facts for the GCC shows interesting patterns. During the 1970s oil boom, as the OPEC-led oil shocks led to higher oil prices, the GCC countries launched ambitious programs of public spending on infrastructure and the welfare system. The boom in oil prices led to a corresponding boom in spending, with strong correlations between expenditure changes and revenue changes (figure 5.5). With the declines in oil prices during the 1980s and 1990s, budgets contracted somewhat as the economies adjusted. By the 2000s, GCC governments were more careful with fiscal policy, and the correlation between revenue changes and expenditure changes declined. Thus, a significant part of revenues has been saved, although spending on wages and salaries has increased. It is important to note in this regard that the post-2000 boom has been more pronounced in terms of revenue expansions, while the booms in the 1970s were more short lived.

Fiscal policy in the GCC in the 2000s has been significantly different from what it was during the 1970s boom, with important implications for growth and diversification. In the 1970s, GCC governments spent more than two-thirds of their oil revenues, but by the 2000s, they had put about one-fourth into savings and stabilization funds, or sovereign wealth funds, which increased exponentially over the 2000s. (By contrast, much of the money in the 1970s was put into international banks, which engaged in reckless lending.) The prudent management in the wake of the 2000 commodity boom led to a decline in the combined public debt of the GCC countries, from 60 percent of GDP in the early 2000s to less than 15 percent by 2010, with Saudi Arabia reducing its debt overhang by close to $100 billion. Many of the GCC countries maintained fiscal surpluses, rather than the deficits they ran in the earlier period, and some

Figure 5.5   GCC Government Fiscal Policy

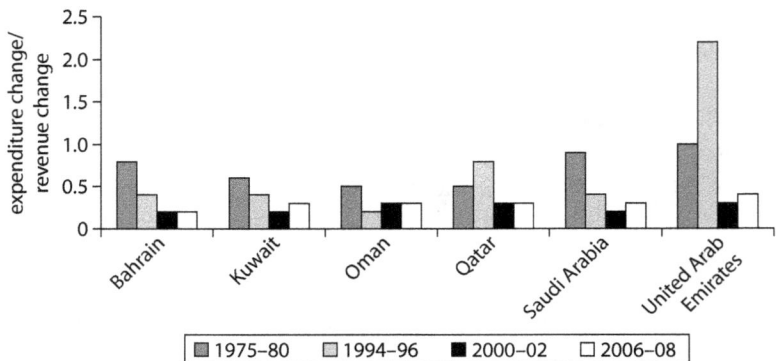

Legend: ■ 1975–80   □ 1994–96   ■ 2000–02   □ 2006–08

y-axis: expenditure change/revenue change (0, 0.5, 1.0, 1.5, 2.0, 2.5)

x-axis: Bahrain, Kuwait, Oman, Qatar, Saudi Arabia, United Arab Emirates

Sources: Fassano 2002; IMF database.

countries had surpluses in the double digits. It is fair to say that macro-economic management of the commodity booms was better in the 2000s than in the 1970s.

Over the past decade, one of the major fiscal policy successes of the GCC governments has been the buildup of savings in the sovereign wealth funds, which demonstrates their countercyclical fiscal behavior. The SWFs were originally started in 1980 to cushion the effects of vola-tile oil revenue and build up reserves. Their growth has been a testament to prudent macroeconomic management in the Gulf. An important ratio-nale behind the formation of the SWFs in the Gulf countries was to cre-ate a source of revenue that could replace oil revenue after the depletion of oil reserves.[7] While each country is different, the SWF has become an instrument for both financing deficits and building long-term financial assets. Given the lack of taxation in the GCC, the funds play an impor-tant role. The overall assets of the various funds are estimated to be more than $1.3 trillion (figure 5.6). Details of the SWF stocks are not publicly available, but the available estimates suggest that the Abu Dhabi Investment Authority has more than $600 billion and that Saudi Arabia has more than $400 billion (although the Saudi fund is technically a monetary account and not an SWF).[8] Despite a strong shock in the wake of the financial crisis, the SWFs remain major players in the Gulf economies. Overall, the use of the reserve funds have helped cushion budgets, protect the economies from volatile oil prices, and help diversify government investments for each country's long-term future.

However, one major issue with the SWFs has been a lack of transparency and accountability. Because they are the main allocators of state capital in the region, the lack of transparent governance of the funds raises some

Figure 5.6   GCC Sovereign Wealth Funds

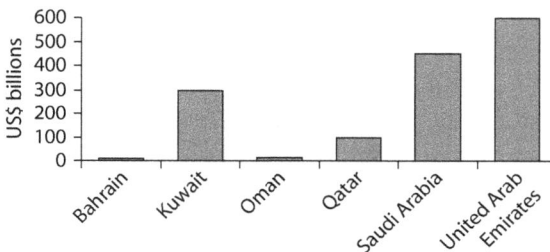

Sources: Government authorities; Goldman Sachs; World Bank.
Note: Technically, the Saudi account is not a SWF but an account in the central bank.

issues in relation to governance and control. Since funding for the SWFs comes from the central bank reserves that accumulate as a result of budget and trade surpluses, proper fiscal rules should be applied to these funds. Recent literature casts doubt on whether this is the case. Truman (2007) finds that many wealth funds, particularly in the MENA region, involve large official holdings of cross-border assets, which are often unknown to the citizens of the countries and to market participants. In a similar vein, Elbadawi and Soto (2011) find that the resource-rich but largely democracy-deficient MENA region has been a fiscal rules-free region, and that fiscal rules can be valuable fiscal stabilization instruments, especially with the nascent democracies demanding more accountability. In a world of greater transparency regarding natural resource management, the resource-rich governments in the MENA region will need to demonstrate more openness and transparency about the use of oil revenues in order to reduce corruption and rebuild trust in government institutions. A more open approach to information on the SWFs will increase the accountability and transparency of these revenues.

The oil exporters have also shown greater efficiency in capital expenditures in the 2000s, especially in their infrastructure investments, than in the earlier periods. The 1970s saw a plethora of investment projects, but without strong project viability or cost efficacy. The available empirical evidence suggests that many of the projects had low rates of return. Some noteworthy investments were made in roads and airports, but the industry consensus is that the level of efficiency in execution of the capital budget was low. Moreover, the lack of savings resulted in slippages in the infrastructure budget in the 1980s and 1990s as oil prices declined.[9] However, the latter period saw much more pronounced government investment in real estate projects, which helped pave the way for additional infrastructure investment. In the post-2001 oil boom period, an inventive mix of government entities—including ministries, municipalities, and national oil companies—has been involved in public-private partnerships, including build-operate-transfer projects and joint ventures. Close to 1,000 government projects have been launched in GCC countries in the past decade, with more than 50 percent completed or in the final execution phase.

Fiscal Policy and Diversification

One of the channels by which fiscal policy affects the economy is through its role in diversification. A growing body of international literature discusses the impact of public expenditure and expenditure composition on growth, but there is no strong consensus on the impact and the sectoral drivers. Devarajan, Swaroop, and Zou (1996) find a positive link between current spending and growth, and a negative link between capital spending and growth, in a sample of 43 developing countries, suggesting problems with capital allocations and investment efficiency. However, Bose, Haque, and Osborn (2007) find a significant positive link between capital spending and growth in a sample of 30 developing countries, with a weak link between current spending and growth. Other studies are similarly mixed. For the MENA region, there are links between fiscal policy and non-oil growth. For the oil producers, this diversification relates to the development of the non-oil sectors and the reduction of the proportion of government revenue and export proceeds from oil and gas sector. For the oil-importers, the story is more complex and depends on a variety of channels of transmission.

Furthermore, the available literature on MENA finds weak links between public infrastructure investment and private growth, although, again, there is not a strong consensus on this issue. Agenor, Nabli, and Yousef (2005) find that public infrastructure expenditure has a small and short-lived impact on private investment in Egypt, Jordan, and Tunisia. Using a relatively sophisticated empirical model, they find that public capital is unproductive and that many MENA countries have a bad investment climate, which is a deterrent to private investment. Other empirical work reaches similar conclusions, both for the MENA region and for non-MENA countries.[10] While public investment can potentially crowd out private capital, the reverse may also occur when public spending on useful infrastructure allows private operators to emerge.

The stylized facts on the links between fiscal policy and diversification are interesting. First, an examination of public expenditure trends in the MENA region shows that fiscal policy is oriented more toward subsidies and consumption and less toward public investment. The MENA region historically has underinvested in infrastructure—MENA spending on infrastructure amounted to less than 5 percent of GDP in 2010 compared with 15 percent of GDP in East Asia. The World Bank finds that the spending has been so limited that the region's actual infrastructure needs are between $75 billion and $100 billion a year from 2012 onward, in contrast to the low investment volume of $6 billion that flowed to MENA in 2009. This low investment has impeded diversification. In MENA countries, 55 percent of businesses identify lack of reliable power networks as a main constraint to running their enterprises; in Egypt,

Jordan, and Morocco, road congestion is also a significant obstacle—the average speed of vehicles in Cairo is as low as 9 kilometers an hour.

The limited investment in infrastructure in MENA is the mirror image of the large public spending in subsidies and public consumption. Most MENA countries have much higher subsidies than their international comparators, with subsidies in Egypt, Jordan, Morocco, and Tunisia equivalent to more than 3 percent of GDP in the late 2000s (figure 5.7). The region's water scarcity means that food production is low and that the region is dependent on imported food. In parallel, fuel subsidies have been used to build support for governments among their people. As a result, the region has had very high food and fuel subsidies, sometimes even bigger than the country's allocations to education, health, or infrastructure. Unfortunately, these subsidies are generally poorly targeted and fail to reach lower-income people, with questionable cost-effectiveness in terms of social protection. Many subsidies, especially fuel, generally go to middle-class urban residents, and less than 50 percent of the subsidies actually reach the poor (figure 5.8). For obvious reasons, food subsidies are better targeted than fuel subsidies.

One contentious area is the nature of the linkages between public spending and private sector investment. An examination of the econometric evidence about such links leads to mixed and ambiguous conclusions. Overall, the relationship appears weak and short lived. In many of the countries, there are periods of congruence and periods of divergence between the two series. Gross fixed capital formation in the

Figure 5.7   Level of Subsidies, 2006–10 Average
(percent of GDP)

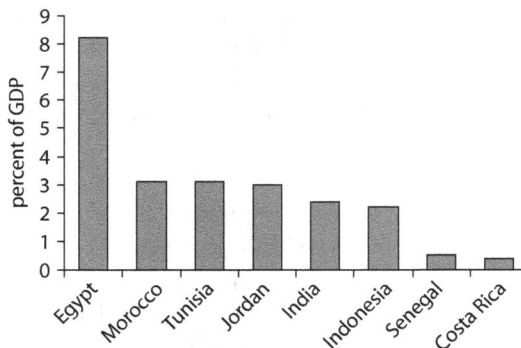

Figure 5.8   Distribution of Subsidies to Poorest 40 percent

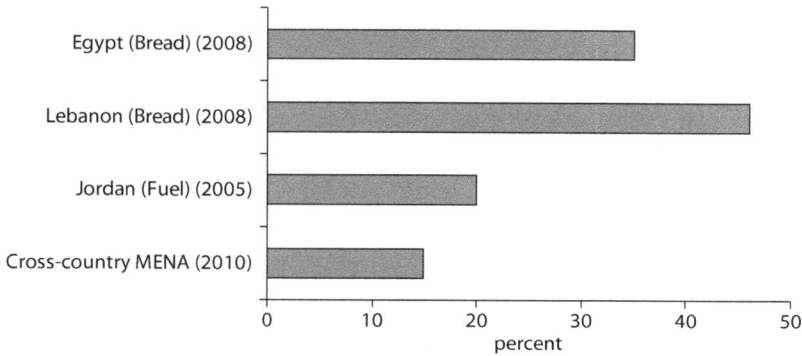

Source: IMF 2011.

private sector seems more closely correlated with investment climate data than with any metric of government capital spending. In Egypt, from 1982 to 2009, investment expenditure by the state declined while private capital formation increased (figure 5.9a). Many of the intervening years show a mixed and uncertain path. Dobronogov and Iqbal (2005) find that while some reduction in public investment was justifiable during the period, the reduction of budget deficits in the first half of 1990s was achieved largely through a fall in public investment. In Jordan, the relationship between public and private capital is similarly ambiguous, suggesting difficulty in finding a correlation (figure 5.9b). Overall, there seems to be little empirical evidence for either crowding in or crowding out of private investment over the long run, but there may be particular spending in individual countries that can play a catalytic role.

Fiscal Management and Diversification: Case Studies
While the key channels through which fiscal policy influences diversification appear to be infrastructure spending and the provision of fiscal incentives for business expansion, this is difficult to test empirically for a large sample of countries. Because of the paucity of long-term time series on fiscal policy and diversification, this section reviews the experience from three case studies—Saudi Arabia (a large oil producer in the GCC), Algeria (a smaller oil producer in the Maghreb), and Jordan (an oil importer in the Mashreq). In some cases, fiscal policy can act as a brake on growth by crowding out the private sector, although the evidence is not strong in that regard.

Figure 5.9   Public and Private Capital, 1982–2010

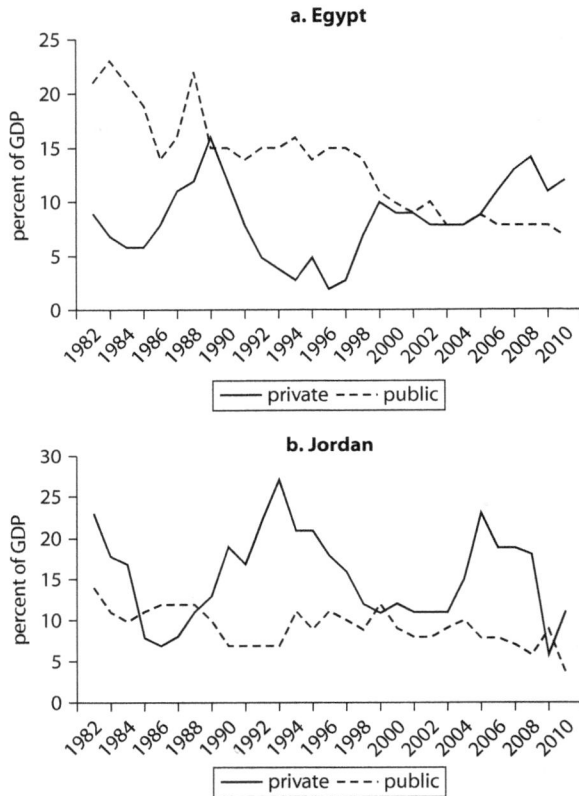

a. Egypt

b. Jordan

Source: World Development Indicators.

Case study 1: Saudi Arabia. Saudi Arabia's macroeconomic performance has remained strong over the past few decades. As the world's largest oil exporter, Saudi Arabia has benefited from protracted windfalls from the large increases in oil prices in recent years. As a result of the sharp rise in petroleum revenues in 1974 following the 1973 Arab-Israeli war, Saudi Arabia became one of the richer economies in the world. Real GDP growth has averaged more than 5 percent from 1970 onward, and real annual growth in the non-oil sector has also been strong, averaging close to 7 percent between 1975 and 2010. The petroleum sector is very strong, accounting for roughly 75 percent of budget revenues, 40 percent of GDP, and 90 percent of export earnings in the past two decades.

Current account surpluses became a stable feature of the Saudi economy, and the government built up a huge reserve. For many years, ample government revenues were available for development, as reflected in the various five-year plans.[11] Given the limited tax regime and the strong reliance on oil receipts and customs duties to produce government revenue, Saudi Arabia has been historically very sensitive to oil price fluctuations. In many ways, Saudi Arabia mirrors the behavior of other GCC countries in its growth and macro management.

After the oil boom, there was a strong budget surplus, which was replaced by deficits during the 1980s decline in oil prices. The decrease in Saudi oil production, from 10 million barrels a day (b/d) during 1980–81 to less than 2 million b/d in 1985, had a fiscal impact on the budget. However, rising prices and strong macroeconomic management led to a decline in budget deficits as a share of GDP, from 25.3 percent in 1987 to 2.9 percent in 1997. By 2000, the country had reached a strong fiscal surplus for the first time in 17 years and achieved solid internal and external balances. Since the mid-2000s, the government has used higher revenue from oil to fuel the non-oil economy, especially construction and infrastructure development.

In relation to fiscal management, Saudi Arabia has improved its ability to confront crisis, partly due to lessons learned in the 1980s in the aftermath of the oil price collapses. The buildup of both the SWF and fiscal surpluses indicates that Saudi fiscal policy has become quite prudent and effective.[12] The Saudi central bank also has been prudent in monitoring inflation, and countercyclical macro-prudential policy became a defining parameter of central bank management.

In parallel, over the years, the Saudi economy has undergone a structural transformation. Difficulties in diversifying the economy have given way to greater success in recent years. The private sector response, both domestic and foreign, has been strongly positive, laying the foundation for continued economic health beyond the oil price boom. The domestic private sector has grown, from about 20 percent of GDP in the 1970s to about 30 percent of GDP by 2010 (figure 5.10). Resilience in the non-oil sectors, particularly real estate, construction, tourism, and trade, has been helpful for the country's economic growth. Mostly, the private sector in Saudi Arabia involves the growth of heavy industry—petrochemicals, fertilizer, and steel, although the nontradable service sector and, to a lesser extent, the small-scale manufacturing sector, are relatively strong. Non-oil exports of goods from both the private and the public sectors (as a share of imports of goods) have increased to 40 percent in the first half of 2012.

Figure 5.10   Saudi Arabia's GDP Decomposition

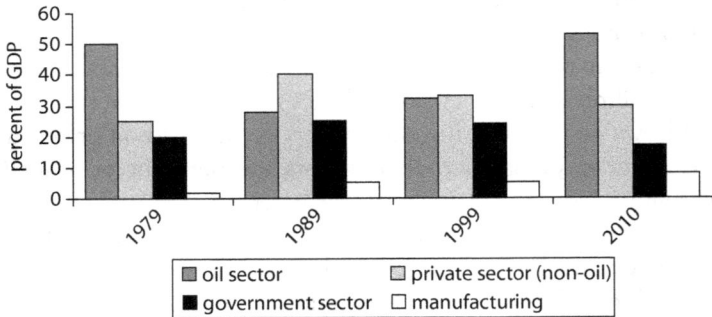

Source: Government of Saudi Arabia.
Note: Government sector includes drilling and oil refining.

A casual analysis of the correlation between fiscal policy and diversification (especially that resulting from the rise of the private sector) shows a clear link. When fiscal policy has been strong and focused, infrastructure development has followed, and diversification has deepened. During periods of contraction, as in the 1980s and late 1990s, fiscal control has hurt diversification efforts. Oil windfalls have been used to help promote diversification and boost growth. In the 1970s, Saudi fiscal policy was essentially procyclical, as 90 percent of the income from the commodity booms was spent with mixed results. With the income from the oil booms, Jubail on the Persian Gulf coast and Yanbu on the Red Sea, once fishing villages, were built into large industrial cities; since the mid-1970s, they have helped attract total investments of close to $150 billion. In parallel, there were many projects, some of dubious investment quality. By the mid-1980s, the oil price collapse led to a deficit and a strong decline in infrastructure spending. Government estimates show a 25 percent decline in infrastructure expenditure in the 1980s, because it was easier to cut than other sectors. Many of the cuts related to capital expenditure and maintenance. The annual growth rate in the transport sector, which reached 19.3 percent between 1975 and 1979, had fallen to a bit more than 1 percent by the late 1980s and early 1990s.

During the 2000s boom, Saudi authorities manifested a more prudent and focused attitude toward diversification. Fiscal policy changed positively. There was significant investment in infrastructure, especially roads, health care, water, power generation, telecom, and air transport. More than $40 billion was spent on infrastructure in the 2000s, representing only half the revenues from the commodity boom, while the rest was saved or used to pay down the debt stock. There was also a greater emphasis on the quality of investment expenditure. Saudi Arabia's 2009 budget increased investment spending by 36 percent, in line with these objectives. The largest projected growth in infrastructure spending is in education, with many new universities and schools being built and old facilities being revamped. Finally, the goal has been to increase the government's partnership with the private sector in providing infrastructure. Very generous fiscal incentives, especially cheap land, low corporate taxes, and no income taxes have also served to attract FDI.

The prevailing modality with which the Saudi government is currently promoting diversification is through public-private partnerships. Essentially, the government sets policies and procedures, while the private sector takes responsibility for the technical aspects of project delivery. The government is planning to spend more than $70 billion on infrastructure development between 2010 and 2015. It is planning the construction of six new urban centers (Eastern province, Hail, Jizan, Madinah, Rabigh, and Tabuk). Public-private partnerships are being formed to address infrastructure needs such as transportation, energy, and water.[13] Under these arrangements, the government provides a percentage of the cost, while the remainder is financed by the private sector and commercial banks. Saudi Arabia has also reduced its dependence on fiscal policy by allowing companies to access the debt capital markets for project finance. Overall, the Saudi story shows that focused fiscal policy can help diversification efforts.

Case study 2: Algeria. Another interesting case study is Algeria, an oil producer in the Maghreb, where diversification has been very limited. Algeria is an oil exporter with close proximity to Europe and far from the GCC, and it has a checkered political history. The story of Algeria is one of missed opportunities for diversification and growth, although recent evidence suggests a change of policy. Throughout Algerian history, the government has not been able to diversify away from hydrocarbons. In addition to the poor business climate, fiscal policy played a central role in not allowing the private sector the necessary infrastructure to expand. Only recently, as a result of strong oil windfalls and careful fiscal expansion in infrastructure, is Algeria seeing private sector growth and a strengthening of domestic and foreign investment.

A relatively large economy in North Africa, Algeria has the 14th-largest oil reserves and the 7th-largest reserves of natural gas in the world. The hydrocarbon sector is the mainstay of the economy, accounting for about 60 percent of budget revenues, 45 percent of GDP, and more than 95 percent of export earnings. After years with a centrally planned economy, Algeria is slowly attempting to dismantle the socialist edifice and install a market economy, but it has not been an easy journey.

For a variety of reasons, diversification has not been very successful in Algeria. The share of oil exports in the economy has remained roughly constant. Manufacturing output remains a low percentage of GDP, even for an oil economy. The growth of labor-intensive industries such as textiles, manufacturing, and food production has been minimal. The private sector share in GDP has not been strong and has frequently decreased over the past three decades.[14] Hausmann, Klinger, and Lopez-Calix (2010) find that the country is overspecialized in oil given its small endowment; its non-oil export basket is small and highly unsophisticated and offers little growth potential (figure 5.11). The private sector share of GDP was still only 12 percent in 2010. The failure of diversification can be seen in the country's unemployment rate, which currently is close to 30 percent. Moreover, unemployment among those under age 25 has reached 70 percent. In a strange twist, the country has moved from having state-controlled, centrally planned industries to having a model with an inefficient, hydrocarbon export–dependent public sector. The Algerian model has been one of using public employment programs to create jobs, and although these programs created 1.4 million jobs between 1997 and 2001, they are mostly temporary (Ait Youness and Annane 2004).

Fiscal policy in Algeria has remained a challenge. Despite favorable oil prices, the country has experienced pronounced fiscal imbalances, a result

Figure 5.11   Number of Exported Products Compared across Four Countries, 2007

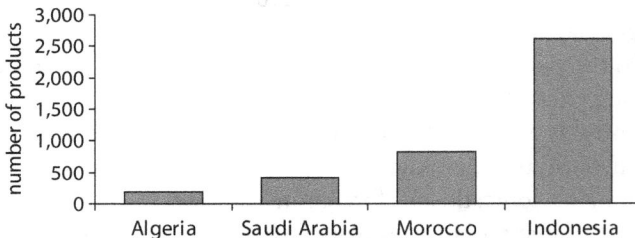

Source: Hausmann, Klinger, and Lopez-Calix 2010.

of poor fiscal policy and lending to weak public enterprises. In the 1980s and 1990s, deficits averaged more than 55 percent of GDP, and the lack of resources for infrastructure hurt diversification prospects. However, much more prudent fiscal management over the past decade has led to a string of surpluses. In 2009, Algeria posted its first overall fiscal deficit in a decade, at 8 percent of GDP, following a surplus of 8 percent in 2008 (IMF 2009). Annual overall and nonhydrocarbon GDP growth has been respectable, averaging close to 4 and 5 percent, respectively, largely driven by public spending, along with low inflation, averaging around 3 percent. A good share of hydrocarbon export revenues was saved in reserves and in the oil stabilization fund or used to drastically reduce external debt. After years of negative or low productivity, by the mid-2000s, the Algerian economy had started turning the corner with regard to fiscal management.[15]

The low level of government investment in infrastructure in the 1990s, amounting to less than 0.5 percent of GDP a year, contributed to weaknesses in the private sector.[16] An analysis of Algerian public expenditure data shows a correlation between low government investment and limited diversification. Only recently has fiscal policy made a distinct shift toward infrastructure, with investment increasing to more than 3 percent of GDP. Since 2006, after the last oil boom, the government has pushed to build roads, railways, dams, houses, and airports. As a result, public investment in infrastructure remained strong in 2009.

With more attention to the provision of infrastructure, the Algerian private sector has generated more than 50 percent of GDP in the past few years and accounts for a growing percentage of imports. The country also has implemented strong corporate tax relief, which has acted as a catalyst to bring in valuable FDI. Moreover, the country is building a 1,200-kilometer east-west motorway, most of which has been operational since 2009; and tramways are being constructed in the major cities of Algiers, Constantine, and Oran.[17]

Case study 3: Jordan. Jordan is another interesting case study because it is a small oil-importing economy in the Mashreq with a degree of diversification. Despite having one of the smallest economies in the Middle East along with a weak resource environment, Jordan has crafted a positive and ambitious development strategy to achieve rising standards of living in recent decades. Growth was close to 7 percent annually in 2000–08. Although highly dependent on foreign aid, the country has emerged as the business capital of the Levant. Relying on foreign trade to solve its energy requirements, the country has one of the most liberal economic regimes in the Middle East. Many international ratings give Jordan high numbers for a competitive business climate. Unlike Algeria and Saudi Arabia, Jordan cannot rely on hydrocarbons to provide the bulk of its revenues and thus has had to forge strong trade and finance links with the outside world. Jordan has a good track record with economic diversification, and it now exports varied goods such as phosphates, pharmaceutical products, textiles, and fruits.[18] A resilient service economy, including tourism and construction, and a growing industrial sector have also helped Jordan become a diversified and vibrant economy (figure 5.12). Although defined as a lower-middle-income country with significant levels of poverty, Jordan has displayed vitality and innovation in recent years despite limited access to the sea and other geographical disadvantages.

Jordan's fiscal regime has improved following a severe fiscal crisis in the late 1980s (which saw the debt-to-GDP ratio reach more than 200 percent) and has helped support the government's development objectives. Like Saudi Arabia and Algeria, Jordan suffered from persistent deficits in the 1970s and 1980s. Large aid inflows and poor fiscal management, partly stemming from high subsidies, had led to sharp increases in external debt. By the 1990s, however, the country succeeded in reducing its deficit and achieving successful growth. By the 2000s, the government's strong fiscal policy with regard to infrastructure lending helped to spur the rise of manufacturing.

Fiscal policy has been key to Jordan's diversification program. In the wake of the oil boom in the 1970s, the Jordanian government received grants from its neighbors, with which it increased spending to a high of

Figure 5.12   Jordanian Diversification

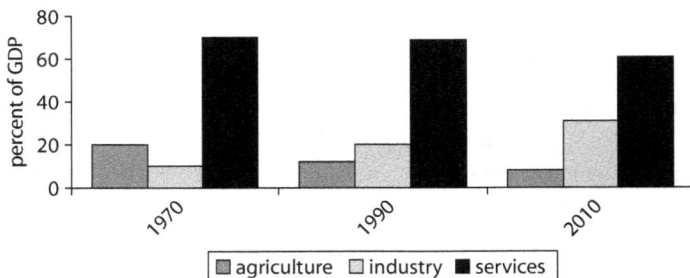

Sources: Government authorities; World Bank staff.

40 percent of GDP, with some emphasis on military and wages. However, the government had to retrench as the grants declined, and it cut vital capital expenditure. Infrastructure investment was then neglected for decades, until the government started investing heavily in infrastructure again in the 2000s. The public sector also began supporting private sector industrial activity in Jordan's qualified industrial zones.

As the government began to address historically neglected sectors, it also began to enact fiscal measures to attract foreign investors and stimulate business activity. These included a reduction in corporate taxes for industry, long-term tax breaks for foreign direct investment in industrial and free zones, and a strengthened state fiscal system. Jordan has also announced a massive $30 billion plan to invest in infrastructure projects by 2030, starting with a water desalination plant. Overall, government investment in infrastructure has helped the rise of the manufacturing sector and has accelerated diversification. However, increases in spending on salaries, food, and energy subsidies in the wake of the Arab Spring threaten to lessen fiscal stability and reduce resources for long-term public investment in infrastructure. In 2011, the fiscal deficit, excluding grants, reached 12 percent of GDP and the debt-to-GDP ratio increased to 65 percent from 59 percent in 2010. Jordan has no fiscal space to cover current expenditures fully, not to mention capital spending, which was curtailed by 29 percent in 2011. The country will be unable to realize its ambitious infrastructure program in the medium to long term without seriously jeopardizing fiscal stability.

Comparison among the Three Countries

A comparison among the three case studies yields some important insights. Each study provides a typical story regarding the relationship between fiscal policy and diversification among a specific set of countries. Saudi Arabia shows the dilemmas of the large oil exporters, Algeria shows the challenges faced by the smaller oil exporters, and Jordan reveals the difficulties of the oil importers in the MENA region. It is important to note that while all three have faced shocks, the impact of the shocks has been asymmetric depending on each country's resource endowment.

- Over the past decades, all three countries improved their fiscal policies through better expenditure control and debt management. In parallel, the boom-and-bust cycles caused difficulties for each government's diversification efforts. Since 2000, however, diversification efforts have been more successful in Saudi Arabia and Jordan than in Algeria.

- All three experiences show increased allocation to infrastructure investment in recent years, along with greater reliance on the private sector, stronger fiscal incentives for domestic and foreign investment, and more focus on the efficiency of interventions. In the absence of strong cross-country econometric evidence of crowding out and crowding in, a cursory examination of the evidence shows no strong relationships between public and private capital, suggesting questions about the quality of public investment.

- In all the case studies, infrastructure expenditure expanded when oil prices were high (1970s and 2000s) and was cut back when oil prices were low (1980s and 1990s). The earlier wave of infrastructure investment was uneven and sporadic, with greater success in Saudi Arabia. Infrastructure remained a neglected sector until the 2000s in Algeria and Jordan.

- A comparison between the Saudi and Algerian experiences suggests that the former's role as a strong oil producer gives it greater investment capital and its policy makers have a greater degree of freedom to invest in the necessary infrastructure. Jordan's experience suggests that diversification is easier for an oil importer given the right government policy mix.

- The case studies suggest that although the relationship between fiscal policy and diversification is not linear, there are clear links. The optimal policy is one that provides a modicum of subsidies but does not neglect good public investment.

The Behavior of Fiscal Policy in MENA: Econometric Evidence

Procyclical fiscal policy has been viewed as pernicious to long-term growth. By leading to high output variability, it can have detrimental effects on the aggregate economy and social welfare. Moreover, during revenue slumps, the first cuts are often to public investment. This section empirically measures the cyclicality of fiscal policy. The theoretical rationale is well defined in a growing literature (Perry, Serven, and Suescon 1998).[19] The analysis seeks to understand the degree of volatility in MENA fiscal expenditures and the various drivers of that volatility. The precise objective of the analysis is to examine the link between fiscal behavior and macroeconomic fluctuations. The goal is to document empirically the properties of cyclical fiscal policy. According to a well-developed body of theoretical and empirical work, the goal of fiscal policy should be to save during good times to prepare for a rainy day, and to be expansionary during bad times to stimulate economic activity.

Fiscal policy should, in essence, be countercyclical to help to dampen business cycle swings.[20] While literature is scant on fiscal policy in the MENA region, there are a few important contributions. Studying the fiscal policies in 19 oil-exporting countries over the period 1965–2005, Sturm et al. (2009) find support for the existence of procyclical conduct of fiscal policy, including a more pronounced response during the 1985–2005 subperiod. Modeling cyclical fluctuations (output gaps) by comparing actual production data with the Hodrick-Prescott smoothed series, the authors find strong fiscal response to oil prices increase.[21] Abdih et al. (2010), in a recent review of fiscal policy in oil economies, find positive average fiscal policy responses of oil-producing countries to the recent oil price hike. Their estimates show that non-oil primary balances worsened substantially in the oil economies during 2003–08, driven by an increase in primary spending, but this trend was partially reversed when oil prices went down in 2009. Macroeconomic volatility in the region has historically been the highest in the world in large part because of oil price changes. Aizenman and Marion (1993) find that macroeconomic volatility has an adverse impact on investment and economic growth. Expenditure volatility associated with fluctuations in oil revenue was found to be a key factor explaining slower growth in oil-producing countries compared with resource-poor countries (Auty and Gelb 2001).

Concluding Remarks

The long-term challenge for the MENA region is to ensure that fiscal policy is used to promote growth and diversification. The GCC countries will need to implement policy reforms to accelerate non-oil growth and create employment opportunities for a rapidly increasing labor force in a sustained fashion. For oil importers in the Mashreq and Maghreb, fiscal management must ensure that the pressing demands on the state from the citizenry must be accommodated without jeopardizing longer-term macroeconomic stability. Reorientation of public expenditure, away from subsidies that do not go to the poor and toward both conditional cash transfers and effective public investment programs, must be encouraged. Through fiscal policy targeted toward infrastructure, MENA countries can help lay the foundation for successful diversification.

Notes

1. In the past, current account and fiscal surpluses had reached large proportions, and there had been a large expansion of sovereign wealth funds. International Monetary Fund (IMF) estimates suggest that sovereign wealth funds, or SWFs, control as much as $3 trillion, and that a significant part of this investment has been in the Gulf states.

2. Preliminary IMF and government estimates from Egypt projected a fiscal deficit of more than 9 percent for 2011. The general perception among industry experts is that the deficit will be manageable in the short term but will lead to higher debt-servicing costs in the medium term and endanger the country's sovereign rating.

3. The massive spending packages include a 15 percent pay raise and two-month salary bonus for government workers.

4. In the GCC countries, the dollar peg prevents the use of independent monetary policy. The central banks of the GCC countries, which are in charge of monetary policy formulation and implementation, keep the peg to maintain price stability, with the medium-term objective of having a monetary union with the other GCC countries. While GCC member countries officially pegged their national currencies to the U.S. dollar on January 1, 2003, as an explicit step toward monetary integration, and have defined a series of convergence criterion, the common currency still faces a number of obstacles.

5. However, as seen in chapter 3, the real exchange rates—that is, the price of tradable versus nontradable goods—were often overvalued in 1980–2010. The nontradable sectors' prices (including wages) are so high in the GCC that no tradable industries other than oil and gas and related industries survive. Thus, there has been an adverse impact on competitiveness. Using the methodology explained by Zafar (2007), there are various ways to detect the extent of GCC misalignment, including purchasing power parity (PPP) and time series econometrics. GCC states have tried to resolve some of these exchange rate issues through a policy of importing labor, which has allowed them to have very flexible labor markets with strong nominal wage adjustment.

6. This is not systematic for all oil importers. Although there have been episodic overvaluations in Tunisia, in 2000–08, the policy has been to depreciate the currency by about 4 percent per year vis-à-vis the euro.

7. Most of the oil economies in the Gulf use conservative oil price estimates to protect the budget, and use excess revenues to pay down debt.

8. These buildups in the SWFs have been aided by unprecedented relatively high oil prices, which have persisted postcrisis. Projected to rise to nearly $70, the price levels are much higher than the $35–50 price range assumed by the GCC authorities during the budget planning process.

9. In the 1980s and 1990s, in the wake of the oil price declines, the GCC faced a slump and made systematic cuts in infrastructure expenditures, especially for development projects, land purchases, and equipment. Smaller cuts were also made in the wage bill and in operations and maintenance.

10. It is a challenge to obtain reliable disaggregated fiscal data for a range of countries over a large enough time series. However, the available data show that the quality of governance is vital in explaining the efficacy of public expenditures.

11. In the first two five-year plans (1970–80), the government emphasized infrastructure, with the building of highways and power generation plants and expanding seaports. In the third plan (1980–85) two industrial cities—Jubail and Yanbu—were constructed for the production of steel, petrochemicals, fertilizer, and refined oil products. The seventh plan (2000–05) focused on diversification and an increased role for the private sector in the Saudi economy. The eighth plan (2005–10) included economic and social infrastructure, with a focus on transportation, energy, and water.

12. While a discussion of Saudi oil policy is beyond the scope of this paper, it is important to note that the policy has been guided by a strong desire to maintain market and quota shares and to support stability in the international oil market.

13. This is best illustrated with a typical example. In July 2008, the Saudi government licensed the establishment of Saudi Landbridge Company, which was to build a freight and passenger rail network between Riyadh and Jeddah, and Dammam and Jubail on a build-operate-transfer (BOT) basis, for an investment of $7–$9 billion. In April 2008, the Tarabot consortium, consisting of seven Saudi companies and Asciano of Australia, was selected as the preferred bidder for the 50-year BOT concession for the Landbridge project.

14. In an interesting study on Algerian diversification, Hausmann, Klinger, and Lopez-Calix (2010) find that the conventional Dutch Disease explanations for oil dependence, leading to an appreciated real exchange rate and strong macroeconomic volatility, are not strong arguments. On the contrary, they argue that Algeria's limited diversification is due to a poor business climate, a highly protected internal market, and strong competition for oil rents, which dulls the incentives for private sector investment in new export activities.

15. The country also has a restrictive attitude toward foreign investment. There are tight restrictions on imports, and new foreign investment must be in the form of joint ventures, with Algerian partners owning at least a 51 percent share.

16. This reflects, to a great extent, the civil war during that period.

17. International calls for tender have been issued for the construction of a 1,300-kilometer high-speed train line. In addition, existing railways are

undergoing modernization and electrification, and work has begun on 400 kilometers of new railways.

18. In a study, Nassif and Walkenhorst (2006) find that Jordan was very successful with the creation of qualified industrial zones (QIZs), which accounted for almost a quarter of total exports and helped exports surge to close to $1 billion by 2005. In the process, the number of employees in QIZ enterprises increased to more than 46,000, or almost 30 percent of the country's manufacturing workforce.

19. The work follows a growing literature on fiscal policy and volatility. Gavin and Perotti (1997) find that, in sharp contrast to industrial countries, procyclical fiscal policy has been the norm in several developing countries, particularly in Latin America.

20. A methodology used by the IMF to link macroeconomic output and fiscal policy looks at the change in the non-oil primary fiscal balance when it is decomposed into the change in the cyclically adjusted non-oil primary balance (fiscal impulse) plus the change in the cyclical non-oil primary balance (automatic stabilizers). While the construction of such a cyclically adjusted fiscal balance is laudable, in practice it is problematic given the technical and econometric difficulties in establishing a benchmark indicator such as an output gap. Overall, fiscal policy in oil economies has often been defined as expansionary/contractionary when the change in the non-oil primary balance is negative/positive. Following Barnett and Ossowski (2002), the non-oil primary balance is calculated by subtracting the non-oil revenue from total government expenditure.

21. Several of the studies use public consumption rather than public expenditure due to data difficulties.

References

Abdih, Y., P. Lopez-Murphy, A. Roitman, and R. Sahay. 2010. "The Cyclicality of Fiscal Policy in the Middle East and Central Asia: Is the Current Crisis Different?" IMF/WP/10/68, International Monetary Fund, Washington, DC.

Agenor, P-R., M. K. Nabli, and T. Yousef. 2005. "Public Infrastructure and Private Investment in the Middle East and North Africa." World Bank, Washington, DC.

Ait Younes, A., and S. Annane. 2004. "La question de l'emploi et de l'intermédiation sur le marché du travail." International Labour Organization, Algiers.

Aizenman, J., and N. Marion. 1993. "Macroeconomic Uncertainty and Private Investment." *Economics Letters* 41 (2): 207–10.

Auty, R., and A. Gelb. 2001. "The Political Economy of Resource-Abundant States." In *Resource Abundance and Economic Development*, ed. R. Auty. Oxford, U.K.: Oxford University Press.

Barnett, S. A., and R. Ossowski. 2002. "Operational Aspects of Fiscal Policy in Oil-Producing Countries." IMF Working Paper, International Monetary Fund, Washington, DC (October).

Bose, N., M. E. Haque, and D. R. Osborn. 2007. "Public Expenditure and Economic Growth: A Disaggregated Analysis for Developing Countries." *Manchester School* 75 (5, September): 533–56.

Devarajan, S., V. Swaroop, and H. Zou. 1996. "The Composition of Public Expenditures and Economic Growth." *Journal of Monetary Economics* 37 (2, April): 313–44.

Dobronogov, A., and F. Iqbal. 2005. "Economic Growth in Egypt: Constraints and Determinants." World Bank, Washington, DC.

Elbadawi, I. A., and R. Soto. 2011. "Fiscal Regimes in and outside the MENA Region." Documentos de Trabajo 398, Instituto de Economia. Pontificia Universidad Católica de Chile.

Fassano, U. 2002. "Testing the Relationship between Government Spending and Revenue: Evidence from GCC Countries." IMF/WP02/201, International Monetary Fund, Washington, DC.

Gavin. M., and R. Perotti. 1997. "Fiscal Policy in Latin America." In *NBER Macroeconomics Annual 1997*, 11–72. Cambridge, MA: National Bureau of Economic Research.

Hausmann, R., B. Klinger, and J. Lopez-Calix. 2010. "Export Diversification in Algeria." In *Trade Competitiveness of the Middle East and North Africa*, ed. J. Lopez-Calix, P. Walkenhorst, and N. Diop. Washington, DC: World Bank.

IMF (International Monetary Fund). 2009, 2011. *Regional Economic Outlook: Middle East and Central Asia*. Washington, DC.

Khan, M., et al. 2008. "The GCC Monetary Union—Choice of Exchange Rate Regime." International Monetary Fund, Middle East and Central Asia Department, Washington, DC.

Nassif, C., and P. Walkenhorst. 2006. "Trade, Competitiveness, and Employment in Jordan." World Bank, Washington, DC.

Perry, G., L. Serven, and R. Suescon. 1998. "Fiscal Policy, Stabilization, and Growth: Prudence or Abstinence." World Bank, Washington, DC.

Sturm, M., et al. 2009. "Fiscal Policy Challenges in Oil Exporting Countries: A Review of Key Issues." European Central Bank, Frankfurt.

Truman, E. 2007. "Sovereign Wealth Funds: The Need for Greater Transparency and Accountability." Policy Brief, Institute of International Economics, Washington, DC.

Zafar, Ali. 2007. "The Impact of the Strong Euro on the Real Effective Exchange Rates of the Two Francophone African CFA Zones." Working Paper 3751, World Bank, Washington, DC.

CHAPTER 6

Natural Resource Heterogeneity and the Incentives for and Impact of Regional Integration

Celine Carrère, Julien Gourdon, and Marcelo Olarreaga

At low levels of development, economic growth is often accompanied by a diversification of the production structure (Imbs and Wacziarg 2003; Cadot, Carrère, and Strauss-Kahn 2011). In resource-abundant countries, however, rising commodity prices can slow down the process of economic diversification, at least when rising foreign exchange is not properly managed (see chapter 2). The development of regional markets in MENA has therefore been seen as a potential (second-best) solution to resource-dependence-induced low diversification, at least since the creation of the Arab League in 1945.[1]

Despite numerous regional trade agreements, intraregional trade in MENA is only a 10th of the region's total trade and is below the level that a standard gravity model[2] would predict (Miniesy, Nugent, and Yousef 2004; Péridy, 2007). This chapter explores the extent to which regional trade agreements have contributed to intraregional trade in MENA, and whether this contribution has been at the expense of trade diversion and therefore of broader economic efficiency.

In a recent theoretical paper, Venables (2011) argues that some degree of trade diversion is expected when a resource-rich country enters into a preferential trade agreement with a relatively labor-abundant country. In such a situation, the preferential agreement will create incentives for labor-intensive goods to be sourced from the resource-poor country. This will help the resource-poor country diversify its production bundle and reach a higher level of economic growth. But this diversification process will be achieved at the expense of the resource-rich country, which will experience trade diversion, as it replaces imports from the relatively more efficient rest of the world with those from the regional partner.

To empirically test this assumption, this chapter builds on a standard panel gravity model where aggregate imports of MENA countries are explained using bilateral fixed effects and year-specific importer and exporter fixed effects. These fixed effects control for, among other things, the traditional determinants of a gravity equation, such as distance, colonial links, and common language, as well as gross domestic product (GDP), population, and most-favored-nation (MFN) tariffs of the exporter and the importer. Different types of dummies are then introduced to capture the impact of the creation of trade agreements on intraregional imports and imports from the rest of the world (as in Carrère 2006). The coefficient on the variable capturing the impact on intraregional imports measures the extent of *trade creation* (in the Lipsey rather than Viner sense),[3] and the coefficient on the variable capturing the impact on imports from the rest of the world measures the extent of *trade diversion* (again, in the Lipsey sense).

The results of our basic specification suggest that there is trade creation in most agreements, and that trade diversion may be a problem only in the Pan-Arab Free Trade Area (PAFTA),[4] in particular when considering non-oil imports. As predicted by Venables (2011), trade diversion seems to be concentrated in resource-rich importers. These are generally countries that export only a few products and that have a highly concentrated export bundle. Interestingly, these countries have also significantly increased their exports of non-oil goods to resource-poor countries, but these increases were not accompanied by trade diversion in resource-poor countries.

Thus, MENA's regional integration has been mainly trade-creating, and both resource-poor and resource-rich countries have seen increases in their exports of non-oil goods to other countries in the region. Trade diversion has been observed only in resource-rich countries, suggesting that MENA's preferential agreements have been associated with income redistribution from resource-rich to resource-poor countries.

Trade Agreements in MENA: An Analytical Setup

Our theoretical setting is a three-country world with two countries that have abundant natural resources and form a preferential trade agreement.[5] If the two countries have a comparative advantage in the same natural resource, there is no reason for these countries to trade, and therefore little trade creation or trade diversion should be expected from such an agreement. If the countries are abundant in different natural resources, however, then trade creation can be expected and will be accompanied by little trade diversion. Thus, the first prediction for regional integration among natural-resource-abundant countries is that integration should be accompanied by no trade diversion and mild levels of trade creation.

If, on the other hand, the preferential trade agreement is signed by a natural-resource-abundant country and a natural-resource-poor country with a small but developing manufacturing sector, then the introduction of tariff preferences will probably lead to some trade creation in the resource-poor country, because it will be able to import more natural resources from the resource-rich country. There is little scope for the resource-poor country to suffer from trade diversion if the resource-abundant country is specialized in the natural resource good. On the other hand, the resource-rich country may suffer from a significant amount of trade diversion, because the resource-poor country benefiting from the preferential access can increase its exports of manufacturing goods to the resource-rich country while continuing to export labor-intensive goods to the rest of the world.

As suggested by Fouquin, Langhammer, and Scweickert (2006) and Venables (2011), the fact that resource-poor countries benefit more from preferential trade agreements than resource-rich countries explains why the latter have not been a driver of regional integration schemes in the developing world. Such schemes would imply income redistribution from resource-rich to resource-poor countries. Indeed, preferential access allows producers in resource-poor countries to benefit from higher prices in the resource-rich country, which increases producer surplus in the exporting resource-poor country while reducing tariff revenue in the importing resource-rich country. Therefore, while the resource-poor country is better off, the resource-rich country tends to be worse off.

Whether this effect is desirable for the region as a whole is an empirical question. In the pure trade-diverting case, where the increase in exports from the resource-poor country to the resource-rich country is accompanied by an equivalent decline in resource-rich-country imports from the rest of the world, the region will unambiguously be worse off. Thus, a necessary condition for the region to be better off is that the increase in intraregional trade be larger than the decline in trade with the rest of the world.

We use the empirical model presented here to test Venables's (2011) theoretical proposition that when resource-rich countries sign preferential trade agreements with resource-poor countries, the former are more likely to suffer from trade diversion than the latter. We then investigate whether in such a case, the increase in exports from the resource-poor country to the resource-rich country is larger than the fall in the resource-rich country imports from the rest of the world.

The Empirical Model

A standard gravity equation approach is applied here to assess the extent of trade creation and diversion associated with MENA's preferential trade agreements. Bilateral imports of MENA countries with respect to each of their regional and nonregional partners are explained by a series of bilateral fixed effects that capture the effects of distance, colonial links, and any other time-invariant characteristic of each bilateral pair, as well as year-specific importer and export fixed effects that capture the impact of the evolution of GDP, population, most-favored-nation (MFN) tariffs, or any other importer and year or exporter and year characteristic. In particular, the importer-year and exporter-year fixed effects make it possible to avoid the bias associated with the omission of exporter and importer remoteness terms (Anderson and VanWincoop 2003). More formally:

$$\ln M_{ijt} = \alpha_{ij} + \delta_{it} + \gamma_{jt} + \sum_k \phi_1^k \text{RTAintra}_{ijt}^k + \sum_k \phi_2^k \text{RTArow}_{ijt}^k + v_{ijt} \quad (6.1)$$

where M_{ijt} is country i ($\in$MENA) imports from j in year t; $\text{RTAintra}_{ijt}^k = 1$ if i and j belong to the same regional trade agreement (RTA) k in t, otherwise 0 (intraregional trade); and $\text{RTArow}_{ijt}^k = 1$ if i but not j belongs to the RTA k in t, otherwise 0. The coefficient of the first term (Φ_1^k) captures trade creation in the Lipsey sense, and the second term (Φ_2^k) trade diversion. α_{ij} is bilateral fixed effects, δ_{it} is the importer and year-specific effects, and γ_{jt} is the exporter and year fixed effects. v_{ijt} is an independent and identically distributed error term.

The k regional trade agreements explored here include PAFTA; the Gulf Cooperation Council (GCC), involving Bahrain, Kuwait, Oman, Qatar, Saudi Arabia, and United Arab Emirates, or UAE; the Agadir

Agreement (involving the Arab Republic of Egypt, Jordan, Morocco, and Tunisia); the Common Market of Eastern and Southern Africa (COMESA), which also involves some Sub-Saharan African countries; all Euromed (Euro-Mediterranean Partnership) agreements signed by MENA countries; all free trade agreements (FTAs) with European Free Trade Agreement countries; and all FTAs with Turkey (for a complete list of these agreements, see annex table 6A.1).

As a further step, we explored, within the same gravity setup, the variation in patterns of trade creation and trade diversion across bilateral pairs, one resource rich and one resource poor. This could be done only for PAFTA, because that is the only trade agreement within MENA involving both types of countries.[6] PAFTA is also one of the few well-functioning regional trade agreements in MENA. Indeed, as argued by Hoekman and Zarrouk (2009), intra-PAFTA trade barriers have come down substantially since the agreement was initiated.[7] The gravity equation becomes:

$$\ln M_{ijt} = \alpha_{ij} + \delta_{it} + \gamma_{jt} + \beta_1 \left[RR_i \cdot RR_j \cdot PAFTA\text{intra}_{ijt} \right] + \beta_2 \left[RR_i \cdot RP_j \cdot PAFTA\text{intra}_{ijt} \right]$$
$$+ \beta_3 \left[RP_i \cdot RP_j \cdot PAFTA\text{intra}_{ijt} \right] + \beta_4 \left[RP_i \cdot RR_j \cdot PAFTA\text{intra}_{ijt} \right]$$
$$+ \beta_5 \left[RR_i \cdot PAFTA\text{row}_{ijt} \right] + \beta_6 \left[RP_i \cdot PAFTA\text{row}_{ijt} \right]$$
$$+ \sum_k \phi_1^k RTA\text{intra}_{ijt}^k + \sum_k \phi_2^k RTA\text{row}_{ijt}^k + v_{ijt} \tag{6.2}$$

where RR and RP capture whether the importer or the exporter is considered resource rich or resource poor. As before, $RTA\text{intra}_{ijt}^k = 1$ if i and j belong to the same RTA k in t, otherwise 0, and $RTA\text{row}_{ijt}^k = 1$ if i but not j belongs to the RTA k in t, otherwise 0. The intravariables of PAFTA are then interacted with RR_i and RP_i, as well as with RR_j and RP_j, to explore the degree of heterogeneity on trade creation within MENA depending on whether the importer and exporter are resource rich or poor. Then β_1 captures trade creation between resource-rich countries in PAFTA; β_2 when the importer is resource rich and the exporter is resource poor within PAFTA; β_3 when both PAFTA countries are resource poor; and β_4 when the importer is resource poor but the exporter is resource rich.

The specification in equation 6.2 also allows for heterogeneity in trade diversion within PAFTA depending on whether the importer or the exporter is resource rich or poor. The term β_5 captures the extent of trade diversion if the PAFTA importer is resource rich, and β_6 if resource poor. Since within PAFTA we can further distinguish between resource-rich labor-abundant (that is, developing oil exporter) and resource-rich labor-importing (that is, GCC oil exporter) countries, the heterogeneity in

trade creation and diversion after this further decomposition is also investigated. The robustness of the results to the use of alternatives to the
World Bank's resource-poor and resource-rich categories is tested.

As a last addition, a variable capturing the degree of export concentration of the exporter and the importer is also introduced. The rationale is
that countries that are relatively abundant in natural resources will tend
to have a more concentrated export bundle, whereas countries less abundant in natural resources will have a more diversified export bundle. This
will lead to effects similar to the ones described in Venables (2011), with
more concentrated countries suffering from trade diversion and more
diversified countries benefiting from trade diversion to their more concentrated partners. As proxies for the degree of concentration of the
export bundle, we apply the Herfindahl index of export concentration,
and the average number of exported goods at the six-digit level of the
Harmonized System (HS) over the three-year period preceding the
entrance in force of the PAFTA agreement. The estimated gravity equation then becomes:

$$\ln M_{ijt} = \alpha_{ij} + \delta_{it} + \gamma_{jt} + \lambda_1 \left[PAFTA\text{intra}_{ijt} \right] + \lambda_2 \left[\frac{CI_{jt_0}^{export}}{CI_{it_0}^{export}} \cdot PAFTA\text{intra}_{ijt} \right]$$

$$+ \lambda_3 PAFTArow_{ijt} + \lambda_4 \left[CI_{it_0}^{export} \cdot PAFTArow_{ijt} \right]$$

$$+ \sum_k \phi_1^k RTA\text{intra}_{ijt}^k + \sum_k \phi_2^k RTArow_{ijt}^k + v_{ijt} \qquad (6.3)$$

where CI_{jt_0} is the measure of the exporter's export bundle concentration
(Herfindahl index or number of lines exported) in year t_0, with t_0 being
an average over the three years preceding the entry of country j in the
agreement. When the CI is indexed I, it captures the concentration of the
export bundle of the importer in the three years previous to the signing
of the agreement. Thus, λ_2 captures the extent to which one could expect
a strong degree of trade creation when the exporter is relatively more
concentrated than the importer (if $\lambda_2 > 0$). And λ_4 captures whether
trade diversion is expected to be larger (if $\lambda_4 < 0$) when the importer has
a highly concentrated production structure.

Finally, because all specifications imply controlling for a very large
number of dummy variables, it was decided for computational reasons not
to introduce thousands of fixed effects, but to compute deviations from
the mean for each of these variables. But because there are several dimensions in the fixed effects (bilateral, importer-year, and exporter-year), the

calculation of the deviations to the mean is not straightforward. Each variable was transformed as follows:

$$\tilde{y}_{ijt} = \left[y_{ijt} - y_{ij.} - y_{t.t} + y_{.jt} + y_{i..} + y_{.j.} + y_{..t} - y_{...} \right] \qquad (6.4)$$

A simple ordinary least squares (OLS) estimator was applied to the transformed variables in each of the specifications in equations 6.1, 6.2, and 6.3. To control for potential correlation of the error term within country pairs, standard errors were corrected for clustering within the country pairs. Indeed, the country pair i–j has the same determinants as the country pair j–I, which may lead to correlation of the errors for these observations.

Data and Variable Construction

Bilateral import data for 18 MENA countries (all except Iraq and West Bank and Gaza) and 239 partners are from the COMTRADE database and were obtained through the World Bank's web platform, World Integrated Trade Solution. Data were used for the 20-year period 1990–2009, because MENA regionalism did not exist in the 1980s. Data for Libya are mirrored because Libya does not report to the United Nations system. These differences in data sources for Libya are partly controlled for in the empirical specification by the importer-year and exporter-year fixed effects.

Total import data were used, as well as data on non-oil imports. In a robustness check, data that subtract re-exports from bilateral import data were also used, but results are almost identical to the ones reported in the next section.

World Trade Organization (WTO) notifications were used as a proxy to capture the year of entry into force of the agreement (see annex table 6A.1). It was decided not to include dummies for the FTAs signed by some MENA countries and the United States because these are too recent to meaningfully estimate their impact. In addition, we did not control for the Economic Cooperation Organization (ECO), for three reasons. First, the only MENA country in ECO is the Islamic Republic of Iran. Second, ECO starts in 1992 and therefore captures almost the entire time variation. Including ECO would require expanding the time frame. Third, and most important, it is well known that ECO has suffered from serious implementation problems, and therefore not much should be expected (Pomfret 1997). It is worth noting, however, that the results reported in the next section are robust to the inclusion of ECO.

Data used to define countries as resource poor, resource rich labor abundant, or resource rich labor importing were taken from World Bank (2008). Of all trade agreements, only one includes both resource-poor and resource-rich MENA countries, and that is PAFTA. The Herfindahl indexes of export concentration and the number of export lines at the six-digit HS level before the entry into force of the agreement are computed using HS six-digit data from COMTRADE on exports of each country to the world.

Empirical Results

Table 6.1 reports the results of the estimation of equation 6.1 for seven preferential trade agreements involving MENA countries. Both intraregional and rest-of-the-world effects are reported for each of the seven agreements. The first column reports results using total imports, whereas the second column reports results for non-oil imports. The first point to notice is that there are no statistically significant differences between the coefficients reported under the two columns for total imports and non-oil imports.

In all agreements except Agadir and GCC, a positive, large, and statistically significant coefficient on intraregional trade was found. That Agadir and GCC do not show a statistically significant coefficient for intraregional trade can be partly explained by the fact that all Agadir and GCC countries are part of PAFTA and entered into the other agreements after PAFTA was in force. So the advantages in terms of intraregional liberalization that Agadir and GCC offer may be limited.

The only agreement to show a negative and statistically significant coefficient for imports from the rest of the world is PAFTA, and that is for non-oil imports only. For all other trade agreements, the coefficient is either positive or statistically insignificant, suggesting that trade diversion is not an important problem.

In the case of PAFTA, the coefficient on imports from the rest of the world is statistically significant at the 11 percent level. It is much smaller than the coefficient on trade creation. Indeed, the estimated percentage increase in intraregional trade due to PAFTA is around 195 percent $(e^{1.082} - 1 = 1.95)$.[8] The percentage decline in imports from the rest of the world is 18 percent. It is important, however, to caution about the basis on which these numbers are calculated. Intra-PAFTA imports are only 11 percent of PAFTA imports from the world. So an 18 percent decline in something that is almost 10 times larger is not too far off a

Table 6.1   Trade Creation and Diversion for Each Agreement Involving MENA Countries, 1990–2009

Trade agreement	$\ln (M_{ijt})$	
	Total imports	Non-oil imports
PAFTA		
Intra	1.039***	1.082***
	(0.17)	(0.17)
Rest of world	−0.181	−0.195*
	(0.12)	(0.12)
GCC		
Intra	0.166	0.260
	(0.17)	(0.17)
Rest of world	0.954***	0.956***
	(0.12)	(0.12)
AGADIR		
Intra	−0.051	0.042
	(0.24)	(0.23)
Rest of world	−0.383	−0.247
	(0.22)	(0.21)
COMESA		
Intra	0.532***	0.522**
	(0.20)	(0.21)
Rest of world	0.469***	0.395***
	(0.12)	(0.12)
Euromed		
Intra	0.325**	0.266**
	(0.15)	(0.15)
Rest of world	0.102	0.041
	(0.14)	(0.14)
FTA with EFTA		
Intra	0.535**	0.570**
	(0.24)	(0.24)
Rest of world	0.237	0.218
	(0.19)	(0.19)
FTA with TUR		
Intra	0.619***	0.512*
	(0.30)	(0.29)
Rest of world	0.226	0.073
	(0.22)	(0.21)
Observations	31,054	31,016
Number of importers[a]	18	18
Number of exporters	239	239
Years	1990–2009	1990–2009
Fixed effects (ij)	Yes	Yes
Fixed effects (it)	Yes	Yes
Fixed effects (jt)	Yes	Yes

Source: Authors.
Notes: Estimation with OLS; standard errors in parentheses: heteroscedasticity consistent and adjusted for country-pair clustering; for a list trade agrements, see annex table 6A.1; * $p = 0.1$, ** $p = 0.05$, *** $p = 0.01$.
a. Only MENA countries; mirror data for Libya; no data for Iraq and West Bank and Gaza.

195 percent increase in something that is 11 times smaller. In other words, most of the increases in intraregional trade within PAFTA appear to be simply substituting for imports from the rest of the world and could therefore be an important source of inefficiency.

If the increase in intra-PAFTA trade is fully compensated by a fall in PAFTA imports from the rest of the world, then it is clear that PAFTA has been welfare reducing for the region. This is a hypothesis that the estimates for PAFTA in the second column of table 6.1 cannot statistically reject.

To assess the degree to which trade diversion in PAFTA may be concentrated in resource-rich countries, table 6.2 reports results of the estimation of the specification in equation 6.2. Again, the first column reports results for total imports and the second column for non-oil imports only.

Table 6.2   Decomposition of Intra-PAFTA Trade Creation and Diversion According to Natural Resources Endowment, 1990–2009

	$ln\ (M_{ijt})$	
PAFTA	Total imports	Non-oil imports
Intra		
RRi-RRj	1.09***	1.21***
	(0.24)	(0.23)
RRi-RPj	0.80***	0.84***
	(0.20)	(0.21)
RPi-RRj	1.45***	1.40***
	(0.26)	(0.24)
RPi-RPj	0.79***	0.91***
	(0.23)	(0.23)
Rest of world		
RRi	−0.29***	−0.32***
	(0.13)	(0.1274)
RPi	0.005	0.01
	(0.15)	(0.1485)
Observations	31,054	31,016
Number of importers[a]	18	18
Number of exporters	239	239
Years	1990–2009	1990–2009
Fixed effects (ij)	Yes	Yes
Fixed effects (it)	Yes	Yes
Fixed effects (jt)	Yes	Yes

Source: Authors.
Notes: All regressions include, in addition to PAFTA, all other agreements; dummies also introduced in table 6.1, but coefficients are not reported to save space; estimation with OLS; standard errors in parentheses: heteroscedasticity consistent and adjusted for country-pair clustering; * p = 0.1, ** p = 0.05, *** p = 0.01
a. Only MENA countries; mirror data for Libya; no data for Iraq and West Bank and Gaza.

Results are not statistically different from each other across columns. The intra-PAFTA trade creation is now disentangled into four possible categories: trade creation among resource-rich countries in the first row; trade creation when the importer is resource rich and the exporter is resource poor in the second row; trade creation when the importer is resource poor and the exporter is resource rich in the third row; and finally, trade creation among resource-poor countries in the last row.

The coefficients on intra-PAFTA trade creation are all positive and statistically different from zero. They are not very different from each other, and after performing the six possible tests of equality among intra-PAFTA trade creation coefficients, only two were found rejecting the null hypothesis that they are equal. Those were the tests for H_0: $RP_i - RR_j = RR_i - RP_j$, and for H_0: $RP_i - RR_j = RP_i - RP_j$. Note, however, that a joint test of the six equalities simultaneously cannot be rejected, suggesting that the coefficients on intraregional trade creation may not be statistically different from each other after all.

Interestingly, the largest coefficients are found for imports of resource-poor countries from resource-rich countries. The coefficient when the importer is resource rich and the exporter is resource poor (the second row) is 0.84, and the coefficient when the importer is resource poor and the exporter is resource rich (the third row) is 1.40; the difference is statistically significant, as discussed above. This finding implies that intra-PAFTA trade when the importer is resource rich and the exporter is resource poor increased by 132 percent, whereas the increase in intra-PAFTA trade when the importer is resource poor and the exporter is resource rich increased by 305 percent—or more than two times larger.

Venables's (2011) main prediction is that resource-rich countries are more likely to experience trade diversion. This prediction is supported by the data from MENA, which show a decline in non-oil imports from the rest of the world of around 38 percent in the case of resource-rich PAFTA countries, and no trade diversion at all in the case of resource-poor countries.

Table 6.3 reports results of the same specification as in table 6.2, but the resource-rich countries are disaggregated further into GCC oil exporters and developing oil exporters. As expected, there are no significant differences from the results reported in table 6.2, but the decomposition is interesting in itself. The top panel reports results for total imports and the bottom panel for non-oil imports. Again, there are no statistical differences between the coefficients in the two panels. The decomposition suggests that the main driver of the large trade creation coefficient

Table 6.3   Decomposition of Intra-PAFTA Trade Creation and Diversion According to Natural Resources and Labor Endowment, 1990–2009

Total imports	Importer		
	RPLA	RRLA	RRLI
Exporter			
RPLA	0.66	1.78	0.25
	(0.26)**	(0.65)***	(0.22)**
RRLA	0.75	0.17	0.38
	(0.37)**	(1.23)	(0.46)
RRLI	1.54	2.81	0.26
	(0.24)***	(0.61)***	(0.29)***
Rest of world	0.01	−0.41	−0.26
	(0.12)	(0.20)**	(0.11)**

Non-oil imports	Importer		
	RPLA	RRLA	RRLI
Exporter			
RPLA	0.78	1.91	0.53
	(0.26)***	(0.65)***	(0.24)**
RRLA	0.76	1.73	0.77
	(0.36)**	(1.22)	(0.37)**
RRLI	1.48	1.62	0.89
	(0.24)***	(0.61)**	(0.25)***
Rest of world	0.03	−0.43	−0.29
	(0.12)	(0.20)**	(0.11)***

Source: Authors.
Notes: All regressions include, in addition to PAFTA, all other agreements; dummies also introduced in table 6.1, but coefficients are not reported in order to save space; estimation with OLS; standard errors in italics: heteroscedasticity consistent and adjusted for country-pair clustering; RRLA = resource-rich labor-abundant (that is, developing oil exporter) countries; RRLI = resource-rich labor importing (GCC oil exporter) countries; RPLA =resource-poor labor-abundant countries; * p = 0.1, ** p = 0.05, *** p = 0.01.
a. Only MENA countries; mirror data for Libya; no data for Iraq and West Bank and Gaza.

in table 6.3 for imports of resource-poor countries from resource-rich countries comes from imports of GCC countries.

The largest trade diversion effects are to be found in developing oil exporters, not in GCC oil exporters, and the extent of trade creation in the GCC is also much smaller than in developing oil exporters. Thus, in GCC countries, the increase in imports from other PAFTA countries is, on average, 107 percent, whereas the decline in imports from the rest of the world is estimated at 25 percent. However, to assess the relative importance of these two reductions, it is necessary to consider the difference in the base. Given that initial non-oil imports from the rest of the world are at least five times the imports of non-oil imports from other PAFTA countries, this again suggests a fully trade-diverting PAFTA for GCC members.

In the case of developing oil exporters, the percentage decline in imports from the rest of the world is in fact much larger: around 35 percent for non-oil imports. But the average increase in intra-PAFTA trade is much larger as well: around 479 percent. Given that non-oil imports from the rest of the world are nine times imports from PAFTA at the beginning of PAFTA's implementation, this implies that the increase in intra-PAFTA trade is not fully compensated by the decline in imports from the world in the case of developing oil exporter PAFTA members.[9]

Resource-poor PAFTA members experience no trade diversion and quite significant trade creation. While the trade creation is not a prediction of the Venables (2011) model, the model does predict the absence of trade diversion among resource-poor PAFTA members.

To check whether our results regarding trade diversion and trade creation are sensitive to the use of predetermined categories of countries (resource rich, resource poor, and so forth), the estimation of the specification in equation 6.3 was recalculated—instead of using predetermined categories of countries, measures of the extent of concentration in the export bundle of each country before the creation of PAFTA are interacted with the PAFTA variable. The results are shown in table 6.4. Two measures of concentration of exports are applied: a Herfindahl concentration index, and the number of HS six-digit goods that the country exports (the latter being a measure of diversification rather than concentration). The first two columns of table 6.4 report results for total imports and non-oil fuel imports using the Herfindahl concentration index as a measure of concentration. The last two columns report results for total imports and non-oil imports using the number of HS six-digit goods that the country exports as a measure of the diversification of exports before PAFTA was signed. The idea is simply to explore whether there is some heterogeneity in trade creation and trade diversion when countries with different degrees of concentration in their export bundle sign a preferential trade agreement.

Results suggest very little heterogeneity in trade creation, with the coefficients on trade creation being all positive and statistically different from zero, but not statistically different from each other across the estimates in the four columns. The interaction of relative concentration of the importer and the exporter is not statistically different from zero. This suggests that there is little evidence of heterogeneity in trade creation across country pairs with different relative degrees of export concentration.

However, there is some statistically significant heterogeneity in trade diversion, as illustrated by the fact that all the coefficients in the fourth row of table 6.4 are statistically significant. More concentrated countries

Table 6.4   Decomposition of Intra-PAFTA Trade Creation and Diversion

PAFTA	In (M_{ijt})			
	Total imports	Non-oil imports	Total imports	Non-oil imports
Intra	1.051***	1.083***	1.186***	1.247***
	(0.18)	(0.17)	(0.20)	(0.20)
Clj/Cli.intra	0.009	0.013	−0.009	−0.028
	(0.01)	(0.01)	(0.06)	(0.06)
Rest of world	−0.005	0.017	−0.656***	−0.647***
	(0.15)	(0.14)	(0.15)	(0.15)
Cli.row	−0.383**	−0.461***	0.0003***	0.000***
	(0.18)	(0.18)	(0.00)	(0.00)
Concentration index	Herfindahl	Herfindahl	Number of lines	Number of lines
Observations	31,054	31,016	31,054	31,016
Number of importers[a]	18	18	18	18
Number of exporters	239	239	239	239
Years	1990–2009	1990–2009	1990–2009	1990–2009
Fixed effects (*ij*)	Yes	Yes	Yes	Yes
Fixed effects (*it*)	Yes	Yes	Yes	Yes
Fixed effects (*jt*)	Yes	Yes	Yes	Yes

Source: Authors.
Notes: All regressions include, in addition to PAFTA, all other agreements; dummies also introduced in table 6.1, but coefficients are not reported in order to save space; estimation with OLS; standard errors in parentheses: heteroscedasticity consistent and adjusted for country-pair clustering; * p = 0.1, ** p = 0.05, *** p = 0.01.
a. Only MENA countries; mirror data for Libya; no data for Iraq and West Bank Gaza.

(as measured by a higher Herfindahl index, or a lower number of products exported) tend to suffer from a larger degree of trade diversion. It is difficult to interpret the size of the coefficients because the variables are multiplied by the Herfindahl index or the number of exported lines, but figure 6.1 provides an idea of the size of trade diversion in the PAFTA countries, as well as the standard error of the estimate for each country.

When concentration is measured using the Herfindahl index, Kuwait, Libya, Oman, Saudi Arabia, UAE, and the Republic of Yemen all have levels of trade diversion that are statistically different from zero, with a more than 20 percent average decline in imports from the rest of the world. When the number of export lines is instead used as a measure of diversification of exports before the agreement was signed, Bahrain, Jordan, Kuwait, Lebanon, Libya, Oman, Qatar, Sudan, and the Republic of Yemen all have levels of trade diversion that are statistically different from zero, with an average 30 percent decline in imports from the rest of the world.[10]

Figure 6.1 Predicted Non-Oil Trade Diversion by MENA Countries Given the Pre-PAFTA Concentration Index Value

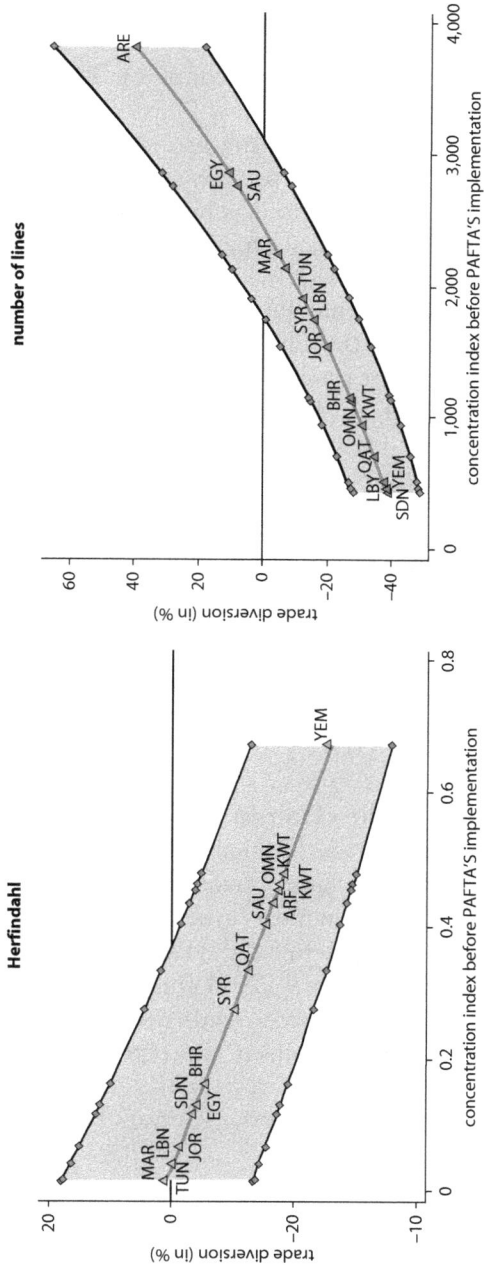

Source: Authors.

Note: The figure shows predicted values: exponential of coefficients for trade diversion presented in table 6.4, columns 2 and 4.

Finally, to understand the types of goods in which we observe trade creation and trade diversion in resource-rich and resource-poor countries, we report the distribution of export growth by sector between resource-rich countries in PAFTA and the rest of the world in the top panel of figure 6.2, and between resource-poor countries in PAFTA and the rest of the world in the bottom panel.

Interestingly, the bottom panel suggests that exports of resource-poor countries to GCC countries are not as well correlated with their exports to the world as they are to developing oil exporters, or to other resource-poor countries. This again suggests that some significant trade diversion could be taking place when GCC countries import from resource-poor countries within PAFTA. The correlation between the distribution of export growth from resource-rich countries to resource-poor countries with export growth from resource-rich countries to the world in the top panel is also quite strong, suggesting again that resource-poor countries within PAFTA may not be subject to a significant amount of trade diversion.[11]

Concluding Remarks

Regional integration is sometimes seen as an instrument to help diversify the economies of resource-abundant MENA countries. A recent theoretical study by Venables (2011) suggests, however, that when resource-rich and resource-poor countries give preferences to each other, the resource-rich country is very likely to suffer from trade diversion.

This chapter explores the extent to which MENA's different integration schemes have led to trade creation and trade diversion. Significant evidence of increase in intraregional trade following the entry into force of the agreements was found in most cases, while evidence of trade diversion appeared in only one agreement, the PAFTA.

Consistent with what Venables (2011) predicts in theory, the empirical work presented in this chapter confirms that the main source of trade diversion in PAFTA has been the replacement of imports of resource-rich countries from the rest of the world by imports from other PAFTA members. Resource-poor counties have suffered no trade diversion.

This finding seems to suggest that the main beneficiaries from PAFTA have been resource-poor countries, which experienced only trade creation and benefited from the trade diversion of resource-rich countries. In

Figure 6.2   Regional Distribution of Export Growth by Sector for Resource-Rich and Resource-Poor Countries
percentage

a. from resource-rich countries

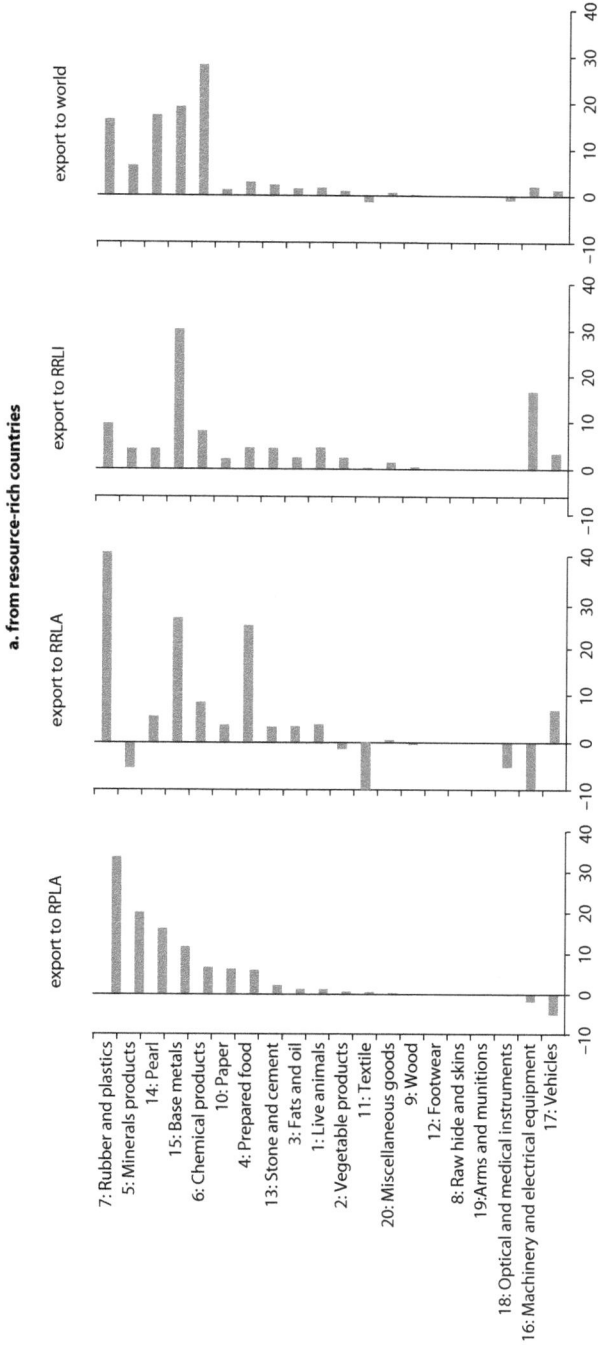

export to RPLA

export to RRLA

export to RRLI

export to world

7: Rubber and plastics
5: Minerals products
14: Pearl
15: Base metals
6: Chemical products
10: Paper
4: Prepared food
13: Stone and cement
3: Fats and oil
1: Live animals
2: Vegetable products
11: Textile
20: Miscellaneous goods
9: Wood
12: Footwear
8: Raw hide and skins
19: Arms and munitions
18: Optical and medical instruments
16: Machinery and electrical equipment
17: Vehicles

(continued next page)

Figure 6.2 *(continued)*

b. from resource-poor countries

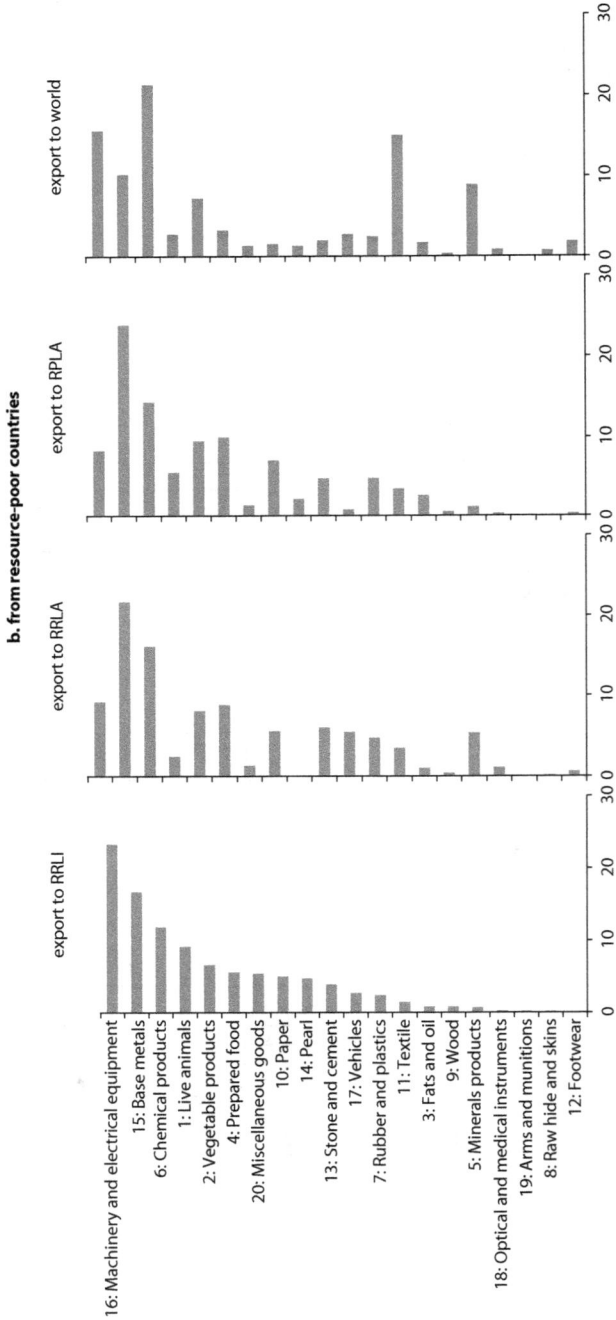

export to RRLI | export to RRLA | export to RPLA | export to world

16: Machinery and electrical equipment
15: Base metals
6: Chemical products
1: Live animals
2: Vegetable products
4: Prepared food
20: Miscellaneous goods
10: Paper
14: Pearl
13: Stone and cement
17: Vehicles
7: Rubber and plastics
11: Textile
3: Fats and oil
9: Wood
5: Minerals products
18: Optical and medical instruments
19: Arms and munitions
8: Raw hide and skins
12: Footwear

Source: COMTRADE.

192

Annex Table 6A.1 Agreements Involving MENA Countries as Importer

Name	Member countries	Coverage	Type	Date of notification	WTO legal cover	Date of entry into force
FTA intra-MENA						
Pan-Arab Free Trade Area (PAFTA)	Bahrain; Egypt, Arab. Rep; Iraq; Jordan; Kuwait; Lebanon; Libya; Morocco; Oman; Qatar; Saudi Arabia; Sudan; Syrian Arab Republic; Tunisia; United Arab Emirates; Yemen, Rep.	Goods	FTA	3-Oct-06	GATT Art. XXIV	1-Jan-98
Gulf Cooperation Council (GCC)	Bahrain; Kuwait; Oman; Qatar; Saudi Arabia; United Arab Emirates	Goods	CU	6-Oct-09	GATT Art. XXIV	1-Jan-03
AGADIR	Egypt, Arab. Rep.; Jordan; Morocco; Tunisia	Goods		3-Oct-06	GATT Art. XXIV	1-Jan-04
Arab Magheb Union (UMA)	Algeria; Libya; Morocco; Tunisia; Mauritania	Goods				2-Jan-12
BTA intra-Mena (and not already included in intra-MENA FTAs above)						
Algeria-Jordan	Algeria-Jordan	Goods	FTA			2-Jan-02
FTA with non-MENA countries						
Economic Cooperation Organization (ECO)	Afghanistan; Azerbaijan; Iran, Islamic Rep, Kazakhstan; Kyrgyz; Pakistan; Tajikistan; Turkey; Turkmenistan; Uzbekistan	Goods	PTA	10-Jul-92	Enabling Clause	17-Feb-92
Common Market for Eastern and Southern Africa (COMESA)	Angola; Burundi; Comoros; Djibouti; Egypt, Arab. Rep. (1999), Eritrea; Ethiopia; Kenya; Lesotho; Libya (2005); Madagascar; Malawi; Mauritius; Rwanda; Sudan; Swaziland; Tanzania; Uganda; Zambia; Zimbabwe	Goods	PTA	4-May-95	Enabling Clause	8-Dec-94
COMESA Free Trade	Burundi (2004); Comoros (2006); Djibouti; Egypt, Arab. Rep., Kenya; Libya (2006); Madagascar; Malawi; Mauritius; Rwanda (2004); Sudan; Zambia; Zimbabwe	Goods	FTA			22-Jun-00
Euromed Agreements						
EC Treaty	Austria (1995); Belgium; Bulgaria (2007); Cyprus (1995); Czech Republic (1995); Denmark (1973); Estonia (2004); Finland (1995); France; Germany; Greece (1981); Hungary (2004); Ireland (1973); Italy; Latvia (2004); Lithuania (2004); Luxembourg; Malta (2004); Netherlands; Poland (1995); Portugal (1986); Romania (2007); Slovak Republic (2004); Slovenia (2004); Spain (1986); Sweden (1995); United Kingdom (1973)	Goods	FTA	24-Jul-06	GATT Art. XXIV	1-Sep-05
EC - Algeria	EC - Algeria	Goods	FTA	24-Jul-06	GATT Art. XXIV	1-Sep-05

(continued next page)

Annex Table 6A.1 *(continued)*

Name	Member countries	Coverage	Type	Date of notification	WTO legal cover	Date of entry into force
EC - Egypt, Arab. Rep.	EC - Egypt, Arab. Rep.	Goods	FTA	3-Sep-04	GATT Art. XXIV	1-Jun-04
EC - Jordan	EC - Jordan	Goods	FTA	17-Dec-02	GATT Art. XXIV	1-May-02
EC - Lebanon	EC - Lebanon	Goods	FTA	26-May-03	GATT Art. XXIV	1-Mar-03
EC - Morocco	EC - Morocco	Goods	FTA	13-Oct-00	GATT Art. XXIV	1-Mar-00
EC - Palestinian Authority	EC - Palestinian Authority	Goods	FTA	29-May-97	GATT Art. XXIV	1-Jul-97
EC - Syrian Arab Republic	EC - Syrian Arab Republic	Goods	FTA	15-Jul-77	GATT Art. XXIV	1-Jul-77
EC - Tunisia	EC - Tunisia	Goods	FTA	15-Jan-99	GATT Art. XXIV	1-Mar-98
FTA with EFTA						
European Free Trade	Iceland; Liechtenstein; Norway; Switzerland	Goods	FTA	30-Jan-70	GATT Art. XXIV	1-Mar-70
EFTA - Egypt, Arab. Rep.	EFTA - Egypt, Arab. Rep.	Goods	FTA	17-Jul-07	GATT Art. XXIV	1-Aug-07
EFTA - Jordan	EFTA - Jordan	Goods	FTA	17-Jan-02	GATT Art. XXIV	1-Jan-02
EFTA - Lebanon	EFTA - Lebanon	Goods	FTA	22-Dec-06	GATT Art. XXIV	1-Jan-07
EFTA - Morocco	EFTA - Morocco	Goods	FTA	20-Jan-00	GATT Art. XXIV	1-Dec-99
EFTA - Palestinian Authority	EFTA - Palestinian Authority	Goods	FTA	23-Jul-99	GATT Art. XXIV	1-Jul-99
EFTA - Tunisia	EFTA - Tunisia	Goods	FTA	3-Jun-05	GATT Art. XXIV	1-Jun-05
EFTA - Turkey	EFTA - Turkey	Goods	FTA	6-Mar-92	GATT Art. XXIV	1-Apr-92
BTA with Turkey						
Turkey - Morocco	Turkey - Morocco	Goods	FTA	10-Feb-06	GATT Art. XXIV	1-Jan-06
Turkey - Palestinian Authority	Turkey - Palestinian Authority	Goods	FTA	1-Sep-05	GATT Art. XXIV	1-Jun-05
Turkey - Syrian Arab Republic	Turkey - Syrian Arab Republic	Goods	FTA	15-Feb-07	GATT Art. XXIV	1-Jan-07
Turkey - Tunisia	Turkey - Tunisia	Goods	FTA	1-Sep-05	GATT Art. XXIV	1-Jul-05
BTA with US						
US - Bahrain	US - Bahrain	Goods & services	FTA & EIA	8-Sep-06	GATT Art. XXIV & GATS V	1-Aug-06
US - Jordan	US - Jordan	Goods & services	FTA & EIA	15-Jan-02	GATT Art. XXIV & GATS V	17-Dec-01
US - Morocco	US - Morocco	Goods & services	FTA & EIA	30-Dec-05	GATT Art. XXIV & GATS V	1-Jan-06
US - Oman	US - Oman	Goods & services	FTA & EIA	30-Jan-09	GATT Art. XXIV & GATS V	1-Jan-09

Source: Authors, based on WTO data.

Note: FTA = free trade agreement; BTA = bilateral trade agreement; CU = customs union; PTA = preferential trade agreement; EIA = economic integration agreement.

this way, the trade agreement has helped redistribute income from resource-rich countries to resource-poor countries within PAFTA itself. It also explains why resource-rich countries may be reluctant to further deepen these types of agreements. Indeed, there are certainly more efficient means of redistributing income to resource-poor countries in the region than through trade diversion.

Notes

1. Clause 2 of the Arab League protocol reads: "the Arab States. . . shall closely cooperate in . . . commercial exchange, customs. . . ." In 1982, league members reached an agreement for the development of intraregional trade (Decree 848 of 27/2/1982).

2. The model explains bilateral trade using distance between two partners and their economic size.

3. Trade creation in the Viner sense occurs only when the regional partner is the lowest cost supplier. This is not necessary to observe trade creation according to Lipsey's definition; trade creation will be observed whenever intraregional trade increases are conditional on not displacing imports from the rest of the world. Thus, trade creation in the Viner sense is a sufficient but not necessary condition to observe trade creation in the Lipsey sense

4. PAFTA was signed in 1996 and entered into force in 1998. It was signed by Bahrain, Arab Republic of Egypt, Iraq, Jordan, Kuwait, Lebanon, Libya, Morocco, Oman, Qatar, Saudi Arabia, Syrian Arab Republic, Tunisia, United Arab Emirates, and Republic of Yemen. See annex table 6A.1 for more detail.

5. This section draws heavily from Venables (2011) and WTO (2010).

6. According to World Bank classification, resource-poor countries in PAFTA include Djibouti, Egypt, Jordan, Lebanon, Morocco, Sudan, Tunisia, and West Bank and Gaza. Resource-rich countries can be divided into two subcategories. GCC oil exporters include Bahrain, Kuwait, Oman, Qatar, Saudi Arabia, and United Arab Emirates. Developing oil exporters include Algeria, Islamic Republic of Iran, Iraq, Libya, Syrian Arab Republic, and Republic of Yemen.

7. Although, as argued by Hoekman and Zarrouk (2009) and Chauffour (2011), there is still some important work to be done to reduce nontariff barriers.

8. Because the left-hand variable (imports) is in logs and the right-hand variable is a dummy (trade agreements by different types of countries), the percentage increase in imports is given by the exponent of the coefficient minus 1. All percentage changes discussed below are computed as discussed here.

9. More precisely, 67 percent of the intraregional trade increase is at the expense of the rest of the world, allowing for one-third of pure trade creation.

10. In the case of the United Arab Emirates, imports from the world seem to increase after the creation of PAFTA, with the use of a number of export lines as a measure of diversification. However, this could be partly explained by the country's large amount of re-exports.

11. The goods with the higher growth in exports of resource-poor countries to other PAFTA countries are machinery and equipment and base metals and equipment. Rubber and plastics seem to dominate exports of resource-rich countries to other PAFTA countries.

References

Anderson, J., and E. VanWincoop. 2003. "Gravity with Gravitas: A Solution to the Border Puzzle." *American Economic Review* 93 (1): 170–92.

Cadot, O., C. Carrère, and V. Strauss-Kahn. 2011. "Export Diversification: What's Behind the Hump?" *Review of Economics and Statistics* 93 (2): 590–605.

Carrère, C. 2006. "Revisiting the Effects of Regional Trade Agreements on Trade Flows with Proper Specification of the Gravity Model." *European Economic Review* 50 (2): 223–47.

Chauffour, J. P. 2011. "Trade Integration as a Way Forward for the Arab World." Policy Research Working Paper 5581, World Bank, Washington, DC.

Fouquin, M., R. Langhammer, and R. Scweickert. 2006. "Natural Resource Abundance and Its Impact on Regional Integration: Curse or Blessing?" Paper presented at the ELSNIT/Fundacao Getulio Vargas Conference in Sao Paulo.

Hoekman, B., and J. Zarrouk. 2009. "Changes in Cross-Border Trade Costs in the Pan-Arab Free Trade Area, 2001–2008." Policy Research Working Paper 5031, World Bank, Washington, DC.

Imbs, J., and R. Wacziarg. 2003. "Stages of Diversification." *American Economic Review* 93 (1): 63–86.

Miniesy, R. S., J. B. Nugent, and T. M. Yousef. 2004. "Intra-Regional Trade Integration in the Middle East: Past Performance and Future Potential." In *Trade Policy and Economic Integration in the Middle East and North Africa: Economic Boundaries in Flux*, ed. H. Hakimian and J. B. Nugent. London: Routledge.

Péridy, N. 2007. "Toward a Pan-Arab Free Trade Area: Assessing Trade Potential Effects of the Agadir Agreement." *The Developing Economies* 43 (3): 329–45.

Pomfret, R. 1997. The Economic Cooperation Organization: Current Status and Future Prospects." *Europe-Asia Studies* 49 (4): 657–67.

Venables, A. 2011. "Economic Integration in Remote Resource-Rich Regions." In *Costs and Benefits of Economic Integration in Asia,* ed. R. Barro and J. W. Lee. New York: Oxford University Press.

World Bank. 2008. *MENA Economic Developments and Prospects: Regional Integration and Global Competitiveness.* Washington, DC: World Bank.

WTO (World Trade Organization). 2010. *World Trade Report, 2010. Trade in Natural Resources.* Geneva.

Country Grouping Classifications

This appendix defines the different classifications used in the text. For most comparisons, countries are classified into three groups: resource-poor labor-abundant (RPLA) countries (Arab Republic of Egypt, Jordan, Lebanon, Morocco, and Tunisia); resource-rich labor-abundant (RRLA) countries (Algeria, Islamic Republic of Iran, Iraq, Libya, Syrian Arab Republic, and Republic of Yemen); and resource-rich labor-importing (RRLI) countries (Bahrain, Kuwait, Oman, Qatar, Saudi Arabia, and United Arab Emirates).[1] This last group corresponds to the members of the Gulf Cooperation Council (GCC) countries.[2] Because there is no ambiguity, we refer to the groups as resource rich (6), resource poor (5), and GCC (6). To signal missing data leading to a reduced sample, we indicate each time how many countries are included in the group in parenthesis.

This three-group classification captures only some of the diversity in the region. For example, in the GCC grouping, half of the countries have a population of approximately 1 million, two of 3 million–4 million, and Saudi Arabia has 25 million. To account for the importance of market size and the exploitation of economies, we constitute a group of LARGE (48, 6) developing countries with a population over 20 million. (The numbers in parentheses indicate the number of large developing countries in the world and then the number in the Middle East and

North Africa) Likewise, we build an OIL (18, 10) group that includes all the major oil exporters (that is, those with oil exports accounting for 80 percent or more of total merchandise exports). Although they are not included in the OIL group, Morocco, Syria, and Tunisia have natural resources and qualify as "point-source natural resource" countries in the classification proposed by Isham et al. (2005).[3] This classification distinguishes natural-resource-rich countries according to whether these resources are "diffuse" (such as the United States) and do not give rise to rents, or "point-source," like Morocco (phosphates), that do give rise to rents. The resulting group, POINT (43, 8), is large, with half of the MENA countries, including Egypt.

Finally, for the mobility analysis, we use the World Bank four-group income classification: low (L), lower middle (LM), upper middle (UM), and high (H). We break MENA countries into these four categories in an extended sample that also includes member countries of the Organisation for Economic Co-operation and Development (OECD) countries (but excludes the former socialist countries of Europe and Central Asia).

The list of countries in each grouping (except income) is given in table A1. It corresponds to the groupings used in table 2.3 in chapter 2.

Table A.1   Comparator Groups

	Countries
Middle East and North Africa (MENA) (17)[a]	Algeria, Bahrain, Arab Republic of Egypt, Islamic Republic of Iran, Iraq, Israel, Jordan, Kuwait, Lebanon, Libya, Morocco, Oman, Qatar, Saudi Arabia, Syrian Arab Republic, Tunisia, United Arab Emirates, Republic of Yemen.
Resource-rich, labor-abundant (6)	Algeria, Islamic Republic of Iran, Iraq, Libya, Syria, Republic of Yemen
Resource-poor labor-abundant (5)	Egypt, Jordan, Lebanon, Morocco, Tunisia
Resource-rich labor-importing, or GCC (6)	Bahrain, Kuwait, Oman, Qatar, Saudi Arabia, United Arab Emirates
LARGE Large countries (48, 6)[b]	Afghanistan, Algeria, Argentina, Bangladesh, Brazil, Canada, China, Colombia, Egypt, Ethiopia, France, Germany, India, Indonesia, Islamic Republic of Iran, Iraq, Italy, Japan, Kenya, Republic of Korea, Morocco, Mexico, Myanmar, Malaysia, Nigeria, Nepal, Pakistan, Peru, Philippines, Poland, Dem. Rep. of Congo (Zaire), Dem. Rep. of Korea, Romania, Russian Federation, Spain, Saudi Arabia, South Africa, Sudan, Tanzania, Thailand, Turkey, Uganda, Ukraine, United Kingdom, United States, Uzbekistan, República Bolivariana de Venezuela, Vietnam

(continued next page)

Table A.1   *(continued)*

	Countries
OIL Oil exporters (18, 10)[c]	Angola, Algeria, Bahrain, Canada, Islamic Republic of Iran, Iraq, Kazakhstan, Kuwait, Libya, Mexico, Nigeria, Norway, Russian Federation, Oman, Saudi Arabia, United Arab Emirates, República Bolivariana de Venezuela. Republic of Yemen
POINT Point source natural resources (43, 8)[d]	Algeria, Angola, Benin, Bolivia, Botswana, Burkina Faso, Chad, Chile, Republic of Congo, Dem. Rep. of Congo, Dominican Republic, Ecuador, Egypt, Fiji, Gabon, Guinea, Guyana, Indonesia, Islamic Republic of Iran, Iraq, Jamaica, Jordan, Liberia, Malawi, Mauritania, Mauritius, Mexico, Morocco, Namibia, Niger, Nigeria, Oman, Papua New Guinea, Paraguay, Peru, Saudi Arabia, Sierra Leone, South Africa, Sudan, Syria, Togo, Trinidad and Tobago, Tunisia, República Bolivariana de Venezuela, Zambia

Notes: When comparisons are made with countries in the LARGE, OIL, and POINT groups, MENA members belonging to the group are excluded.
a. Middle East and North Africa definition is based on the World Bank definition of the MENA region. Number of MENA countries in the group is indicated.
b. Large countries are those with a population of at least 20 million in 2000. The category excludes OECD countries except for the Republic of Korea, Mexico, and Turkey.
c. Oil exporters are the 15 major oil crude exporters listed by the U.S. Energy Information Administration in 2005, to which we added Bahrain (80 percent), Oman (90 percent), and Republic of Yemen (93 percent); share of oil in merchandise exports in parenthesis.
d. Classification taken from Isham et al. (2005).

Notes

1. This three-group classification was introduced in World Bank (2004, ch. 2).
2. The GCC was founded in 1981 with security and economic cooperation as main objectives. Regional integration picked up around 2000, with a quasi–common market status reached in 2008.
3. The objective of this classification is to capture the idea that natural riches produce institutional weaknesses (the "voracity effect" associated with the attempt at rent-capture by different social groups—see Tornell and Lane (1999). "Point source" natural resources such as oil, minerals, and plantation crops are extracted from a narrow economic base, while "diffuse" natural resources are extracted from a large base. While this voracity effect extends to all sources of rents (natural monopolies, foreign aid, nontariff barriers, and financial elites), over the long haul, it makes sense to include a classification of countries along this dimension.

References

Isham, J., M. Woolcock, L. Pritchett and G. Busby. 2005. "The Varieties of Resource Experience: Natural Resource Export Structures and the Political Economy of Economic Growth." *World Bank Economic Review* 19 (2): 141–74.

Tornell, A., and P. R. Lane. 1999. "The Voracity Effect." *American Economic Review* 89 (1): 22–46.

www.ingramcontent.com/pod-product-compliance
Lightning Source LLC
Chambersburg PA
CBHW061730270326
41928CB00011B/2177